Apple Watch App Development

Build real-world applications for the Apple Watch
platform using the WatchKit framework and Swift 2.0

Steven F. Daniel

BIRMINGHAM - MUMBAI

Apple Watch App Development

First published: April 2016

Production reference: 1250416

Published by Packt Publishing Ltd.
Livery Place
35 Livery Street
Birmingham B3 2PB, UK.

ISBN 978-1-78588-636-2

www.packtpub.com

Credits

Author
Steven F. Daniel

Reviewer
Dylan Marriott

Commissioning Editor
Amarabha Banerjee

Acquisition Editor
Reshma Raman

Content Development Editor
Priyanka Mehta

Technical Editor
Taabish Khan

Copy Editor
Shruti Iyer

Project Coordinator
Izzat Contractor

Proofreader
Safis Editing

Indexer
Rekha Nair

Graphics
Abhinash Sahu

Production Coordinator
Melwyn Dsa

Cover Work
Melwyn Dsa

About the Author

Steven F. Daniel is the CEO and founder of GENIESOFT STUDIOS, a software development company that is based in Melbourne, Victoria, which focuses primarily on developing games and business applications for iOS, Android, and Mac OS X. Steven is a software developer with more than 14 years of experience developing desktop and web-based applications for a number of companies, including ANZ, Department of Justice, BP Australia, and AXA Australia.

Steven is always interested in emerging technologies, and he is a member of the SQL Server Special Interest Group (SQLSIG), Melbourne CocoaHeads, and the Java Community. He was the co-founder and Chief Technology Officer (CTO) of SoftMpire Pvt Ltd., a company that focused primarily on developing business applications for the iOS and Android platforms.

Steven is the author of various book titles: *Xcode 4 iOS Development Beginner's Guide*, *iOS 5 Essentials*, *iPad Enterprise Application Development Blueprints*, *Xcode 4 Cookbook*, and *Android Wearable Programming*.

Check out his blog at http://www.geniesoftstudios.com/blog/, or follow him on Twitter at http://twitter.com/GenieSoftStudio.

Acknowledgements

No book is the product of just the author; he just happens to be the one with his name on the cover. A number of people have contributed to the success of this book, and it would take more space than I have to thank each one individually.

I would personally like to thank two special people who have been an inspiration and who have provided me with so much support during the writing of this book. The first is Reshma Raman, my Senior Acquisition Editor, who is the reason that this book exists, and the second is Priyanka Mehta for her understanding and support as well as her brilliant suggestive approaches during the chapter rewrites. I would like to thank both of you for everything and making the writing process enjoyable.

To my reviewers, thank you so much for your valued suggestions and improvements to make this book what it is, I am truly grateful to each and every one of you.

Thank you to the entire Packt Publishing team for working so diligently to help bring out a high quality product. A big shout out to the engineers at Apple for creating the Apple Watch and the WatchKit Platform to provide developers with the tools to create fun and sophisticated applications.

Finally, I would like to thank all of my friends for their support, understanding, and encouragement during the book writing process. I am extremely grateful to have you as my friends, and it is a privilege to know each and every one of you.

About the Reviewer

Dylan Marriott is a young iOS developer from Switzerland. At the start of his career, he worked with web technologies, but he soon got involved with mobile and never went back. He started off with Android and then transitioned toward iOS. He currently works at Evernote, where he gets to work with the newest iOS technologies. In his free time, he has published a number of iOS and Apple Watch apps.

www.PacktPub.com

eBooks, discount offers, and more

Did you know that Packt offers eBook versions of every book published, with PDF and ePub files available? You can upgrade to the eBook version at www.PacktPub.com and as a print book customer, you are entitled to a discount on the eBook copy. Get in touch with us at customercare@packtpub.com for more details.

At www.PacktPub.com, you can also read a collection of free technical articles, sign up for a range of free newsletters and receive exclusive discounts and offers on Packt books and eBooks.

https://www2.packtpub.com/books/subscription/packtlib

Do you need instant solutions to your IT questions? PacktLib is Packt's online digital book library. Here, you can search, access, and read Packt's entire library of books.

Why subscribe?
- Fully searchable across every book published by Packt
- Copy and paste, print, and bookmark content
- On demand and accessible via a web browser

This book is dedicated to:

My favorite uncle Benjamin Jacob Daniel, thank you for always making me smile and for inspiring me to work hard and achieve my dreams. You are a true inspiration, and I couldn't have done this without your love, support, and guidance. Thank you.

Chan Ban Guan, for the continued patience, encouragement, and support, and most of all, for believing in me during the writing of this book.

I would like to thank my family for their continued love and support and for always believing in me throughout the writing of this book. This book would not have been possible without your love and understanding, and I would like to thank you from the bottom of my heart.

Table of Contents

Preface   **vii**

Chapter 1: Introducing the Swift Programming Language   **1**

Registering as an Apple developer   **2**

Getting and installing Xcode development tools   **5**

Introduction to Xcode playgrounds   **7**

Introduction to the Swift language   **10**

  Variables, constants, strings, and semicolons   10

    Variables   10

    Constants   12

    Strings   13

    Semicolons   15

  Numeric types and conversion   16

  Booleans, tuples, and string interpolation   17

    Booleans   18

    Tuples   20

    String interpolation   23

  Controlling the flow   25

    The for...in loops   25

What's new in Swift 2.0   **27**

  Error handling   27

  Binding   29

  Protocol extensions   30

Summary   **31**

Chapter 2: Understanding Apple Watch   **33**

Introduction to the WatchKit platform   **34**

  Introducing the WatchKit application architecture   35

  Introducing the WatchKit application life cycle   36

  Introducing the WatchKit classes   39

  Limitations of the WatchKit platform   40

Apple Watch Human Interface Guidelines	**41**
What's new in watchOS 2	**42**
Watch faces	43
Photos	43
Time-Lapse	43
Time travel	43
Nightstand mode	44
Activation Lock	44
FaceTime audio	44
Social features	44
Summary	**46**
Chapter 3: Exploring WatchKit Controls	**47**
Building the Guessing Game application	**48**
Using Interface Builder to create the watch user interface	50
Adding our user interface controls – text and labels	52
Creating Outlets to our Interface Builder objects	55
Creating Actions that respond to user actions	60
Building and running the Guessing Game application	65
Summary	**67**
Chapter 4: Using the Core Location and Watch Connectivity	
Frameworks	**69**
Creating the navigation tracking application	**70**
Building the Watch Tracker application – iPhone	72
Adding and removing annotation placeholders	81
Handling requests for background location updates	82
Building and running the Watch Tracker application	84
Building the Watch Tracker application – WatchKit	86
Limitations of using Core Location within watchOS 2	86
Using Interface Builder to create the Watch Tracker UI	87
Creating the Outlets for our Interface Builder objects	91
Creating an Action event to handle our map zooming	93
Using Core Location with the WatchKit extension	95
Communicating between the iPhone app and the WatchTracker	
WatchKit extension	99
Integrating the Watch Connectivity framework – iPhone app	100
Integrating the Watch Connectivity framework – WatchKit extension	102
Building and running the Watch Tracker application	104
Summary	**106**
Chapter 5: Navigating Around in WatchKit	**107**
Building the Health Monitor application	**108**
Understanding page-based interfaces and navigation	111
Understanding modal interfaces and navigation	112

Understanding hierarchical interfaces and navigation 112
Integrating the HealthKit framework to handle updates 113
Integrating the HealthKit framework – iPhone app 114
Building the Health Monitor application – WatchKit 115
   Creating the profile details interface controller's WatchKit class 125
   Creating the Outlets for our Interface Builder objects 128
Creating an Action event to handle our Start Monitoring button 135
Using HealthKit to obtain heart rate and pedometer information 137
Using HealthKit to obtain biological personal information 144
Building and running the Health Monitor application **150**
Summary **152**
Chapter 6: Implementing Tables within Your App **153**
  Building the Shopping List application **154**
Setting up and provisioning your app for Apple Pay 156
Configuring our Shopping List app to work with Apple Pay 162
Understanding the WatchKit table object 163
Building the Shopping List application – WatchKit 164
   Creating the table row interface controller's WatchKit class 167
   Configuring our product table row controller class 169
   Creating the product class structure to hold product items 172
   Creating the ProductsList property list 175
   Populating our WatchKit table controller with row information 180
   Responding when a row has been selected within our table 182
Running the Shopping List application – WatchKit 184
Handling payment requests with the PassKit framework 185
Building and running the Shopping List application **194**
Summary **195**
Chapter 7: Adding Menus to Your App **197**
  Introduction to gestures and the menu interface **198**
Understanding WatchKit context menu gestures 198
Understanding the WatchKit context menu interface 201
Design considerations for WatchKit context menu icons **202**
Understanding the default WatchKit context menu actions 204
Adding a menu to our Shopping List application – WatchKit **205**
Establishing the WatchKit context menu connections **209**
Design considerations when using Taptic Engine **213**
Learning how to integrate Apple Watch haptics within an app 213
Running the Shopping List application – WatchKit 218
Summary **220**

Chapter 8: Incorporating the Glance Interface in Your App   221

Introduction to working with WatchKit glances   222
    Understanding the glance controller life cycle   222
Adding a glance to our Shopping List application – WatchKit   224
    Creating a glance build scheme for our Shopping List app   226
    Creating the glance interface controller WatchKit class   228
Configuring our glance controller using templates   231
Establishing glance interface controller connections   234
Storing information to show within your glance controller   237
Displaying information within your glance controller   239
Understanding the glance interface guidelines   240
Running the Shopping List application – WatchKit   242
Summary   244

Chapter 9: Incorporating Notifications within Your App   245

Working with WatchKit notifications   246
    Understanding the notification controller life cycle   247
Configuring the notification scheme for our Shopping List app   248
Adding Action buttons to your dynamic notifications   252
    Responding to actions within your custom notifications   255
    The difference between static and dynamic interface controllers   257
    Configuring our Shopping List app's dynamic notification controller   258
Establishing our notification controller connections   262
Configuring a category for our static interface controller   264
Scheduling notifications with your notification controller   266
Displaying messages within the notification interface   269
Understanding the notification interface guidelines   272
Running the Shopping List application – WatchKit   273
Summary   275

Chapter 10: Image Compression and Animation   277

Building the animation application – WatchKit   278
    Setting up and adding images to the assets catalog   281
    Configuring our app to use App Transport Security   284
    Using Interface Builder to create the watch user interface   286
      Establishing connections to our interface controller   290
      Establishing our Action events that respond to user actions   292
      Animating your images within the WatchKit interface   295
      Loading and compressing images within the WatchKit interface   296
      Building and running the Animation Example application   298
Summary   300

Chapter 11: Packaging and Deploying Your App — 301

Creating and setting up your iOS development team — 302
Creating the iOS development certificate — 306
Obtaining the development certificate from Apple — 307
Creating App IDs for your WatchKit applications — 309
Creating development provisioning profiles — 311
Profiling your application using Xcode Instruments — 317
Preparing your app for submission using iTunes Connect — 320
Submitting an app to iTunes Connect using Xcode — 325
Summary — 327

Index — 329

Preface

With the increasing amount of new wearable devices hitting the market, wearables are the next wave of mobile computing technology. After the release of Apple's WatchKit SDK, a whole new world of exciting development possibilities awaits us.

Apple Watch App Development provides you with a practical approach that shows you how to develop and build Apple Watch apps using the Xcode Integrated Development Environment. You will be introduced to the architecture and limitations of the Apple Watch platform, followed by an in-depth look at the Swift programming language, where we talk about closures, tuples, protocols, delegates, and how to work with Xcode playgrounds.

We also discuss more advanced topics, such as notifications, glances, Apple Pay, as well as the Core Location and Watch Connectivity frameworks to synchronize data between the Apple Watch and the iPhone using the WatchKit platform. By the end of this book, you will have a good understanding of how to build real-world applications for the Apple Watch platform using the WatchKit framework and Swift 2.0.

In this book, I have tried my best to keep the code simple and easy to understand by providing a step-by-step approach with lots of screenshots at each step to make it easier to follow. You will soon be mastering the different aspects of Apple Watch wearable programming, as well as mastering the technology and skills that are needed to create your own applications for the Apple Watch platform.

Feel free to contact me at support@geniesoftstudios.com for any queries, or just drop me an e-mail to say "Hello".

What this book covers

Chapter 1, Introducing the Swift Programming Language, focuses on how to go about signing up to the Apple Developer program, as well as downloading and installing the Xcode development tools. We will cover Xcode playgrounds before moving on to learning the basics of the Swift programming language and some of the new additions to Swift with Swift 2.

Chapter 2, Understanding Apple Watch, introduces you to the WatchKit platform architecture and the application life cycle, as well as a list of the WatchKit classes that make up the WatchKit platform. You'll learn about some of the limitations behind the WatchKit platform architecture, as well as some of the new additional features that are a part of watchOS 2. You will then go on to learn about the Apple Watch Human Interface Guidelines.

Chapter 3, Exploring WatchKit Controls, introduces you to some of the controls that come as a part of the WatchKit platform. You will learn how to work with Xcode's Interface Builder to build the visual interface for our first WatchKit application. You will also learn how to use Outlets to bind objects to the Interface Builder objects and create some Action events to respond to these objects when tapped by the user to provide visual feedback.

Chapter 4, Using the Core Location and Watch Connectivity Frameworks, delves deeper into learning more about the WatchKit framework and the new layout system using groups. You'll learn about the MapKit and `WKInterfaceMap` frameworks. You will also learn how you can use these to incorporate mapping capabilities within your WatchKit apps using the Watch Connectivity framework to send geographical location-based coordinates between your iOS app and WatchKit to display the user's current location on the Apple Watch.

Chapter 5, Navigating Around in WatchKit, introduces you to some of the ways that you can navigate within the watch face user interface. You'll learn the differences between page-based, modal, and hierarchical navigation, and when to use them. You will then learn how to use the HealthKit framework to access health-related information and share this information between the iOS device and the WatchKit extension to display a user's current heart rate, blood type, and number of steps taken for a particular day.

Chapter 6, Implementing Tables within Your App, focuses on teaching you how to create applications that handle Apple Pay payments using the PassKit framework. You will learn how to pass information between the iOS device and the WatchKit extension. You will also learn how to use the `WKInterfaceTable` controller, how to set it up and configure it, as well as how to display information from a JSON file.

You will learn how to use the `WKInterfaceTable` methods to determine when a row has been selected by the user and respond to this action.

Chapter 7, Adding Menus to Your App, introduces you to WatchKit menus, and how you can incorporate them into your own applications, as well as respond to them based on what the user has chosen. We end the chapter by covering how you can use the Taptic Engine to integrate haptic feedback in your own applications.

Chapter 8, Incorporating the Glance Interface in Your App, shows you how to effectively incorporate WatchKit glances within an existing WatchKit application by creating a custom `GlanceInterfaceController` class to display information within the glance interface. You'll learn about the glance interface guidelines, which outline the guidelines and principles that you need to follow when designing your layouts for the different Apple Watch screen sizes.

Chapter 9, Incorporating Notifications within Your App, explains how to incorporate and configure local and remote notifications within an existing Apple Watch application. You will learn about the notifications life cycle and the differences between static and dynamic interfaces.

You will learn about the Apple Push Notification service (APNs) and how you can use this to send and receive information by responding to button actions when a user taps on the button. You will learn about the notification interface guidelines, which outlines the guidelines and principles that you need to follow when designing your notifications.

Chapter 10, Image Compression and Animation, shows you how to add images to the image assets catalog, and then start to build a simple WatchKit application that showcases how to animate a series of images within the WatchKit user interface.

You'll learn about the Application Transport Security (ATS) protocol that Apple introduced with the release of iOS 9, which forces developers to provide secure connections between your Apple Watch apps that communicate over HTTPS. We will also be covering how to properly configure our Apple WatchKit extension, as well as learn the best ways of handling and compressing large image files when these are downloaded from an external website so to increase performance.

Chapter 11, Packaging and Deploying Your App, focuses on how to submit your application to the Apple App Store, and share your creations with the rest of the community. You'll learn how to set up your iOS development team as well as the development and distribution certificates.

Finally, you will learn how to use the Instruments application to profile your application to eliminate performance bottlenecks. You will also learn how to package your application using Xcode and deploy this to iTunes Connect so that you can download and test on your Apple Watch device.

What you need for this book

The minimum requirement for this book is an Intel-based Macintosh computer running OS X El Capitan 10.11. We will be using Xcode 7.3, which is the Integrated Development Environment (IDE) that is used to create applications for iOS, watchOS, and tvOS. Almost all projects that you will create with the help of this book will work and run on the iOS Simulator. However, some projects will require an Apple Watch and an iPhone to work correctly.

You can download the latest version of Xcode from `http://developer.apple.com/ xcode/`.

Who this book is for

This book is intended for developers who have a working experience of application development principles on the Mac OS X and/or iOS platforms and wish to expand their knowledge to develop applications for the Apple Watch using the Swift programming language and the WatchKit framework. It is assumed that you are familiar with object-oriented programming (OOP) and have some experience with Swift.

Conventions

In this book, you will find a number of text styles that distinguish between different kinds of information. Here are some examples of these styles and an explanation of their meaning.

Code words in text, database table names, folder names, filenames, file extensions, pathnames, dummy URLs, user input, and Twitter handles are shown as follows: "Launch the Keychain Access application, which can be found in the `/Applications/ Utilities` folder."

A block of code is set as follows:

```
Override func willActivate() {
    Super.willActivate()
    guessLabel.setText("Your Guess is: + String(Int(yourGuess)))
    guessLabel.setTextColor(UIColor.yellowColor())
}
```

When we wish to draw your attention to a particular part of a code block, the relevant lines or items are set in bold:

```
// Method to handle the Encryption
func encryptString(str: String, withPassword password: String) throws
-> String {

    guard password.characters.count > 0  else { throw
    EncryptionError.Empty }
    guard password.characters.count >= 5 else { throw
    EncryptionError.Short }

    // Begin constructing our encrypted string
    let encrypted = password + str + password
    return String(encrypted.characters.reverse())
}
```

New terms and **important words** are shown in bold. Words that you see on the screen, for example, in menus or dialog boxes, appear in the text like this: "To run the app, select the **GuessingGame WatchKit App** scheme as shown in the following screenshot and then select your preferred device."

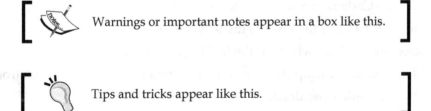

Warnings or important notes appear in a box like this.

Tips and tricks appear like this.

Reader feedback

Feedback from our readers is always welcome. Let us know what you think about this book—what you liked or disliked. Reader feedback is important for us as it helps us develop titles that you will really get the most out of.

To send us general feedback, simply e-mail feedback@packtpub.com, and mention the book's title in the subject of your message.

If there is a topic that you have expertise in and you are interested in either writing or contributing to a book, see our author guide at www.packtpub.com/authors.

Customer support

Now that you are the proud owner of a Packt book, we have a number of things to help you to get the most from your purchase.

Downloading the example code

You can download the example code files for this book from your account at http://www.packtpub.com. If you purchased this book elsewhere, you can visit http://www.packtpub.com/support and register to have the files e-mailed directly to you.

You can download the code files by following these steps:

1. Log in or register to our website using your e-mail address and password.
2. Hover the mouse pointer on the **SUPPORT** tab at the top.
3. Click on **Code Downloads & Errata**.
4. Enter the name of the book in the **Search** box.
5. Select the book for which you're looking to download the code files.
6. Choose from the drop-down menu where you purchased this book from.
7. Click on **Code Download**.

You can also download the code files by clicking on the **Code Files** button on the book's webpage at the Packt Publishing website. This page can be accessed by entering the book's name in the **Search** box. Please note that you need to be logged in to your Packt account.

Once the file is downloaded, please make sure that you unzip or extract the folder using the latest version of:

- WinRAR / 7-Zip for Windows
- Zipeg / iZip / UnRarX for Mac
- 7-Zip / PeaZip for Linux

Errata

Although we have taken every care to ensure the accuracy of our content, mistakes do happen. If you find a mistake in one of our books—maybe a mistake in the text or the code—we would be grateful if you could report this to us. By doing so, you can save other readers from frustration and help us improve subsequent versions of this book. If you find any errata, please report them by visiting `http://www.packtpub.com/submit-errata`, selecting your book, clicking on the **Errata Submission Form** link, and entering the details of your errata. Once your errata are verified, your submission will be accepted and the errata will be uploaded to our website or added to any list of existing errata under the Errata section of that title.

To view the previously submitted errata, go to `https://www.packtpub.com/books/content/support` and enter the name of the book in the search field. The required information will appear under the **Errata** section.

Piracy

Piracy of copyrighted material on the Internet is an ongoing problem across all media. At Packt, we take the protection of our copyright and licenses very seriously. If you come across any illegal copies of our works in any form on the Internet, please provide us with the location address or website name immediately so that we can pursue a remedy.

Please contact us at `copyright@packtpub.com` with a link to the suspected pirated material.

We appreciate your help in protecting our authors and our ability to bring you valuable content.

Questions

If you have a problem with any aspect of this book, you can contact us at `questions@packtpub.com`, and we will do our best to address the problem.

1

Introducing the Swift Programming Language

At WWDC 2014, Apple introduced a brand new programming language called **Swift**. The Swift programming language brings concise syntax, type safety, and modern programming language features to Mac and iOS developers.

Since its release, the Apple developer community has responded with great excitement, and developers are rapidly starting to adopt this new language within their own applications. The Swift language is the future of developing on Apple's platforms.

This chapter includes the following topics:

- Learning how to register as an Apple developer
- Learning how to download and install Xcode development tools
- Introduction to the Swift programming language
- Learning how to work with Xcode playgrounds
- Introduction to the newest additions in Swift 2.0

Registering as an Apple developer

Before you can begin building iOS applications for your iOS devices, you must first join as a registered user of Apple Developer Program in order to download all of the necessary components to your computer. The registration process is free and provides you with access to the iOS SDK and other developer resources that are really useful to get you started.

The following short list outlines some of the things that you will be able to access once you become a registered member of Apple Developer Program:

- It provides helpful "Getting Started" guides to help you get up and running quickly
- It gives you helpful tips that show you how to submit your apps to App Store
- It provides the ability to download the current releases of iOS software
- It provides the ability to beta test the releases of iOS and the iOS SDK
- It provides access to Apple Developer Forums

 Whether you develop applications for the iPhone or iPad, these use the same OS and iOS SDK that allows you to create universal apps that will work with each of these devices. On the other hand, Apple Watch uses an entirely different OS called watchOS.

To prepare your computer for iOS development, you need to register as an Apple developer. This free process gives you access to the basic levels of development that allow you to test your app using iOS Simulator without the ability to sell your app on the Apple App Store. The steps are as follows:

1. To sign up to Apple Developer Program, you will need to go to `https://developer.apple.com/programs/` and then click on the **Enroll** button to proceed, as shown in the following screenshot:

2. Next, click on the **Start Your Enrollment** button, as shown in the following screenshot:

3. Once you sign up, you will then be able to download the iOS SDK and proceed with installing it onto your computer.

You will then become an official member of Apple Developer Program. You will then be able to download beta software so that you can test them on your actual device hardware as well as having the freedom to distribute your apps to your end users.

In the next section, we will look at how to download and install Xcode development tools.

Getting and installing Xcode development tools

In this section, we will take a look at what **Integrated Development Environments (IDEs)** and **Software Development Kits (SDKs)** are needed to develop applications for the iOS platform, which is Apple's operating system for mobile devices. We will explain the importance of each tool's role in the development cycle and the tools required to develop applications for the iOS platform, which are as follows:

- An Intel-based Mac computer running OS X Yosemite (10.10.2) or later with the latest point release and security patches installed is required. This is so that you can install the latest version of the Xcode development tool.

- Xcode 6.4 or later is required. Xcode is the main development tool for iOS. You need Xcode 6.4 minimum as this version includes Swift 1.2, and you must be registered as an Apple developer. The iOS SDK consists of the following components:

Component	Description
Xcode	This is the main IDE that enables you to develop, edit, and debug your native applications for the iOS and Mac platforms using the Objective-C or Swift programming languages.
iOS Simulator	This is a Cocoa-based application that enables you to debug your iOS applications on your computer without the need of having an iOS device. There are many iOS features that simply won't work within Simulator, so a device is required if an application uses features such as the Core Location and MapKit frameworks.
Instruments	These are the analysis tools that help you optimize your applications and monitor memory leaks during the execution of your application in real time.
Dashcode	This enables you to develop web-based iOS applications and dashboard widgets.

Once you are registered, you will need to download and install Xcode developer tools by performing the following steps:

1. Begin by downloading and installing Xcode from Mac App Store at `https://itunes.apple.com/au/app/xcode/id497799835?mt=12`.

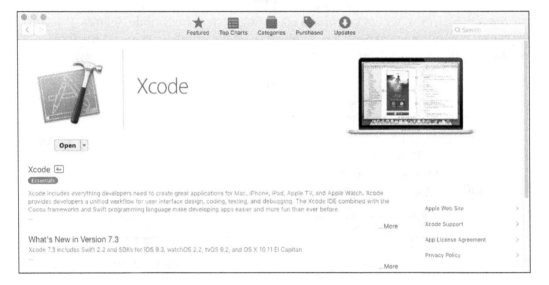

2. Select either the **Free** or **Install** button on the App Store page. Once it completes the installation process, you will be able to launch `Xcode.app` from your `Applications` folder.

 You can find additional development tools from the Apple developer website at `https://developer.apple.com/`.

In the next section, we will be looking at what, exactly, Xcode playgrounds are and how you can use them to experiment with designing code algorithms prior to incorporating the code into your project. So, let's get started.

Introduction to Xcode playgrounds

A playground is basically an interactive Swift coding environment that displays the results of each statement as updates are made without having the need to compile and run a project. You can use playgrounds to learn and explore Swift, prototype parts of your app, and create learning environments for others. The interactive Swift code environment lets you experiment with algorithms, explore system APIs, and even create your very own custom views without the need to create a project. Once you perfect your code in the playground, simply move this code into your project. Given that playgrounds are highly interactive, they are a wonderful vehicle for distributing code samples with instructive documentation and can even be used as an alternative medium for presentations.

With the new Xcode 7 IDE, you can incorporate rich text comments with bold, italic, and bulleted lists with the addition of having the ability to embed images and links. You can even embed resources and support Swift source code in the playground to make the experience incredibly powerful and engaging, while the visible code remains simple.

Playgrounds provide you with the ability to do the following:

- Share curriculum to teach programming with beautiful text and interactive code
- Design a new algorithm and watch its results every step of the way
- Create new tests and verify that they work before promoting them into your test suite
- Experiment with new APIs to hone your Swift coding skills
- Turn your experiments into documentation with example code that runs directly within the playground

Let's begin by opening the Xcode IDE and explore how to create a new playground file for the first time. Perform the following steps:

1. Open the `Xcode.app` application either using the finder in your `Applications` directory or using Apple's Launchpad. If you've never created or opened an Xcode project before, you will be presented with the following screen:

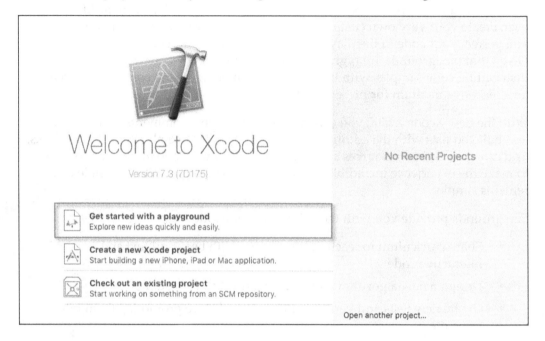

2. In the **Welcome to Xcode** dialog, select the **Get started with a playground** option. If this dialog doesn't appear, you can navigate to **File | New | Playground...** or simply press *Shift + Option + Command + N*.

3. Next, enter `SwiftLanguageBasics` as the name of your playground.

4. Then ensure that you choose **iOS** as the platform that we will target.

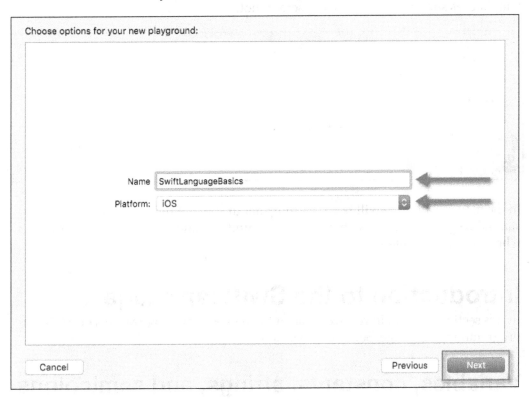

5. Click on the **Next** button to proceed to the next step in the wizard.
6. Specify the location where you would like to save your project.
7. Then click on the **Create** button to save your playground at the specified location.

Once your project is created, you will be presented with the default playground template, as shown in the following screenshot:

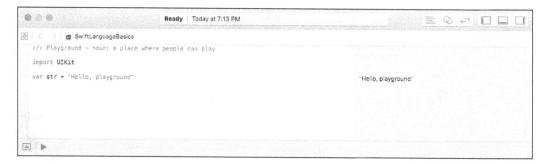

In the next section, you will begin learning about some of the Swift language basics, start adding lines of code within this playground file, and see the results that we get when they are executed.

Introduction to the Swift language

In this section, we will introduce some of the new and exciting features of the Swift programming language. So, let's get started.

Variables, constants, strings, and semicolons

Our next step is to familiarize ourselves with the differences between variables, constants, strings, and semicolons in a bit more detail. We will work with and use Xcode playgrounds to put each of these into practice.

Variables

A **variable** is a value that can change. Every variable contains a name, called the variable name, and must contain a data type. The data type indicates what sort of value the variable represents, such as whether it is an integer, a floating point number, or a string.

Let's take a look at how we can put this into practice and create a variable in Swift.

First, let's start by revealing the console output window by navigating to **View | Debug Area | Show Debug Area**.

Next, clear the contents of the playground template and replace them with the following code snippet:

```
/*:
# Swift Language Basics - Variables
: Created by Steven F. Daniel
: Copyright © 2015 GENIESOFT STUDIOS. All Rights Reserved.
*/

var myGreeting = "Welcome to Learning the basics of Swift Programming"
print(myGreeting, terminator: "")
```

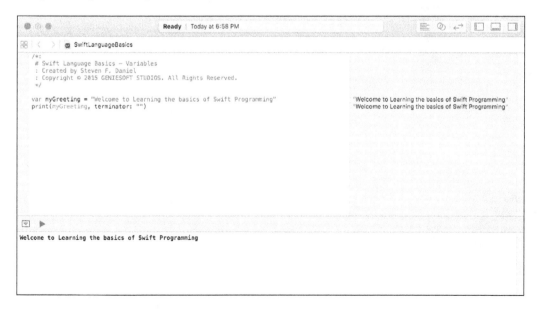

As you begin to type in the code, you should immediately see the **Welcome to Learning the basics of Swift** text magically appear in the right-hand pane in which the assignment takes place and it appears once more for the `print` statement.

The right-hand pane is great for showing you smaller output, but for longer debugging output, you would normally take a look at the Xcode console.

Constants

A **constant** is basically a value that cannot be changed. Creating these constant variables prevents you from performing accidental assignments and can even improve performance.

Let's take a look at how we can put this into practice and create a constant variable in Swift.

Clear the contents of the playground template and replace them with the following code snippet:

```
/*:
# Swift Language Basics - Constants
: Created by Steven F. Daniel
: Copyright © 2015 GENIESOFT STUDIOS. All Rights Reserved.
*/

let myGreeting = "Welcome to Learning the basics"
print(myGreeting, terminator: "")

myGreeting += " of Swift Programming"
```

Take a look at the screenshot now:

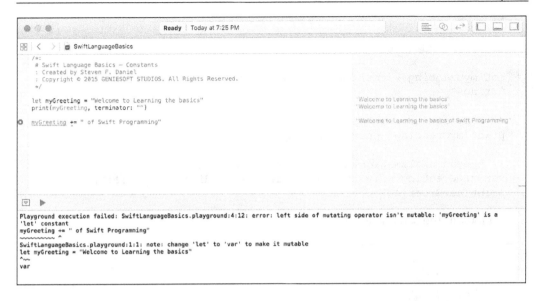

As you begin to type in the code, you will immediately receive an error message stating that you cannot assign myGreeting to our let value because the object is not mutable. In Swift, you can control the mutability of the built-in Swift types by using either the let or var keywords during declaration.

Strings

A **string** is basically an ordered collection of characters, for example, "hello, world". In Swift, strings are represented by the String data type, which represents a collection of values of the char data type.

You can use strings to insert constants, variables, literals, and expressions into longer strings in a process known as **string interpolation**, which we will cover later on this in chapter. This makes it easy to create custom string values for display, storage, and printing.

Let's take a look at how we can put this into practice, create a String variable in Swift, and utilize some of the string methods.

Clear the contents of the playground template and replace them with the following code snippet:

```
/*:
# Swift Language Basics - Strings
: Created by Steven F. Daniel
: Copyright © 2015 GENIESOFT STUDIOS. All Rights Reserved.
```

```
*/

import Foundation

let myGreeting = "Welcome to Swift Language Basics, working with
Strings"

// Make our String uppercase
print(myGreeting.uppercaseString)

// Append exclamation mark at the end of the string
var newGreeting = myGreeting.stringByAppendingString("!!!")
print(newGreeting)
```

Take a look at the screenshot now:

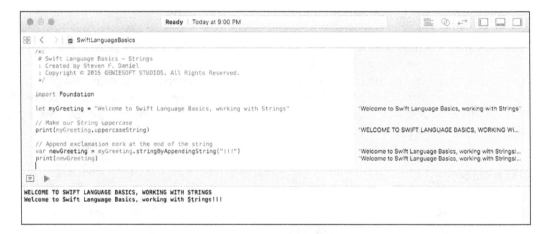

As you can see in the preceding code snippet, we began by importing the
Foundation framework class, which contains several APIs to deal with objects such
as strings and dates. Next, we declared our myGreeting constant variable and then
assigned a default string. We then used the uppercaseString method of the string
object to perform a function to make all of the characters within our string uppercase.
In our next step, we will declare a new variable called newGreeting and call the
stringByAppendingString method to append additional characters at the end of
our string.

For more information on using the String class, you can consult the
Swift programming language documentation at https://developer.
apple.com/library/ios/documentation/Swift/Conceptual/
Swift_Programming_Language/StringsAndCharacters.html.

Semicolons

As you would have probably noticed so far, the code you wrote doesn't contain any **semicolons**. This is because in Swift, these are only required if you want to write multiple statements on a single line.

Let's take a look at a code example to see how we can put this into practice.

Delete the contents of the playground template and replace them with the following code snippet:

```
/*:
# Swift Language Basics - Semicolons
: Created by Steven F. Daniel
: Copyright © 2015 GENIESOFT STUDIOS. All Rights Reserved.
*/

import Foundation

var myGreeting = "Welcome to Swift Language"
let newString = myGreeting + " Basics, ".uppercaseString + "working
with semicolons"; print(newString)
```

Take a look the following screenshot now:

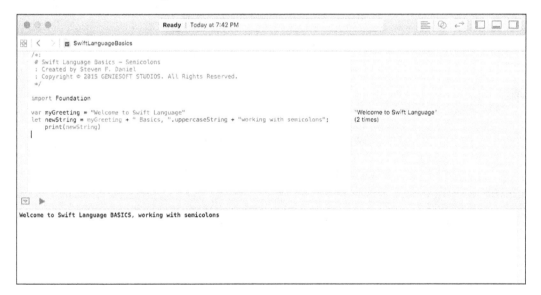

As you can see in the preceding code snippet, we began by declaring our `myGreeting` variable and then assigned a default string. In our next step, we declared a new variable called `newString`, concatenated the details from our `myGreeting` string, and used the `uppercaseString` method, which cycles through each character within our string, making our characters uppercase.

Next, we appended the additional `working with semicolons` string to the end of our string and finally used the `print` statement to output the contents of our `newString` variable to the console window. As you must have noticed, we included a semicolon at the end of the statement; this is because in Swift, you are required to include semicolons if you want to write multiple statements on a single line.

Numeric types and conversion

In this section, we will take a look at how we can perform arithmetic operations on our Swift variables. In this example, we will look at how to calculate the area of a triangle, given a base and height value.

Let's take a look at a code example to see how we can put this into practice.

Clear the contents of the playground template and replace them with the following code snippet:

```
/*:
# Swift Language Basics - Numeric Types and Conversion
: Created by Steven F. Daniel
: Copyright © 2015 GENIESOFT STUDIOS. All Rights Reserved.
*/

import Foundation

// method to calculate the area of a triangle
func calcTriangleArea(triBase: Double, triHeight: Double) -> Double {
    return (triBase * triHeight) / 2
}

// Declare our base and height of our triangle
let base = 20.0
let height = 120.0

// Calculate and display the area of the triangle and
print ("The calculated Area is: " + String(calcTriangleArea(base,
triHeight: height)));
```

Take a look at the following screenshot now:

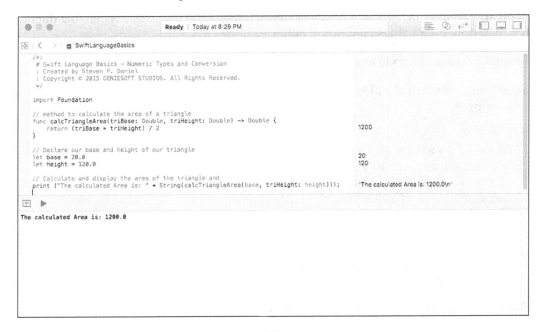

As you can see in the preceding code snippet, we started by creating our `calcTriangleArea` function method, which accepts a base and a height parameter value in order to calculate the area of the triangle. In our next step, we declared two variables, `base` and `height`, which contain the assigned values that will be used to calculate the base and the height of our triangle. Next, we made a call to our `calcTriangleArea` method, passing in the values for our base and height before finally using the `print` statement to output the calculated area of our triangle to the console window.

An important feature of the Swift programming language is that all numeric data type conversions must be explicit, regardless of whether you want to convert to a data type containing more or less precision.

Booleans, tuples, and string interpolation

In this section, we will look at the various features that come with the Swift programming language. We will look at the improvements that Swift has over Objective-C when it comes to using Booleans and string interpolation before finally discussing how we can use tuples to access elements from a string.

Booleans

Boolean variables in Swift are basically defined using the `Bool` data type. This data type can only hold values containing either `true` or `false`.

Let's take a look at a code example to see how we can put this into practice.

Clear the contents of the playground template and replace them with the following code snippet:

```
/*:
# Swift Language Basics - Booleans
: Created by Steven F. Daniel
: Copyright © 2015 GENIESOFT STUDIOS. All Rights Reserved.
*/

import Foundation

let displaySettings : Bool = true
print("Display Settings is: " + (displaySettings ? "ON" : "OFF"))
```

Take a look at the following screenshot now:

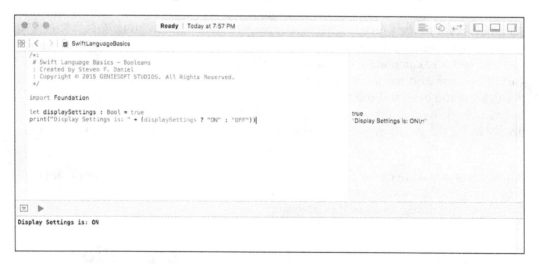

As you can see from the preceding code snippet, we started by declaring our constant variable called `displaySettings` and assigned it a default Boolean value of `true`. Next, we performed a check to see whether the value of our `displaySettings` variable is set to `true` and called our `print` statement to output the **Display Settings is: ON** value to the console window.

In Objective-C, you would assign values of 1 and 0 to denote true and false; this is no longer the case with Swift because Swift doesn't treat 1 as true and 0 as false. You need to explicitly use the actual Boolean values to stay within Swift's data type system.

Let's replace the existing playground code with the following code snippet to take a look at what would happen if we changed our value from `true` to `1`:

```
/*:
# Swift Language Basics - Booleans
: Created by Steven F. Daniel
: Copyright © 2015 GENIESOFT STUDIOS. All Rights Reserved.
*/

import Foundation

let displaySettings : Bool = 1 // This will cause an error!!!
print("Display Settings is: " + (displaySettings ? "ON" : "OFF"))
```

Take a look at the following screenshot now:

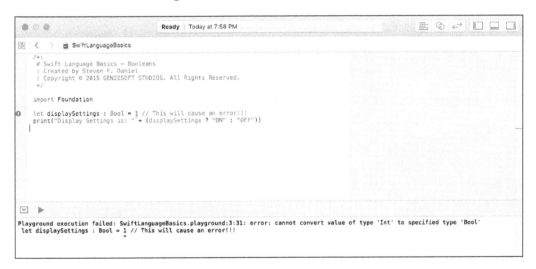

As you can see from the previous screenshot, Swift detected that we were assigning an integer value to our Boolean data type and threw an error message.

Tuples

Tuples provide you with the ability to group multiple values into a single compound value. The values contained within a tuple can be any data type, and therefore are not required to be of the same type.

Let's take a look at a code example, to see how we can put this into practice.

Clear the contents of the playground template and replace them with the following code snippet:

```
/*:
# Swift Language Basics - Tuples
: Created by Steven F. Daniel
: Copyright © 2015 GENIESOFT STUDIOS. All Rights Reserved.
*/

import Foundation

// Define our Address Details
var addressDetails = ("Apple Inc.", "1 Infinite Loop", "Cupertino,
California", "United States");

print(addressDetails.0) // Get the Name
print(addressDetails.1) // Address
print(addressDetails.2) // State
print(addressDetails.3) // Country
```

Take a look at the following screenshot now:

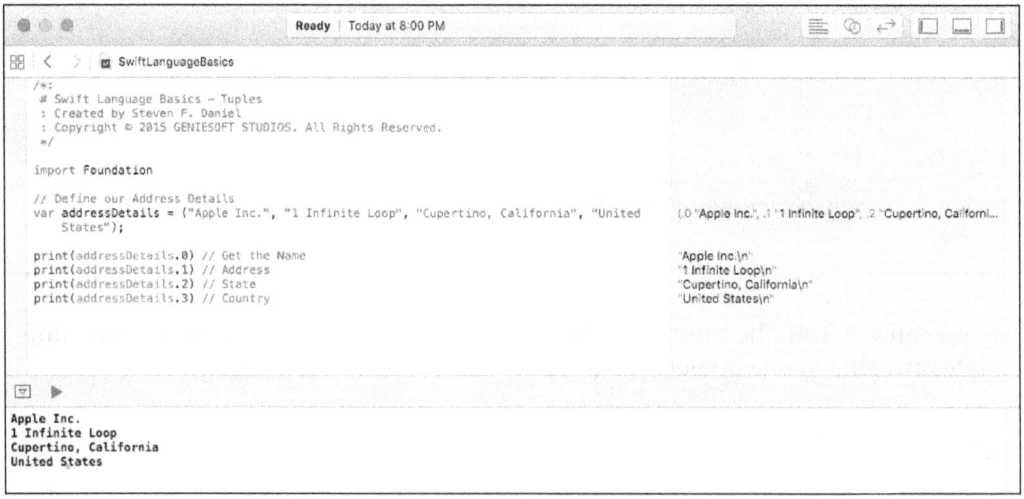

As you can see from the preceding code snippet, we started by declaring a tuple variable called `addressDetails` that contains a combination of strings. Next, we accessed each of the tuple elements by referencing their index values and displayed each of these elements in the console window.

Let's say that you want to modify the contents of the first element within your tuple. Add the following code snippet after your `var addressDetails` variable:

```
// Modify the element within our String
addressDetails.0 = "Apple Computers, Inc."
```

Take a look at the following screenshot now:

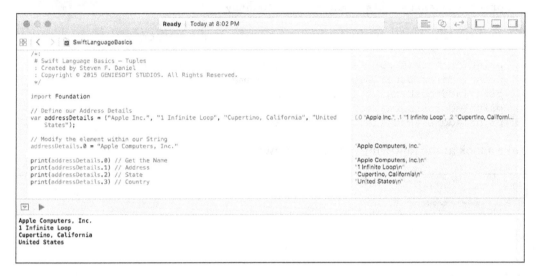

As you can see from the preceding screenshot, we modified our first component within our tuple to the `Apple Computers, Inc` value. If you do not want modifications to be made to your variable, you can just change the `var` keyword to `let`, and the assignment would result in a compilation error.

You can also express your tuples by referencing them using their named elements. This makes it really useful as you can ensure that your users know exactly what the element refers to. If you express your tuples using their named elements, you will still be able to access your elements using their index notation, as can be seen in the following highlighted code snippet:

```
/*:
# Swift Language Basics - Tuples
: Created by Steven F. Daniel
: Copyright © 2015 GENIESOFT STUDIOS. All Rights Reserved.
*/
```

```swift
import Foundation

// Define our Address Details
var addressDetails = (company:"Apple Inc.", Address:"1 Infinite Loop",
City:"Cupertino, California", Country:"United States");

// Accessing our Tuple by using their NAMES

print("Accessing our Tuple using their NAMES\n")
print(addressDetails.company) // Get the Name
print(addressDetails.Address) // Address
print(addressDetails.City)    // State
print(addressDetails.Country) // Country

// Accessing our Tuple by using their index notation

print("\nAccess our Tuple using their index notation:\n")
print(addressDetails.0) // Get the Name
print(addressDetails.1) // Address
print(addressDetails.2) // State
print(addressDetails.3) // Country
```

Take a look at the following screenshot now:

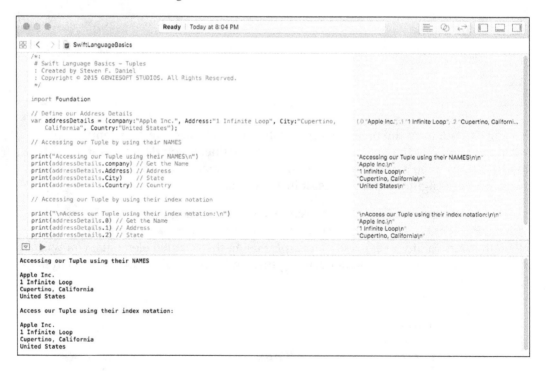

As you can see from what we covered so far about tuples, these are really cool and are basically just like any other data type in Swift; they can be really powerful to use within your own programs. As we progress through this book, you will see tuples being used more frequently.

String interpolation

String interpolation means embedding constants, variables, as well as expressions within your string literals. In this section, we will take a look at an example of how you can use this.

Clear the contents of the playground template and replace them with the following code snippet:

```
/*:
# Swift Language Basics - String Interpolation
: Created by Steven F. Daniel
: Copyright © 2015 GENIESOFT STUDIOS. All Rights Reserved.
*/

import Foundation

// Define our Address Details
var addressDetails = (company:"Apple Inc.", Address:"1 Infinite Loop",
City:"Cupertino, California", Country:"United States");

// Use String Interpolation to format output
print("Apple Headquarters are located at: \n\n" + addressDetails.
company + ",\n"
    + addressDetails.Address + "\n" + addressDetails.City + "\n"
    + addressDetails.Country);
```

Take a look at the following screenshot now:

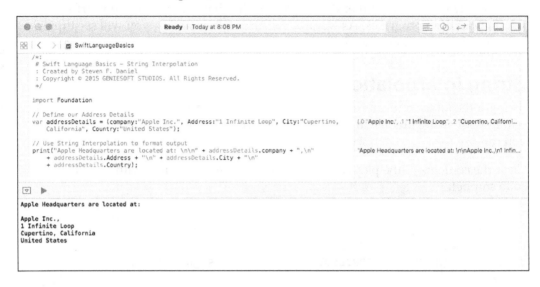

As you can see from the preceding code snippet, we started by declaring a tuple variable called `addressDetails` that contains a combination of strings. Next, we performed a string concatenation to generate our output in the format that we want by accessing each of the tuple elements using their index values and displaying each of these elements in the console window.

Let's take this a step further and use string interpolation to place our address detail information into string variables. The result will still be the same, but I just want to show you the power of using tuples with the Swift programming language.

Clear the contents of the playground template and replace them with the following highlighted code snippet:

```
/*:
# Swift Language Basics - String Interpolation
: Created by Steven F. Daniel
: Copyright © 2015 GENIESOFT STUDIOS. All Rights Reserved.
*/

import Foundation

// Use String Interpolation to place elements into string initializers
var addressDetails = ("Apple Inc.", "1 Infinite Loop", "Cupertino,
California", "United States");
let (Company, Address, City, Country) = addressDetails
```

```
print("Apple Headquarters are located at: \n\n" + Company + ",\n" +
Address + "\n" + City + "\n" + Country);
```

Take a look at the following screenshot now:

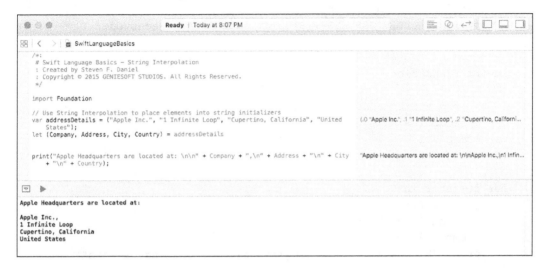

As you can note from the preceding code snippet, we removed the named types from our addressDetails string contents, created a new type using the let keyword, and assigned placeholders for each of our tuple elements. This is very handy as it not only makes your code a lot more readable but you can also continue to create additional placeholders for the additional fields that you create.

Controlling the flow

In this section, we will take a look at how to use the for...in loop to iterate over a set of statements within the body of the loop until a specific condition is met.

The for...in loops

The for...in loops basically perform a set of statements over a certain number of times until a specific condition is met, which is typically handled by incrementing a counter each time until the loop ends.

Let's take a look at a code example to see how we can put this into practice.

Clear the contents of the playground template and replace them with the following code snippet:

```
/*:
# Swift Language Basics - Control Flow
: Created by Steven F. Daniel
: Copyright © 2015 GENIESOFT STUDIOS. All Rights Reserved.
*/


import Foundation


// Perform a fibonacci loop using the For-In Loop
var fibonacci = 0
var iTemp = 1
var jTemp = 0


for iterator in 0...19 {
    jTemp = fibonacci
    fibonacci += iTemp
    iTemp = jTemp
    print("Fibonacci: " + String(fibonacci), terminator: "\n")
}
```

Take a look at the following screenshot now:

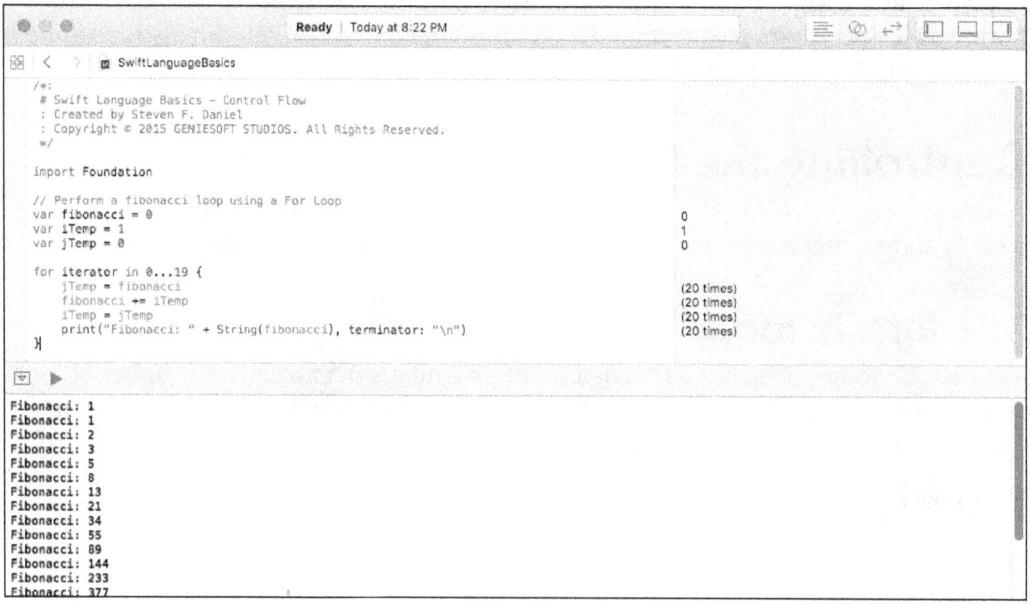

The preceding code demonstrates the `for...in` loop and the closed range operator (`...`). These are often used together, but they are entirely independent.

As you can see from the preceding code snippet, we declared the exact same variables: `fibonacci`, `iTemp`, and `jTemp`. Next, we used the `for...in` loop to iterate over our range, which is from 0 to 19, while displaying the current Fibonacci value in the console window.

What's new in Swift 2.0

In this section, we will take a look at some of the new features that come as part of the Swift 2.0 programming language.

Error handling

Error handling is defined as the process of responding to and recovering from error conditions within your program. The Swift language provides first-class support for throwing, catching, propagating, and manipulating recoverable errors at runtime. In Swift, these are referred to as **throwing functions** and **throwing methods**.

In Swift 2.0, error handling has vastly improved and adds an additional layer of safety to error checking. You can use the `throws` keyword to specify which functions and method are most likely to cause an error. You can implement and use the `do`, `try`, and `catch` keywords to handle something that could likely throw an error.

Let's take a look at a code example to see how we can put this into practice.

Clear the contents of the playground template and replace them with the following code snippet:

```
/*:
# Swift Language Basics - What's new in Swift 2.0
: Created by Steven F. Daniel
: Copyright © 2015 GENIESOFT STUDIOS. All Rights Reserved.
*/

import Foundation

enum EncryptionError: ErrorType {
    case Empty
    case Short
}
// Method to handle the Encryption
func encryptString(str: String, withPassword password: String) throws
-> String {
```

```swift
        if password.characters.count > 0 {
            // Password is valid
        } else { throw EncryptionError.Empty }

        if password.characters.count >= 5 {
            // Password is valid
        } else { throw EncryptionError.Short }

        // Begin constructing our encrypted string
        let encrypted = password + str + password
        return String(encrypted.characters.reverse())
    }

    // Call our method to encrypt our string
    do {
        let encrypted = try encryptString("Encrypted String Goes Here",
    withPassword: "123")
        print(encrypted)
    } catch EncryptionError.Empty {
        print("You must provide a password.")
    } catch EncryptionError.Short {
        print("Passwords must be at least five characters.")
    } catch {
        print("An error occurred!")
    }
```

Take a look at the following screenshot now:

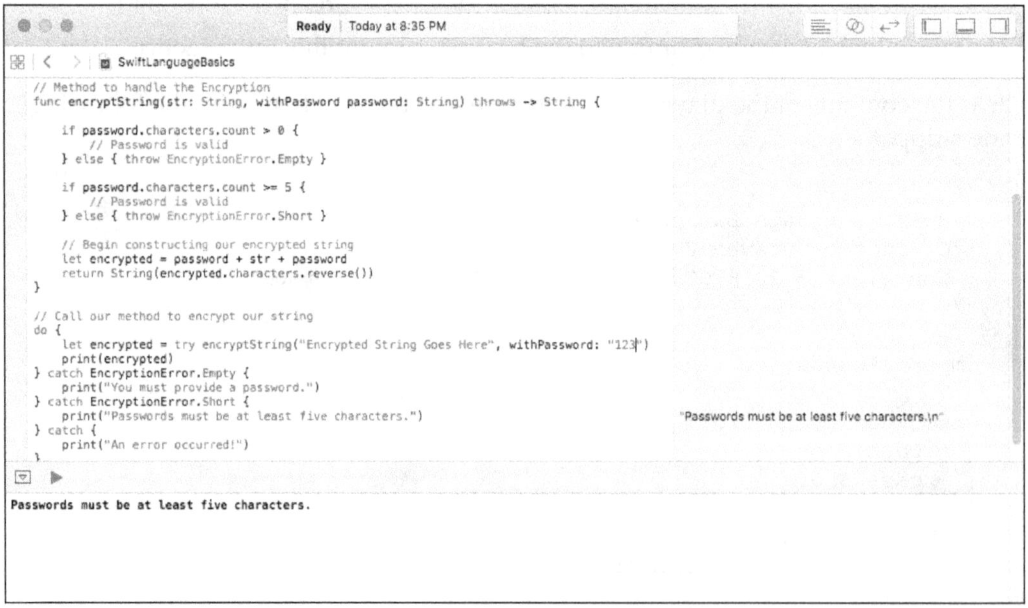

As you can see in the preceding code, we began by creating an enum object that derives from the ErrorType class so that we could create and throw an error. Next, we created a method called encryptString that takes two parameters: str and password. This method performed a check to ensure that we didn't pass an empty password.

If our method determines that we did not specify a valid password, we will automatically throw an error using EncryptionError.Empty and exit from this method. Alternatively, if we provide a valid password and string to encrypt, our string will be encrypted.

Binding

Binding in Swift is something new and provides a means of checking whether a variable contains a valid value prior to continuing and exiting from the method otherwise. Fortunately, Swift 2.0 provides you with exactly this, and it is called the guard keyword.

Let's go back to our previous code snippet and take a look at how we can implement the guard statement to our conditional checking within our encryptedString method.

Modify the contents of the playground template and replace them with the following highlighted sections:

```
// Method to handle the Encryption
func encryptString(str: String, withPassword password: String) throws
-> String {

    guard password.characters.count > 0  else { throw
    EncryptionError.Empty }
    guard password.characters.count >= 5 else { throw
    EncryptionError.Short }

    // Begin constructing our encrypted string
    let encrypted = password + str + password
    return String(encrypted.characters.reverse())
}
```

As you can see in the preceding code snippet, using the guard keyword, you can provide a code block to perform a conditional check within the else statement that will run if the condition fails. This will make your code cleaner as the guard statement lets you trap invalid parameters from being passed to a method. Any conditions you would have checked using if before you can now check using guard.

Protocol extensions

In Swift 2.0, you have the ability to extend **protocols** and add additional implementations for properties and methods. For example, you can choose to add additional methods to the `String` or `Array` classes, as follows:

```
/*
# What's new in Swift 2.0 - Protocol Extensions
The first content line displayed in this block of rich text.
*/

import Foundation

let greeting = "Working with Swift Rocks!"

// Extend the String class to include additional methods
extension CustomStringConvertible {
    var uCaseString: String {
        return "\(self.description.uppercaseString)!!!"
    }
}
print(greeting.uCaseString)
```

Take a look at the following screenshot now:

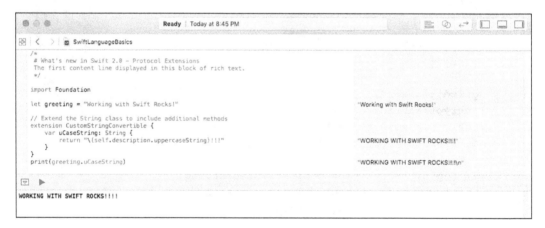

As you can see in the preceding code, we extended the `String` class using the `CustomStringConvertible` protocol, which most of the `Foundation` class objects conform to. Using protocol extensions, they provide you with a wide variety of ways to extend the base classes so that you can add and implement your very own custom functionalities.

Summary

In this chapter, we explored how to go about downloading and installing Xcode development tools and then moved on to discussing and using playgrounds to write Swift code to get to grips with some of the Swift programming language features. Next, we looked at some of the newest features that come as part of the Swift 2.0 language.

In the next chapter, you will learn about the WatchKit platform and its architecture as well as the application's life cycle. You will get accustomed to the WatchKit classes and learn about some of the limitations with the WatchKit platform architecture; then you will learn about Apple Watch Human Interface Guidelines and take a look at what's new in watchOS 2.

2
Understanding Apple Watch

During the launch of WWDC 2015, Apple introduced a new addition to their product lineup called *Apple Watch*, which runs the new watchOS platform. It has been designed and built from the ground up while borrowing design characteristics from iOS 8, with features and apps that take advantage of the hardware within the Apple Watch device.

Apple Watch comes with a variety of apps, such as **Activity** and **Workout**, which read data from the accelerometer and the heart rate sensor, while other apps contain communication features that enable users to send sketches, heartbeats, as well as animated emojis. Notification messages are sent from the iPhone device and delivered to Apple Watch with small haptic taps on the wrist, while **Glances** offers small pieces of information that can easily be digested in a few seconds without having to pull your iPhone out of your pocket.

Since the release of Apple Watch, the Apple developer community has embraced this new piece of technology with great excitement and has already started building applications that target this new platform, with many apps appearing on the Apple App Store daily.

This chapter includes the following topics:

- Introduction to the WatchKit platform
- Introduction to the WatchKit application architecture
- Introduction to the WatchKit application life cycle
- Introduction to the WatchKit classes
- Learning about the limitations of the WatchKit platform
- Understanding the Apple Watch interface guidelines
- Introduction to the newest features of the watchOS 2 platform

Introduction to the WatchKit platform

This section provides you with an overview of the WatchKit platform, which is a fundamental part of Apple Watch. When developing apps for Apple Watch, it takes advantage of the WatchKit framework that happens to be included as part of the iOS SDK, and both are embedded into the watchOS and iOS operating systems.

The WatchKit framework contains the necessary classes that provide the underlying functionality for both the WatchKit extension and the WatchKit application and is responsible for handling all of the communication between the WatchKit extension that runs on the iPhone device and its corresponding WatchKit application that is installed on Apple Watch.

Whenever you begin developing Apple Watch apps, you will notice that your project contains a number of different **targets** that make use of the WatchKit platform.

 A **target** is the final end product that is created by your application, and these can be either an app, a framework, or even a static library. Targets contain a list of classes, resources, as well as any custom scripts to use or include when building your application.

The following table explains each of these projects and what they contain:

Method	Description
Watch extension	This contains the code and resources for the Watch app and is run on the connected iPhone.
Watch app	This is the interface for the Watch application that resides on Apple Watch. This project consists of a storyboard and small resource files, and contains a reference link to the Watch extension.
iOS app	This is the main app that bundles the Watch app and Watch extension into the iPhone application. As a rule, whenever you develop Watch apps, you must have an iOS app that bundles up the Watch app.

In the next section, you will learn about the WatchKit application architecture prior to building Apple Watch applications. You will learn about the associated classes and methods relating to both Apple Watch and the WatchKit framework.

Introducing the WatchKit application architecture

In this section, we must first grasp the importance of this point; in order for Apple Watch applications to function, they require the iPhone to do its work. To understand this, we need to take a closer look at the architecture of an Apple Watch application.

The WatchKit framework basically takes care of all of the essential details for us and automatically pairs the iPhone and Apple Watch as well as handling all of the communication between the Apple Watch application and WatchKit extension.

All of this communication between the iPhone and Apple Watch is handled over Bluetooth. An Apple Watch application is basically the component that runs on Apple Watch and presents the user interface and intercepts touch events from the user. This means that an Apple Watch application is basically rendered useless without the paired device on which the corresponding WatchKit extension runs.

The Apple Watch application and WatchKit extension are part of the iOS application that the user installs on his or her iPhone. The underlying WatchKit architecture consists of your WatchKit app and the associated WatchKit extension that need to work together to implement your application's user interface.

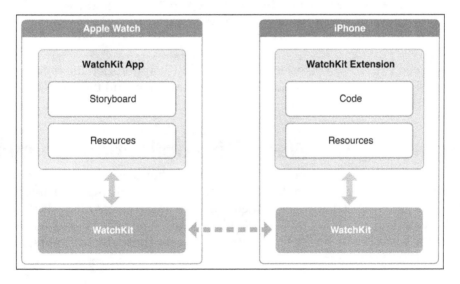

Whenever the user launches an Apple Watch application from the home screen, the paired iPhone initializes and launches the WatchKit extension for the application. Any user interaction is then forwarded and handled by the WatchKit extension, and it is the responsibility of the Apple Watch application to determine how to handle and respond to the user interaction.

The WatchKit app contains the application's **storyboard** as well as the static resources that Apple Watch requires to present the user interface. A storyboard is nothing more than a visual representation containing the flow of how your application will look to the user. Storyboards let you design your application by adding views, view controllers, and segues between them for additional functionality. The WatchKit extension is stored and runs on the iPhone device, and is the iOS device portion of the application that the user has installed on his or her iPhone, which contains all of the business logic.

> One piece of advice to take on board is that an Apple Watch application is nothing more than an extension of an existing iOS application.

As you can see from the previous diagram, the WatchKit framework is responsible for the communication between Apple Watch and the paired iPhone. The Apple Watch section is basically responsible for presenting the user interface and handling the touch events on Watch itself.

> To get more information about the WatchKit architecture, take a look at the *Watch App Architecture* documentation at `https://developer.apple.com/library/prerelease/ios/documentation/General/Conceptual/WatchKitProgrammingGuide/DesigningaWatchKitApp.html`.

In the next section, we will take a look at the WatchKit application life cycle, what happens when an application is launched on Apple Watch, and the associated methods that get called.

Introducing the WatchKit application life cycle

In this section, we will take a look at what happens when a WatchKit application is launched on the Apple Watch device and the method events that get launched. Whenever your WatchKit app is launched, the WatchKit framework loads the initial scene for your app, and, after the scene loads, WatchKit asks the WatchKit extension to create the corresponding interface controller object, which you use to prepare the scene to display to the user.

Your WatchKit app and extension pass information back and forth until the user stops interacting with your app, at which point iOS suspends the extension until the next user interaction. If your app contains Glances and the user decides to view your app's Glances scene, WatchKit will load the Glances scene from your storyboard.

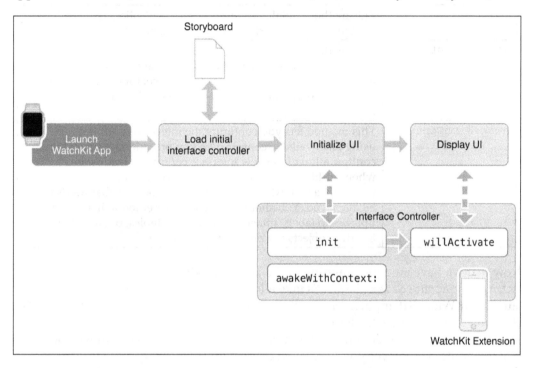

The WatchKit framework consists of a group of entirely new classes. There is a new WKInterfaceController class that acts as the controller using the familiar Model-View-Controller pattern, and there is also a WKInterfaceObjects class that is used to update the user interface. You will notice as you start working with the WatchKit framework that all of the WatchKit classes follow Apple's class naming conventions and are prefixed by WKInterface.

The following table explains the key methods of the `WKInterfaceController` class, which is essentially WatchKit's `UIViewController` class:

Method	Description
`init`	This method initializes your interface controller. This is where the bulk of your interface initialization should occur.
`willActivate`	This method lets you know that your interface will soon be visible to the user. You should only use this method to make small updates to your user interface; for example, you may want to update a label based on new data that has been retrieved.
`awakeWithContext`	This method lets you configure the interface controller using any available context data you provide to assist in the configuration of the new interface controller. For instance, when pushing data to the new interface controller, you need to specify a context object that contains the data that needs to be displayed. You should also use this method to handle any updates to labels, image manipulation, tables, or any other interface objects in your storyboard scene.

Now that we have an understanding of the key methods of our `WKInterfaceController` class, let's take a look at what exactly happens when we launch our WatchKit application. Firstly, we initialized our `WKInterfaceController` class and loaded our controller from the storyboard, and then we called the `awakeWithContext` method that takes a parameter for an optional context object that can contain whatever you like; it can contain an ID, a string, or even a core data model object. Once the `awakeWithContext` method is called, the WatchKit framework sets up all of the `IBOutlet` you may have defined within your application, which is taken care of within our `init` method. The `willActivate` method is called after the `awakeWithContext` method is completed to let you know that the controller is about to be displayed to the user.

Finally, the `didDeactivate` method gets called whenever the user navigates away from the interface controller or Apple Watch terminates the app. If you develop an app that saves details to a database or shared preferences, you should do this within this method.

Introducing the WatchKit classes

In this section, we will take a look at the different WatchKit subclasses that inherit from the `WKInterfaceObject` class. In the coming chapters, we will utilize most of these in the applications that we will create:

Class	Description
WKInterfaceButton	This is basically a standard button similar to the UIButton object that comes with iOS and contains a background and a label.
WKInterfaceDate	This is a class that is unique to the WatchKit framework and is basically a label that is built to display both date and time.
WKInterfaceGroup	This class is unique to WatchKit and is responsible for handling all of the interface layout and grouping of your controls. You can add other objects to a group, lay these out either horizontally or vertically, and apply the necessary spacing and padding between each of the controls.
WKInterfaceImage	This class is almost the same as the UIImageView class that comes with iOS with the exception that when using the WKInterfaceImage class, you can set multiple images and animate them.
WKInterfaceLabel	This class performs the same way as the UILabel class, and you will use this often whenever you need to display text within your interface.
WKInterfaceMap	This class acts a little differently in Apple Watch compared with the MapKit class on iOS. The maps feature on WatchKit is noninteractive, so you will need to use the MKCoordinateRegion class within your controllers (which is basically just a latitude, longitude, and zoom level), and the map will configure a static view of this location. You still have the ability to add additional features, such as drop pins and custom annotations, but these will be noninteractive.
WKInterfaceSeparator	This class is fully configurable and allows you to change the appearance of table separators within tables and views.

Class	Description
WKInterfaceSlider	This class is basically a cut-down version of the UISlider class that comes with iOS but, unfortunately, it comes with limited functionality.
	You still have the ability to customize the slider with the appropriate min and max values as well as number of steps, and you can even change the bar style by setting the **Continuous** property in Interface Builder to make the bar solid. Turning this property off will make the bar appear etched in the number of steps.
WKInterfaceSwitch	This object is also similar to its iOS counterpart, UISwitch, except that with this class, it comes with a built-in label.
WKInterfaceTable	Working with tables in WatchKit is really useful, and you'll most likely use them quite a bit in your applications. When you use the WKInterfaceTable class, these will be automatically paired with WKInterfaceController to handle the interaction events and navigation between segues.
WKInterfaceTimer	This WKInterfaceTimer class is a special WatchKit interface object that contains a label that counts down to a specific date. You have the ability to configure what units to display: seconds, minutes, hours, days, weeks, months, or even years.

Limitations of the WatchKit platform

In this section, we will discuss some of the limitations of the WatchKit platform. With the release of Apple Watch and the WatchKit framework 1.0, this first round of releases is extremely exciting, and developers have utilized these releases to develop apps.

Unfortunately, when developing Apple Watch applications, there are a number of limitations that are important, and you need to keep them in mind as you think about building your first app.

Some of these limitations are as follows:

- There is no way of easily implementing animations in Apple Watch. These need to be created and bundled as a series of images as there is no way to perform the animation dynamically.

- Compared with the iPhone, there is no way of dynamically adding or removing views within the Apple Watch platform.

- There is no ability to run the Watch app or extension without an active connection with the iPhone, and notifications will not appear on the Watch if disconnected.

- However, the last notification received will be available prior to disconnection.

- The Watch app can only handle up to 20 MB of image cached data, and this limit cannot be changed. You need to ensure that you manage and flush out the image cached contents yourself.

- Apple Watch is small and doesn't provide the ability to allow four-finger gestures.

- It does not give you the ability to use advanced features, such as accessing the camera and background fetching of data. Core Location is not supported.

In the next section, we will focus on learning about the Apple Watch interface guidelines. This set of guidelines is particularly useful and will help you when designing apps for Apple Watch as they need to be designed differently due to the amount of space available for you to work with within the Watch face area.

Apple Watch Human Interface Guidelines

When designing apps for Apple Watch, these apps need to be designed differently from how you would go about designing apps for phone or tablets as they provide a different user experience. It is important to keep in mind and follow the Apple Watch interface guidelines documentation that Apple provides.

This document describes guidelines and principles that can help you design consistent user interfaces and experiences for your Watch apps as well as ensure that your applications are running efficiently within the Apple Watch platform. You need to consider the screen sizes for your custom layouts as well as the ease of use your app brings to the platform. Other areas are covered to ensure the consistency of your application while navigating from screen to screen; the principles of designing good user interfaces are also covered.

There is also information related to the proper use and appearance of views and controls for navigation, alerts, notifications, table views, buttons, and images, as well as the creation of custom icons and images.

Some of the Apple Watch interface guidelines are as follows:

- **Gestures**: The gesture system of Apple Watch is far more limited than the generous gesture options that developers have in iOS. These support only vertical and horizontal swipes and taps and, currently, Watch doesn't support multitouch gestures such as pinching.

- **Force Touch**: This is a new gesture that comes with Apple Watch and contains special tiny electrodes around the display to determine whether a tap is light or has more pressure and force behind it.

- **Digital Crown**: The beautifully designed crown on the Apple Watch is a fine tuned scrolling replacement. Since the Watch screen is extremely small, your fingers will most likely hide where you're scrolling. Using the digital crown lets you see the contents that are being scrolled.

- **Side button**: The side button gesture provides you with access to the Friends screen by simply pressing the side button. From this screen, you can call your friends, send messages, or interact with your friends by sending sketches, taps, or even your heartbeat.

- **Glances**: Glances is similar to the Today extensions in iOS, but the main difference is that they are read only. Glances provides the user with relevant information about the Apple Watch extension.

- **Notifications**: This type of feature provides the ability to send customized local and remote notifications as well as the default user interface of local and remote notifications.

- **Action-based events**: This type of events occur whenever a user performs a table-row selection, or when the user taps on a user interface control object, such as `UIButton`.

 To get further information about these guidelines, it is worth checking out the Apple Watch *Human Interface Guidelines* documentation at `https://developer.apple.com/watch/human-interface-guidelines/`.

What's new in watchOS 2

In this section, we will take a look at the differences between watchOS 1.0 and watchOS 2. One of the biggest highlights of the watchOS 2 platform is the support for native apps, which means that the apps will be able to run entirely on Apple Watch without having to rely on iPhone. This allows developers to access the device's built-in heart rate sensor, the Taptic feedback engine, accelerometer, and microphone with the ability to build custom watch faces to display information within the Apple Watch face.

The watchOS 2 version comes with two brand new watch faces called **Time Travel**, which displays information about future complications, such as weather and calendar events, and the **Nightstand** mode, which is activated when Apple Watch charges. There are also several improvements to **Mail** as well as support for FaceTime Audio, and it supports multiple colors for sketches and lets users add more than twelve friends to their list of contacts.

Apple has also made several improvements to Siri under the watchOS 2 platform that allow quickly starting workouts and opening up Glances. It also has iOS 9 features such as transit directions in **Maps** and the addition of **Activation Lock**, which provides safety should we lose or misplace Apple Watch.

Watch faces

The watchOS 2 platform will introduce two new watch face options that will be designed by Apple. These new watch faces, named **Photos** and **Time-Lapse**, are explained here.

Photos

The first one will be the Photo watch face that will take advantage of the photos that are stored on Apple Watch with the ability to let you choose a photo or an album of photos to use as your watch face.

Time-Lapse

The dynamic Time-Lapse face displays videos that are shot over 24 hours from different locations around the world, including Hong Kong, London, New York, Shanghai, and Paris. When you glance at your Apple Watch, the image displayed will be different and is based on the local time.

Time travel

The time travel feature lets you turn the Digital Crown on your Apple Watch to turn time forwards or backwards to display either future or past information on your Apple Watch. This feature is useful for complications, which are basically little pieces of extra information such as weather, calendar events, date, time, and so on, that are displayed on certain Apple Watch faces.

Nightstand mode

The Nightstand mode is a new feature of the watchOS 2 platform that is activated whenever Apple Watch is placed on its side when connected to the charger, which allows it to better function as an alarm clock. When in this mode, the Apple Watch screen becomes illuminated whenever the screen or Digital Crown is pressed to display the current time.

Activation Lock

The Activation Lock feature is already built-in and present in iPhones and iPads, which prevents these devices from being reset or reactivated without the correct Apple ID and password. This effectively renders these devices useless if stolen and therefore cannot be reset using another Apple account.

FaceTime audio

The watchOS 2 version provides you with the ability to accept FaceTime Audio calls on Apple Watch, just as you currently can using your iPhone. There is no ability to answer FaceTime Video calls, but you have the ability to send them to the phone, or reject them.

Social features

In watchOS 2, you have the ability to send sketches, heartbeats, emojis, and more to multiple contacts within your contact list. You also have the ability to create groups and add your friends to this list and organize them through the Apple Watch app on your iPhone.

Take a look at the following diagram:

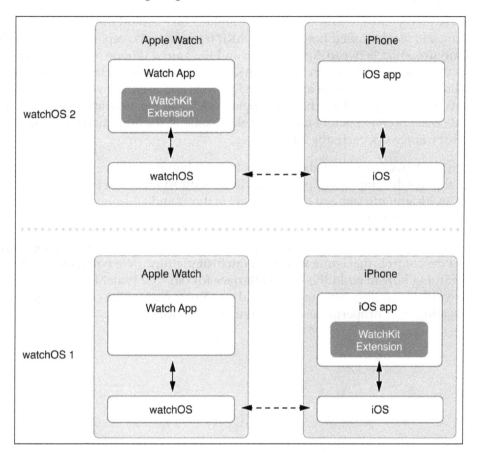

As you can see, watchOS 2 brings the long-awaited feature that will make apps load more quickly and work more smoothly. In watchOS 1, apps were powered by the iPhone over Bluetooth with only the Watch app interface running on Apple Watch.

As you can see from the watchOS 2 equivalent, you will notice that the entire Watch app as well as the WatchKit extension module run independently on the Apple Watch device without the need to pair it with the iPhone. This will make your Apple Watch apps load far more quickly and perform a lot better to provide a better user experience to your customers.

Summary

In this chapter, you were introduced to the architecture behind the WatchKit platform, and we discussed how the WatchKit framework is responsible for handling the communication between Apple Watch and the paired iPhone over Bluetooth as well as the differences between the WatchKit app and extension. We then moved on to discussing the WatchKit application life cycle and took an overview of what happens when an app is launched on Apple Watch and the associated classes and methods that are called before taking a look at some of the limitations that the WatchKit framework currently has.

In our next step, you learned about Apple Watch Human Interface Guidelines to ensure that we develop our apps in accordance with Apple's best practices. Finally, we got an insight into some of the great new features and additions that are coming as part of the watchOS 2 platform.

In the next chapter, you will learn how to work with Xcode's Interface Builder and some of the controls that come with the WatchKit platform. We will then move on to learning how to build the visual interface for our first WatchKit application, which will be a simple guessing game, and customize each of the control objects by interrogating their properties using Attributes Inspector.

Exploring WatchKit Controls

3

In this chapter, you will learn how to build a simple guessing game application for Apple Watch that will allow the watch to randomly generate a number and have the user try and guess the number. You will learn how to use Interface Builder to create the visual user interface for our application using some of the controls that come as part of the WatchKit platform.

You will learn how to customize each of the control objects by interrogating their properties using Attributes Inspector and then learn how to create connections with each of our controls using Outlets so that we can access their getters and setters through code. You will also learn how to create Actions to control objects, which are basically events that are called when a user performs an action.

To end the chapter, you will learn how to compile, build, and run the *Guessing Game* application using the watchOS simulator so that you can test the app and ensure that everything is working correctly. In the later chapters, you will learn how to build an application and deploy it to Apple Watch and App Store.

This chapter includes the following topics:

- Learning how to use Interface Builder to create the watch user interface
- Learning how to add and customize Interface Builder objects
- Learning how to create Outlets for Interface Builder objects
- Learning how to create Actions that respond to user actions
- Learning how to build and run the WatchKit *Guessing Game* application

We have an exciting project ahead of us, so let's get started.

Building the Guessing Game application

In this section, we will take a look at how we can go about designing our user interface for our *Guessing Game* application. We will begin by developing the WatchKit and iOS app portion of our application.

Before we can proceed, we need to create our GuessingGame project. It is very simple to create this using Xcode. Simply follow the steps listed here:

1. Launch Xcode from the /Applications folder.

2. Choose **Create a new Xcode project** or go to **File | New Project**:

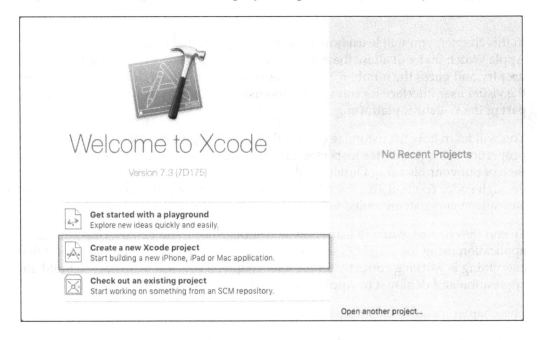

3. Select the **iOS App with WatchKit App** option from the list of available templates under the **watchOS** section, as shown in the following screenshot:

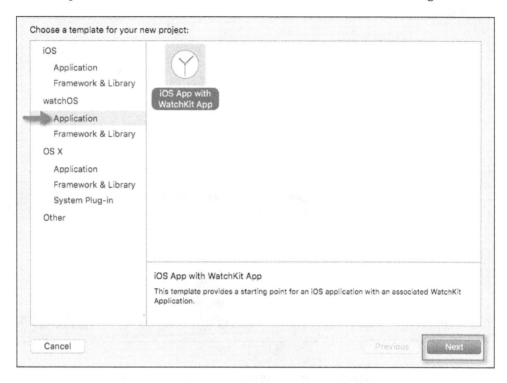

4. Click on the **Next** button to proceed to the next step in the wizard.
5. Next, enter GuessingGame as the name for your project.
6. Select **Swift** in the **Language** drop-down menu.
7. Select **iPhone** in the **Devices** drop-down menu.
8. Ensure that the **Include Notification Scene** checkbox is selected.

9. Click on the **Next** button to proceed to the next step in the wizard.

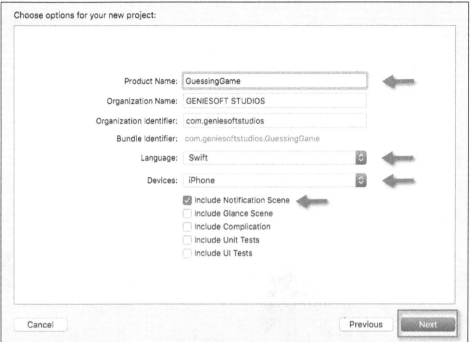

The **Organization Identifier** option for your app needs to be unique. Apple recommends that you use the reverse domain style (for example, `com.domainName.appName`).

10. Specify the location where you would like to save your project.

11. Then, click on the **Create** button to save your project at the specified location.

Once your project is created, you will be presented with the Xcode development environment along with the project files that the template created for you. If you want, you can build and run the application. The iOS simulator will start and show a blank white screen.

Using Interface Builder to create the watch user interface

In this section, we will familiarize ourselves with the Interface Builder application. Interface Builder is a visual tool integrated within the Xcode development IDE that enables you to design the user interface for your iOS and watchOS applications.

Using Interface Builder, you can drag and drop views and objects onto your canvas area from the libraries pane. These objects can then be connected using Outlets and Actions so that they can programmatically interact with your code.

Select the `Interface.storyboard` file from the project navigation window. From the Xcode toolbar, you can select the viewing options, as shown in the following screenshot:

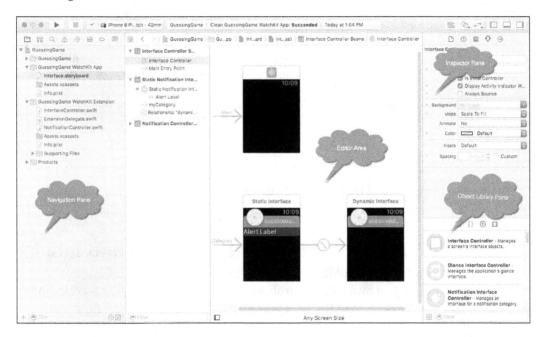

The preceding screenshot shows what Interface Builder looks like when designing interfaces for Apple Watch when the storyboard for our interface is chosen from the project navigation window.

Whenever you use Interface Builder to design user interfaces for your iOS applications, any object that is used from the library pane will be associated with and connected to the project that they belong to.

As you can note from the preceding screenshot, the Interface Builder workspace is divided into three main areas. The following table provides a brief description of which area is used for which function:

Area name	Description
Navigation pane	This area displays all the files that are associated with the current project.
Editor area	This is where we will start designing our user interfaces for our applications.
Inspector pane	This area is used when we want to configure each of our Interface Builder objects—for example, changing the color, font size, or the name of a label or button.
Object library pane	This area is where we can locate objects and drag them onto our design canvas. Such objects are the `WKInterfaceLabel`, `WKInterfaceButton`, `WKInterfaceSwitch`, and so on.

In our next section, we will look at how to design the user interface for our Apple Watch *Guessing Game* application.

Adding our user interface controls – text and labels

In this section, we will begin building the user interface for our *Guessing Game* application by adding text and label controls to our watch area as well as learning how to create the necessary `@Outlets` for our application. Perform the following steps:

1. Select the `Interface.storyboard` file from the project navigation window.

2. From the Object Library pane, drag a `WKInterfaceSlider` control to the watch area canvas.

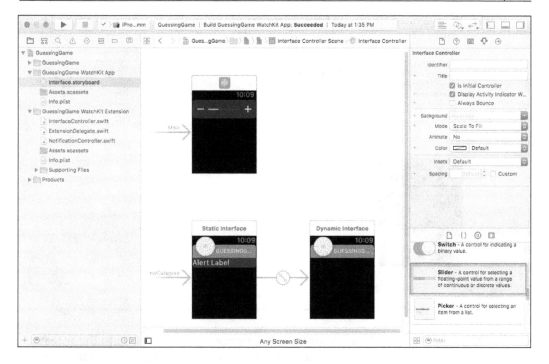

3. Then, from the Attributes Inspector section, change the starting **Value** property for our slider control to **1**.

4. Next, we need to set the **Minimum** property of our slider control to **1** so that it doesn't exceed the minimum set amount.

5. Then, we need to change the **Maximum** value property for our slider control to **10** so that we don't exceed the limit.

6. Lastly, we need to set the **Steps** property for our slider control to show **11** increments (as dashes) when we press the **+** and **–** buttons.

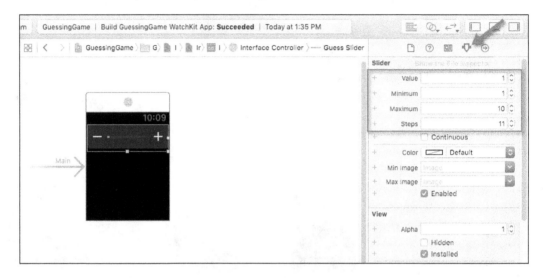

7. Next, from Object Library, drag a `WKInterfaceLabel` control to the watch area canvas and place this under the `WKInterfaceSlider` control that we added previously.

8. Then, in the Attributes Inspector section in the **Text** property, enter `Your guess is ?`.

9. Next, from Object Library, drag a `WkInterfaceButton` control to the watch area canvas and place this under the **Your guess is?** (`WKInterfaceLabel`) control that we added previously.

10. Then, from the Attributes Inspector section, ensure that the **Content** property is set to **Text**, and in the **Title** property for our `WKInterfaceButton` control, type `Guess`.

As you can see, using Interface Builder to build our user interface is not that difficult once you get used to it. Whenever you drag objects from Object Library onto the watch canvas, you will notice that a small cross with a green circle appears on the cursor to indicate that it is safe to drop the object onto the view.

Once you drop the object onto your view, you have the ability to resize the control as well as modify the attributes associated with the control.

Creating Outlets to our Interface Builder objects

In the previous section, we looked at how to add controls to our `Interface.storyboard` canvas to form the construction of our user interface for our *Guessing Game* app as well as set some properties for each of our controls.

In this section, we will look at how to connect each of our controls and access them through code:

1. Open the Assistant Editor window by going to **Navigate | Open in Assistant Editor** or by pressing *Option + Command + ,*. Ensure that the `InterfaceController.swift` file is displayed within the Assistant Editor window, as shown in the following screenshot:

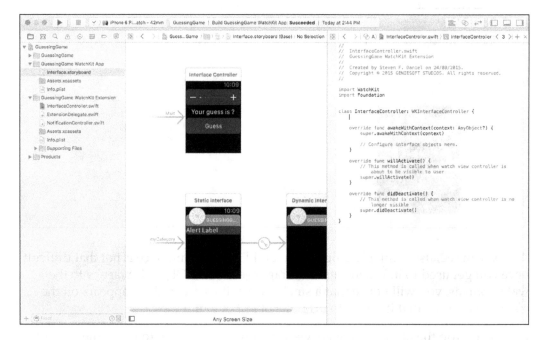

2. Next, select the `WKInterfaceSlider` control, then hold down the *Control* key, and drag it into the `InterfaceController.swift` file within the body of the `InterfaceController: WKInterfaceController` class.

3. Choose **Outlet** from the **Connection** drop-down menu for the type of connection to create and enter `guessValue` for the name of the Outlet property to create.

4. Next, choose **Weak** from the **Storage** drop-down menu and click on the **Connect** button.

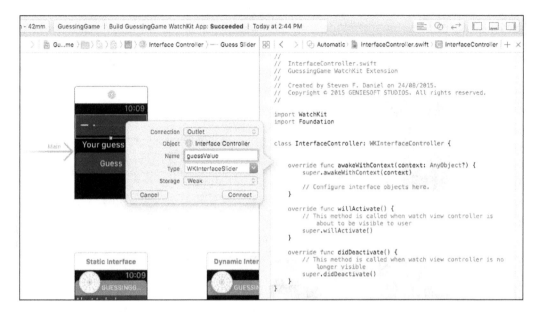

5. Next, select the `WKInterfaceLabel` control, then hold down the *Control* key, and drag it into the `InterfaceController.swift` file as we did for our `guessValue` Outlet.

6. Then, select **Outlet** from the **Connection** drop-down menu for the type of connection to create and enter `guessLabel` for the name of the Outlet property to create.

7. Next, select **Weak** from the **Storage** drop-down menu and click on the **Connect** button.

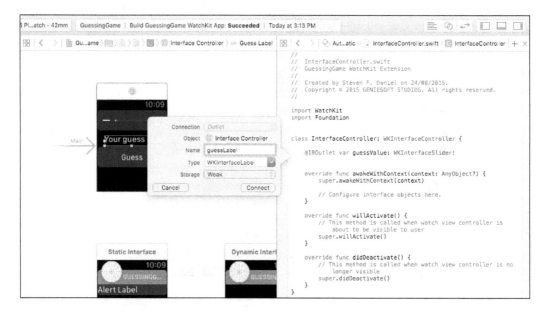

8. Next, select the `WKInterfaceButton` control, then hold down the *Control* key, and drag it into the `InterfaceController.swift` file as we did for our `guessLabel` Outlet.

9. Then, select **Outlet** from the **Connection** drop-down menu for the type of connection to create and enter `guessButton` for the name of the Outlet property to create.

10. Next, select **Weak** from the **Storage** drop-down menu and click on the **Connect** button.

11. Once you create the necessary outlets, it would be good to save your project by navigating to **File | Save** or alternatively pressing *Command + S*.

Whenever you create an Outlet, you must remember to create them within the `InterfaceController` class as these cannot be created outside this class body.

Outlets provide a means of allowing our Interface Builder objects to communicate with the code. This is necessary, and it is the only way in which we can access the user interface objects that are created within the Interface Builder designer environment.

The following code snippet shows the complete implementation of the Outlets that we created in the previous steps:

```
//  InterfaceController.swift
//  GuessingGame WatchKit Extension
//
//  Created by Steven F. Daniel on 24/08/2015.
//  Copyright © 2015 GENIESOFT STUDIOS. All rights reserved.
//

import WatchKit
import Foundation

class InterfaceController: WKInterfaceController {

    @IBOutlet var guessValue:  WKInterfaceSlider!
    @IBOutlet var guessLabel:  WKInterfaceLabel!
    @IBOutlet var guessButton: WKInterfaceButton!
```

As you can see from the preceding code snippet, Interface Builder creates each of our control objects as well as the associated type of control we used. Declaring Outlets also has another advantage associated with them; it basically provides us with access to these controls through their getter and setter methods.

Creating Actions that respond to user actions

In the previous section, we looked at how to add controls to our `Interface.storyboard` canvas to form the construction of our user interface for our *Guessing Game* app and how to connect each of the Outlets for each of our controls.

In this section, we will look at how we can communicate with these Outlets when the **Guess** button is tapped. Perform the following steps:

1. Open the Assistant Editor window by navigating to **Navigate | Open in Assistant Editor** or pressing *Option + Command + ,*.

2. Ensure that the `InterfaceController.swift` file is displayed within the Assistant Editor window, as shown in the following screenshot:

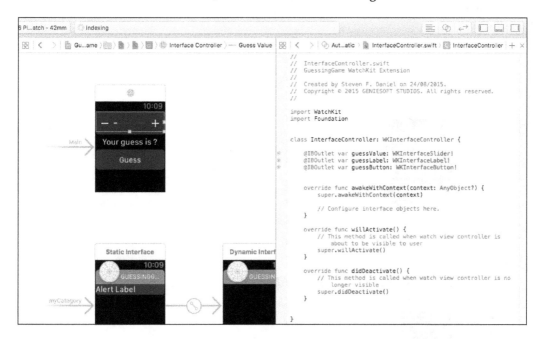

3. Next, select the `WKInterfaceSlider` control, then hold down the *Control* key, and drag it into the `InterfaceController.swift` file under the `didDeactivate` method.

4. Select **Action** from the **Connection** drop-down menu for the type of connection to create and enter `updateGuess` for the name of the action to create.

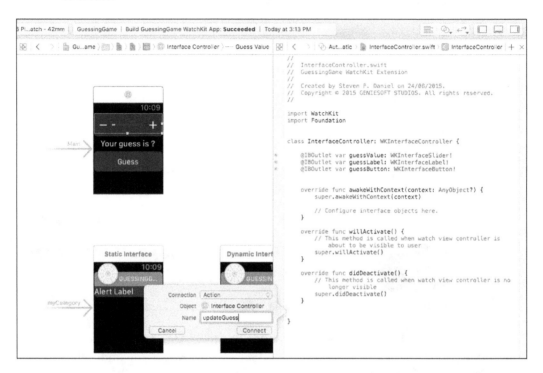

In our next step, we need to create the code that will be responsible when the slider value changes.

5. Open the `InterfaceController.swift` file located within the **GuessingGame WatchKit Extension** group in the project navigation window. Then, locate the `updateGuess:` method and enter the following code snippet:

```
/*
 * method to handle when the slider value changes
 */
@IBAction func updateGuess(value: Float) {
    let yourGuess = Int(value)
    guessLabel.setText("Your Guess is: " +
    String(Int(yourGuess)))
    guessLabel.setTextColor(UIColor.yellowColor())
}
```

As you can see from the preceding code snippet, we began by declaring our `yourGuess` variable and then assigned a default string containing `"Your Guess is: "` before appending the user's chosen guessed value, which we obtained from the slider control. In our next step, we will update our `guessLabel` control with the contents of the `yourGuess` variable and then set the color of our label to display our text in yellow.

6. Next, select the `WKInterfaceButton` control, then hold down the *Control* key, and drag it into the `InterfaceController.swift` file under the `updateGuess:` method.

7. Select **Action** from the **Connection** drop-down menu for the type of connection to create and enter `showGuess` for the name of the action to create.

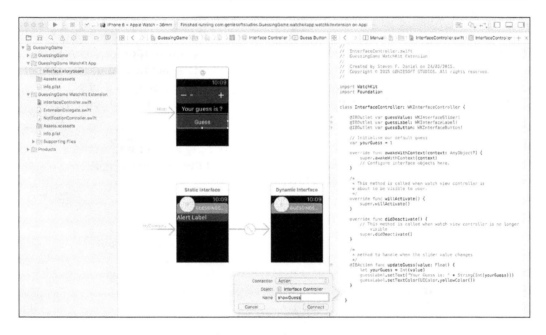

In our next step, we need to create the code that will be responsible when the **Guess** button is pressed and will determine whether the user guessed correctly.

8. Open the `InterfaceController.swift` file located within the **GuessingGame WatchKit Extension** group in the project navigation window. Then, locate the `showGuess:` method and enter the following code snippet:

```
/*
 * method to determine if the user guess correctly
 * by comparing the computers stored number, with the chosen
```

```
    * users value.
    */
    @IBAction func showGuess() {
        // Generate the randomized number
        let computersGuess = Int(arc4random_uniform(11))

        if (yourGuess == computersGuess) {
            guessLabel.setText("You're Correct. Good Job!")
            guessLabel.setTextColor(UIColor.greenColor())
        } else {
            guessLabel.setText("Wrong. The number is " +
            String(computersGuess))
            guessLabel.setTextColor(UIColor.redColor())
        }
    }
}
```

As you can see from the preceding code snippet, we began by declaring our `computerGuess` variable that will be used to store our randomized computer guessed value using `arc4random_uniform(11)` to generate a random number between 0 and 10. Finally, we made a comparison between the user's chosen value from the slider control and the randomized value that the computer stored and displayed the result on the screen.

9. Next, open the `InterfaceController.swift` file located within the **GuessingGame WatchKit Extension** group in the project navigation window and enter the following code snippet:

```
class InterfaceController: WKInterfaceController {

    @IBOutlet var guessValue: WKInterfaceSlider!
    @IBOutlet var guessLabel: WKInterfaceLabel!
    @IBOutlet var guessButton: WKInterfaceButton!

    // Initialize our default guess
    var yourGuess = 1

    override func awakeWithContext(context: AnyObject?) {
        super.awakeWithContext(context)
        // Configure interface objects here.
    }
```

As you can see from the preceding code snippet, we needed to make one final addition before our application is complete. We declared the `yourGuess` variable, which will be responsible for holding the value chosen from our `WKInterfaceSlider` control. This variable is used to make a comparison between the value we choose from our slider control and the value of what the computer thinks when we tap the **Guess** button.

10. Next, open the `InterfaceController.swift` file located within the **GuessingGame WatchKit Extension** group in the project navigation window. Then, locate the `willActivate:` method and enter the following code snippet:

```
/*
 * This method is called when watch view controller is
 * about to be visible to user.
 */
override func willActivate() {
    super.willActivate()
    guessLabel.setText("Your Guess is: " +
String(Int(yourGuess)))
    guessLabel.setTextColor(UIColor.yellowColor())
}
```

As you can see from the preceding code snippet, we began by initializing our `guessLabel` Outlet to show the default value for our slider when our app is loaded and displayed within the Apple Watch area.

Now that we have successfully created our *Guessing Game* application, hooked up all of our controls to their respective Outlets, and created the necessary Actions, we can build and run our application within our Apple Watch area; this is covered in the next section.

Building and running the Guessing Game application

In this section, we will take a look at how to compile and run our application. You have the option of choosing to run your application on the watchOS device or within the simulators of Apple Watch.

The version number of the simulator is dependent on the version of the iOS SDK you install on your computer. In Xcode 4, whenever you open an existing Xcode project or create a new one, Xcode will automatically create a default scheme for you. Perform the following steps:

1. To run the app, select the **GuessingGame WatchKit App** scheme as shown in the following screenshot and then select your preferred device:

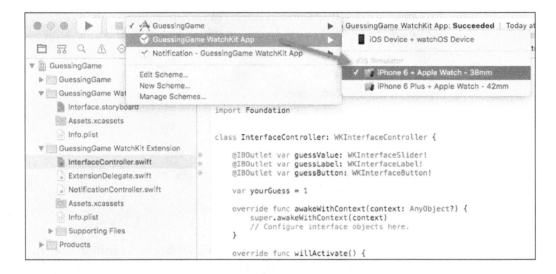

2. Next, build and run the application by going to **Product | Run** from the **Product** menu or alternatively by pressing *Command + R*.

When the compilation is complete, the WatchKit iOS simulator will appear automatically, and the *Guessing Game* application will be displayed, as shown in the following figure:

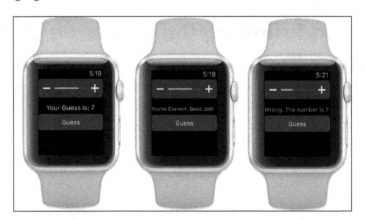

Simply use the **+** and **−** buttons to provide your guess and then click on the **Guess** button to check whether you guessed the same as what the computer was thinking. The preceding screenshot shows you the iterations of what happens when you correctly guess what the computer is thinking and what happens when you guess incorrectly.

 The screenshot is captured using a free developer tool for Apple Watch called **Bezel** by **InfinitApps**. This free developer tool allows developers to run their apps using the iOS simulator and then project the contents of Simulator's window to the Apple Watch simulator's watch window. Bezel can be downloaded for free from `http://infinitapps.com/bezel/`.

Summary

In this chapter, we introduced to some of the WatchKit user interface element controls that come packaged with the WatchKit platform. You learned how to work with Interface Builder and noted how easy it was to design our user interface for our *Guessing Game* application. You learned how to use and customize the `WKInterfaceSlider`, `WKInterfaceLabel`, and `WKInterfaceButton` control properties.

Next, you learned about Outlets and how we can connect and bind them up to control objects within the Interface Builder canvas. We then moved on to learning about creating Action events to our control elements that will be able to respond to user actions when tapped. In our final steps, we looked at how to write the code required for our *Guessing Game* application to respond to actions performed by the user and provide visual feedback to the user using the `WKInterfaceLabel` control.

In the next chapter, we will explore the WatchKit framework more and discuss the new layout system when placing controls within the WatchKit interface as well as how to handle different layouts for different watch screen sizes. You will also get accustomed to the MapKit and `WKInterfaceMap` frameworks to incorporate mapping capabilities within your iOS and WatchKit applications. Finally, you will learn how to use the Watch Connectivity framework in watchOS 2 to share location-based information between your iOS app and WatchKit in order to create annotation pin placeholders to show when the user's location changes directly on the Apple Watch map.

4
Using the Core Location and Watch Connectivity Frameworks

In this chapter, we will build a navigation tracking application for the iPhone and Apple Watch, leveraging both the Core Location and Watch Connectivity frameworks, so that you can share data between your iOS apps and the WatchKit extension.

While developing apps for Apple Watch, you will learn not only about the new layout controls, but also about how to customize these by interrogating their properties using the Attributes Inspector. You will become accustomed to the MapKit framework, which provides APIs to help developers integrate interactive mapping capabilities into their own applications. You will learn how to create annotation pin placeholders, and to represent these directly on the map.

Towards the end of the chapter, you will learn how to compile, build, and run the *Watch Tracker* application using your iPhone and Apple Watch to ensure that everything is working correctly.

This chapter includes the following topics:

- Building a *Watch Tracker* iPhone and WatchKit extension application
- Using MapKit and Core Location frameworks
- Using the Watch Connectivity framework
- Using the NSKeyedArchiver and NSKeyedUnarchiver classes

- Sending messages between an iOS app and the WatchKit extension
- Adding and removing annotation placeholders on the MapView
- Handling background location updates

We have an exciting project ahead of us, so let's get started.

Creating the navigation tracking application

In this section, we will take a look at how to design a user interface for our *Watch Tracker* application. We will begin by developing the WatchKit portion and the iOS app portion of our application.

Before proceeding, we need to create our `WatchTracker` project; this can be created easily using Xcode. Simply follow the steps listed here:

1. Launch Xcode from the `/Applications` folder.

2. Choose **Create a new Xcode project** or go to **File | New Project**:

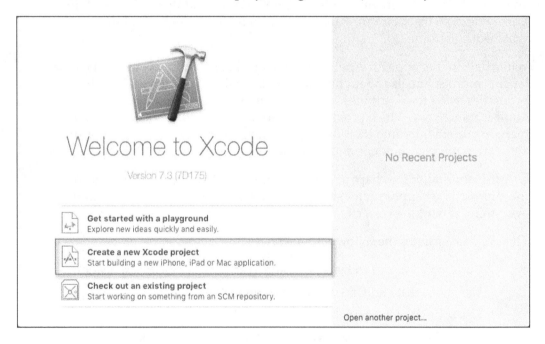

3. Select **iOS App with WatchKit App** from the list of available templates under the **watchOS** section, as shown in the following screenshot:

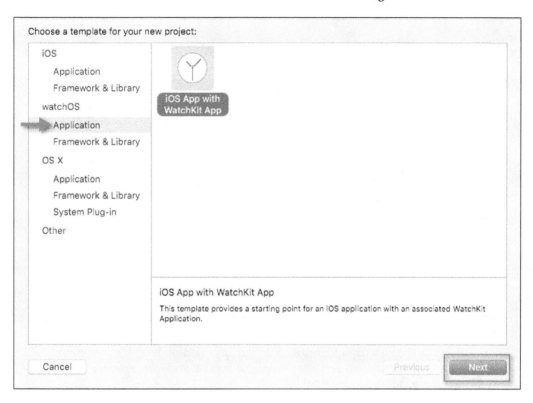

4. Click on the **Next** button to proceed to the next step in the wizard.
5. Next, enter `WatchTracker` as the name of your project.
6. Select **Swift** from the **Language** drop-down menu.
7. Select **iPhone** from the **Devices** drop-down menu.
8. Ensure that the **Include Notification Scene** checkbox has been selected.

9. Click on the **Next** button to proceed to the next step in the wizard:

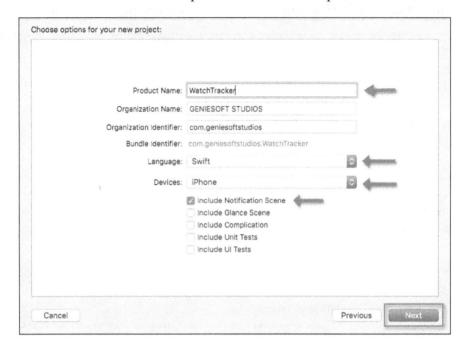

 The **Organization Identifier** for your app needs to be unique. Apple recommends that you use the reverse domain style (for example, com. domainName.appName).

10. Specify the location where you would like to save your project.

11. Then click on the **Create** button to save your project at the specified location.

Once your project has been created, you will be presented with the Xcode development environment, along with the project files that the template created for you.

Building the Watch Tracker application – iPhone

In this section, we will build the iOS portion of our *Watch Tracker* application. You will see how easy it is to use the Core Location framework to begin receiving location update information based on the user's current location.

We will then use the Core Location delegate callback methods to retrieve the user's latitude and longitude coordinates, and represent this information on the map using the MapKit framework:

1. Open the `ViewController.swift` file located within the **WatchTracker** group from the project navigation window, and enter the following code snippet:

```
//
//   ViewController.swift
//   WatchTracker_Starter iPhone App
//
//   Created by Steven F. Daniel on 20/09/2015.
//   Copyright © 2015 GENIESOFT STUDIOS. All rights reserved.
//
import UIKit
import MapKit
import CoreLocation

class ViewController: UIViewController, MKMapViewDelegate,
CLLocationManagerDelegate
{
    var mapView: MKMapView!
    var locationManager: CLLocationManager!
    var lastFoundLocation: CLLocation?

    override func viewDidLoad() {

        super.viewDidLoad()

        // Set up our location manager properties
        locationManager = CLLocationManager()
        locationManager.desiredAccuracy =
kCLLocationAccuracyKilometer
        locationManager.delegate = self

        // allowsBackgroundLocationUpdates is new in iOS 9,
        // perform a check so that it doesn't cause problems
        // on earlier versions of iOS
        switch
           UIDevice.currentDevice().systemVersion.compare("9.0.0",
           options: NSStringCompareOptions.NumericSearch) {
        case .OrderedSame, .OrderedDescending:
           locationManager.requestWhenInUseAuthorization()
```

```
                    locationManager.allowsBackgroundLocationUpdates = true
              case .OrderedAscending:
                 locationManager.requestLocation()
               }

              // Set up our MapView properties and delegate
              mapView = MKMapView(frame: view.bounds)
              mapView.delegate = self
              mapView.showsUserLocation = true
              mapView.zoomEnabled = true

           // Remove the annotations from our mapview
           addRemoveAnnotations(false)

           // Add the map to our View
           view.addSubview(mapView)
        }
```

As you can see from the preceding code snippet, we began by importing our MapKit and Core Location frameworks so that our app can start using it and begin receiving location updates. We then moved on to extend our class to include the class protocols for MKMapViewDelegate and CLLocationManagerDelegate in order to access the protocol's respective methods.

In the next step, we declared our class variables for mapView and locationManager, and created the lastFoundLocation variable to hold the user's last coordinates. We then instantiated the locationManager class, and set its delegate property to conform to the class protocol. Additionally, we set the desiredAccurracy property of the locationManager object to kCLLocationAccuracyKilometer, which specifies the location and heading information provided by the locationManager class.

> The kCLLocationAccuracyKilometer constant doesn't need the user to turn on the GPS or Wi-Fi to get their current location. Instead, it uses the location of the cell tower that the user is connected to. Setting this to anything higher will use a lot more power, and drain your iPhone's battery.

We then moved on to check the iOS version currently running on the user's device, and used the requestWhenInUseAuthorization method call on the locationManager class to request for the user's permission to obtain their current location.

In iOS 9, a new method called `allowsBackgroundLocationUpdates` was added to allow for handling background location updates. If the device is running a version older than iOS 9, we just make a call to the `requestLocation` method of the `locationManager` class to request access.

In our next step, we initialized our `mapView` object to an instance of our `MKMapView` class, and set the `mapView` delegate to point to the `MKMapView` class to begin accessing the class methods. We then specified that we wanted to show the user's location within the map by setting the `showUserLocation` to `true`. The user is allowed to zoom the map by setting the `ZoomEnabled` property to `true`.

Finally, we made a call to the `addRemoveAnnotations` method to remove the existing pin placeholders within our `mapView`, prior to adding our `mapView` object as a sub-view of the main view.

2. Open the `ViewController.swift` file located within the **WatchTracker** group in the project navigation window; locate the `viewWillAppear:` method and enter the following highlighted code snippet:

```
override func viewWillAppear(animated: Bool) {
    super.viewWillAppear(animated)
    locationManager.startUpdatingLocation()
}
```

As you can see from the preceding code snippet, when our `viewController` is about to be displayed on the device's screen, we call the `startUpdatingLocation` method on the `locationManager` object to obtain the user's current fixed location.

3. Then, locate the `viewWillDisappear:` method, and enter the following highlighted code snippet:

```
override func viewWillDisappear(animated: Bool) {
    super.viewWillDisappear(animated)
    locationManager.stopUpdatingLocation()
}
```

As you can see from the preceding code snippet, when our `viewController` is about to be displayed on the device's screen, we proceed to call the `stopUpdatingLocation` method on the `locationManager` object to stop receiving location-related events, and therefore, cease draining the phone's battery.

4. Next, after the `viewWillDisappear:` method, enter the following code snippet:

```
// ********************************************************
// MKMapViewDelegate
// ********************************************************

// Method is called when the user's location gets updated
func mapView(mapView: MKMapView, didUpdateUserLocation
userLocation: MKUserLocation) {
    var region = MKCoordinateRegion()

    // Centre to the user's current location
    region.center = userLocation.coordinate
    region.span = MKCoordinateSpanMake(0.1, 0.1)
    mapView.setRegion(region, animated:true)
}
```

As you can see from the preceding code snippet, the `MKMapView` delegate calls `didUpdateUserLocation` whenever the Core Location manager generates location events, and determines that there has been a change to the user's location. Within this method, we begin by declaring an instance of the `MKCoordinateRegion` class to create a 1 km area span, and then zoom in to the area allocated by the region using the `setRegion` method.

5. Next, after the `mapView:didUpdateUserLocation:` method, enter the following code snippet:

```
// Method is called to check if our location has changed
// since last time.
private func didLocationDistanceChange(updatedLocation:
CLLocation) -> Bool {
    guard let lastQueriedLocation = lastFoundLocation else {
        return true
    }
    let distance =
    lastQueriedLocation.distanceFromLocation(updatedLocation)
    return distance > 400
}
```

As you can see from the preceding code snippet, the `didLocationDistanceChange` method performs a comparison to see if the user's location that was queried last time is the same as their current location. This check basically ensures that if the location is the same, then the user hasn't moved, so it will exit this method. Alternatively, we use the `distanceFromLocation` method of the `CLLocation` class to calculate the distance in meters, and determine if the new location is more than 400 meters from the previous location before returning `true`.

6. Next, after the `didLocationDistanceChange` method, enter the following code snippet:

```
// Method is called to check if our location has changed
// since last time.
private func updateWatchTrackerLocation(location: CLLocation) {

    // Check to see if our distance has changed
    if didLocationDistanceChange(location) == false { return }

    // Store our current location for next time round.
    print("iPhone: Current location has been changed.")
    self.lastFoundLocation = location

    // Get our Coordinate for the location
    let coordinate = location.coordinate

    // Add the Pin Marker at each location
    addRemoveAnnotations(true, coordinate: coordinate)
    locationManager.allowDeferredLocationUpdatesUntilTraveled(400,
    timeout:60)
}
```

In the preceding code snippet, the `updateWatchTrackerLocation` method accepts a location, and then makes a call to the `didLocationDistanceChange` method to see if the user's location has changed significantly since the last time it was queried.

If the distance has changed, the `didLocationDistanceChange` returns `false`, and then the new location is stored in the `lastFoundLocation` variable. We then call the `addRemoveAnnotations` method, which will make use of the `MKPointAnnotation` class to create a new pin placeholder based on the geographic latitude and longitude values to our `mapView` control. The `allowDeferredLocationUpdatesUntilTraveled` method asks the location manager to defer the delivery of location updates until we have travelled the next 400 meters.

7. Next, enter the following code snippet below the `updateWatchTrackerLocation` method :

```
// ****************************************************
// CLLocationManagerDelegate
// ****************************************************
func locationManager(manager: CLLocationManager,
didChangeAuthorizationStatus status: CLAuthorizationStatus) {
    switch status
```

```
        {
            case .AuthorizedAlways:
                manager.requestAlwaysAuthorization()
            case .AuthorizedWhenInUse:
                manager.requestLocation()
            case .NotDetermined:
                manager.requestWhenInUseAuthorization()
            case .Restricted, .Denied:
                let title = "Location Services Disabled"
                let message = "Enable locations for this app via
                            the Settings app on your iPhone."
                let alertController = UIAlertController(title: title,
                    message: message, preferredStyle: .Alert)

                // Set up the action for our Cancel Button
                let cancelAction = UIAlertAction(title: "Cancel", style:
                    .Cancel, handler: nil)
                alertController.addAction(cancelAction)
                presentViewController(alertController, animated: true,
                completion: nil)
        }
    }
```

In the preceding code snippet, whenever the `CLLocationManager` delegate detects a change in the authorization status, you will be notified about those changes. To handle any changes in the authorization status while your app is running, and to prevent your application from crashing unexpectedly, you will need to ensure that the proper authorization is handled accordingly.

If we detect that the user has restricted or denied access to location services on the device, we will need to alert the user to this, and display an alert dialog popup. The following table shows each of the valid authorization status codes and their descriptions, as returned by the `didChangeAuthorizationStatus` method:

Authorization Status	Description
`.AuthorizedAlways` or `.AuthorizedWhenInUse`	Either of these cases can occur whenever the user has granted access to your app to use location services. These statuses are both mutually exclusive, as you can only receive one type of authorization at a time.

Authorization Status	Description
`.NotDetermined`	This generally happens whenever the user hasn't made a choice regarding your iOS app to begin accepting location updates, and can be caused if the user has installed your app for the first time and has not run it yet.
`.Restricted` or `.Denied`	You will generally receive this type of authorization status state whenever the user has explicitly denied access to the use of location services for your app, or when location services are currently unavailable.

For more information on the `CLLocationManager` class, refer to the Apple Developer Documentation located at `https://developer.apple.com/library/ios/documentation/CoreLocation/Reference/CLLocationManager_Class/`.

8. After the `didChangeAuthorizationStatus:` method, enter the following code snippet:

```
// Method is called when updates will no longer be deferred.
func locationManager(manager: CLLocationManager,
  didFinishDeferredUpdatesWithError error: NSError?) {
  if error?.code == CLError.DeferredFailed.rawValue { return }
  print("didFinishDeferredUpdatesWithError: \(error)")
}
```

As you can see from the preceding code snippet, the `CLLocationManager` delegate calls the `didFinishDeferredUpdatesWithError` method whenever the Core Location manager generates location events, and determines that there has been a request to defer location updates for a period of time.

9. Next, after the `didFinishDeferredUpdatesWithError:` method, enter the following code snippet:

```
// Method is called when we have received an updated user location
func locationManager(manager: CLLocationManager,
    didUpdateLocations locations: [CLLocation]) {
    guard let mostRecentLocation = locations.last else { return }
    updateWatchTrackerLocation(mostRecentLocation)
}
```

In the preceding code snippet, the CLLocationManager delegate calls the didUpdateLocations method whenever the Core Location manager generates location events, and determines that there has been a change to the user's current location. Once we have obtained the user's last known location, we then assign the coordinates to our mostRecentLocation variable, and then call our updateWatchTrackerLocation method.

10. Next, after the didUpdateLocations: method, enter the following code snippet:

```
// Method is called whenever we have encountered an issue with
// getting location information
func locationManager(manager: CLLocationManager, didFailWithError
    error: NSError) {
  if error.code == CLError.LocationUnknown.rawValue { return }
  print("Failed to get a valid location: \(error)")
}
```

The didFailWithError class gets called whenever it has been determined that the use of location services is unavailable, or when we are unable to retrieve a location straight away. Next, we use the error property to determine the type of error that occurred, and then call the stopUpdatingLocation method of the locationManager object.

The following table shows each of the valid error codes and their descriptions, as returned by the didFailWithError method:

Core Location error code	Description
kCLErrorLocationUnknown	This error tells you that the location manager was unable to obtain a location at the moment.
kCLErrorDenied	This error lets you know that the user denied access to the location service.
kCLErrorNetwork	This implies that the network was unavailable, or that a network error occurred.
kCLErrorHeadingFailure	This error states that the heading location travelled could not be determined.
kCLErrorRegionMonitoringDenied	This error means that the user denied access to the region monitoring service.

Core Location error code	Description
kCLErrorRegionMonitoringFailure	This error tells you that a registered region could not be monitored.
kCLErrorRegionMonitoringSetupDelayed	This error informs you that Core Location could not initialize the region monitoring service immediately.

> For more information on the didFailWithError error codes of the CLLocationManager class, refer to the Apple Developer Documentation at https://developer.apple.com/ library/ios/documentation/CoreLocation/Reference/ CLLocationManagerDelegate_Protocol/index.html#// apple_ref/occ/intfm/CLLocationManagerDelegate.

In the next section, you will learn how to use the MKPointAnnotation class for adding placeholder markers to our MKMapKit map control.

Adding and removing annotation placeholders

In our app, we would like to place a drop pin to show that the location has changed whenever the location changes. For that, we will add the following code:

```
// Method to add/remove annotations from the MapView
func addRemoveAnnotations(isAdding: Bool, coordinate:
CLLocationCoordinate2D? = nil) {
    if isAdding == false
    {
        // Get an array of all annotations currently present on
        // the map and remove them.
        let allAnnotations = self.mapView.annotations
        if allAnnotations.count > 0 {
            self.mapView.removeAnnotations(allAnnotations)
        }
    }
    else {
        // Add the Pin marker at each location
        let annotation = MKPointAnnotation()
        annotation.coordinate = coordinate!
        self.mapView.addAnnotation(annotation)
    }
}
```

In the preceding code snippet, we begin by checking the isAdding variable to see if we are adding or removing annotations from our MapView. If we are removing annotations, we gather an array of all the annotations that are currently present on the map, determine the number of items by using the count property, and then call the removeAnnotations method of our mapView control, before passing in our allAnnotations array.

Alternatively, if we are adding new pin placeholders to our mapView control, we create an instance of our MKPointAnnotation class, and then assign our location coordinates to our annotation object, prior to passing the geographic location coordinate to our addAnnotation method of our MKMapKit class.

For more information on the MKPointAnnotation class, refer to the Apple Developer Documentation located at https://developer. apple.com/library/prerelease/ios/documentation/MapKit/ Reference/MKPointAnnotation_class/index.html.

In the next section, we will learn how to provide our iOS app the functionality to perform continuous location updates in the background.

Handling requests for background location updates

When working with background location updates to continuously monitor changes to the user location, we will need this functionality to coordinate between the iPhone app and the WatchKit extension; this is due to the fact that watchOS 2 does not support this additional functionality.

Our next step is to provide our app with the ability to monitor location updates in the background:

1. To enable **Background Modes** and select **Location updates**, select the switch for the **Background Modes** option so that Xcode can provision your app to monitor location-based updates in the background.

2. Select the **Location updates** checkbox:

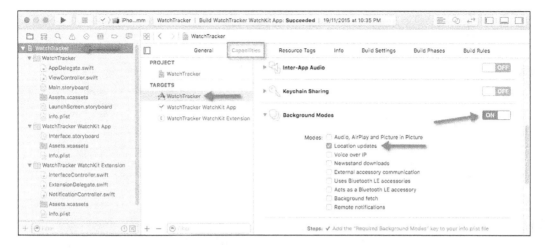

Next, we need to configure our *Watch Tracker* iOS app so that it is able to gain access to location information. The `requestAlwaysAuthorization` method call requires a specific key-value pair to be added to the information property list dictionary.

This dictionary object is contained within the iOS app's `Info.plist` file, and takes the form of a string description, which describes the reason why the application needs to access the user's current location. If you requesting background access to the location information, the `NSLocationAlwaysUsageDescription` key must be added to the property list. The `NSLocationWhenInUseUsageDescription` key already exists, and is required if you don't want to allow location updates to be monitored within the background.

3. Open the `Info.plist` file located within the **WatchTracker** group in the project navigation window.

4. Select the **Information Property List** dictionary within the list.

5. Click on the **+** button to add a new entry to the dictionary.

6. Enter `NSLocationAlwaysUsageDescription` for the **Information Property List** details.

7. Then enter `WatchTracker uses your location to determine your present location.` for the **Value** property.

8. Select the **Information Property List** dictionary within the list.

9. Next, click on the **+** button to add a new entry to the dictionary.

10. Enter in `NSLocationWhenInUseUsageDescription` for the **Information Property List** details.

11. Now +enter `WatchTracker uses your location to determine your present location.` for the **Value** property:

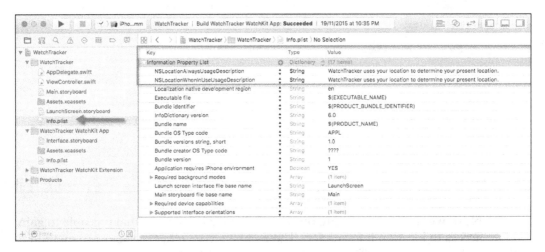

Building and running the Watch Tracker application

In this section, we will take a look at how to compile and run our application. You have the option of running your application on the watchOS device or within the simulators for Apple Watch.

The version number of the simulator is dependent on the version of the iOS SDK that you have installed on your computer. In Xcode 4, whenever you open an existing Xcode project, or create a new one, Xcode will automatically create a default scheme for you.

1. To run the app, select the **WatchTracker** scheme as shown in the following screenshot, and choose your preferred device:

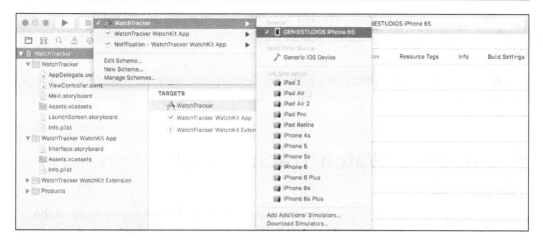

2. Next, build and run the application by selecting **Product | Run** from the **Product** menu, or alternatively, by pressing *Command + R*.

When the compilation completes, the *Watch Tracker* iOS app will be installed on your iOS device, and you will see the following screenshot the first time the application is launched:

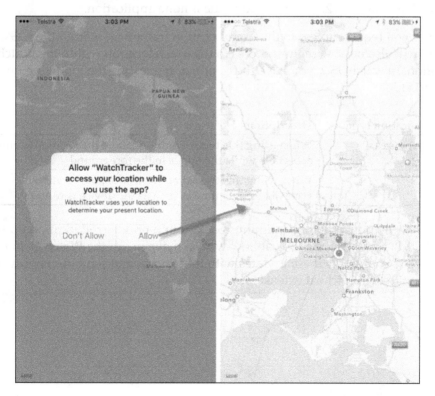

Now that we have successfully created the iPhone portion of our *Watch Tracker* application, you can see how easy it is to create an app that utilizes both the Core Location and MapKit frameworks.

Our next step will be to build the WatchKit counterpart's user interface, and build the functionality that will allow our *Watch Tracker* iPhone app to communicate with the WatchKit extension.

Building the Watch Tracker application – WatchKit

In this section, we will build the user interface as well as the associated code of the WatchTracker WatchKit extension for our *Watch Tracker* application.

Limitations of using Core Location within watchOS 2

Before proceeding with adding location services to the *Watch Tracker* application, it is very important to address some limitations that are part of the Core Location framework in watchOS 2, as compared to the iPhone application.

Whenever you request access to the Core Location framework within the iOS app, you will also need to request access to the user's location within the Watch application. In watchOS 2, you have the option of requesting the following types of authorization:

Core Location type	Description
When in use	When using this type of authorization, the location is only accessible while the app is in the foreground.
Always	When using this type of authorization, the location is accessible at any time as long as the device is running.

Since there is no potential for continuous background or deferred location updates in watchOS 2, we will take a look at how we can make use of the Watch Connectivity framework to coordinate these updates with the iPhone, and send our coordinate information to the WatchKit extension.

Using Interface Builder to create the Watch Tracker UI

Our next step is to design the user interface for our *Watch Tracker* app's UI using Interface Builder. If you remember, in the last chapter, we explained a little bit about Interface Builder, and how it is a visual tool that is integrated within the Xcode development IDE that helps you design user interfaces for iOS and watchOS applications. The steps for designing the UI are as follows:

1. Select the **Interface.storyboard** file from the project navigation window.

2. From the Object Library, drag a WKInterfaceMap control to the watch area canvas:

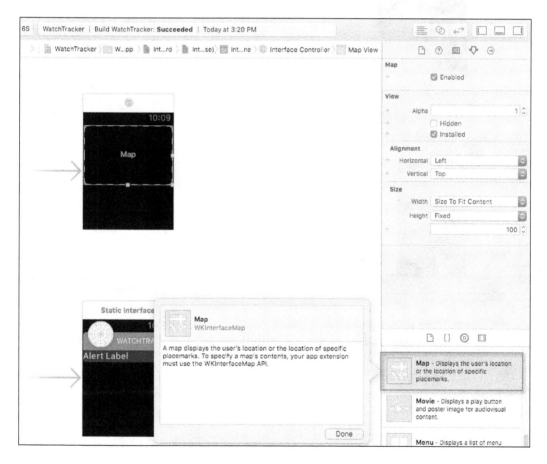

3. Next, from the Object Library, drag a `WKInterfaceGroup` control to the watch area canvas, and place this under the `WKInterfaceMap` control that we added previously:

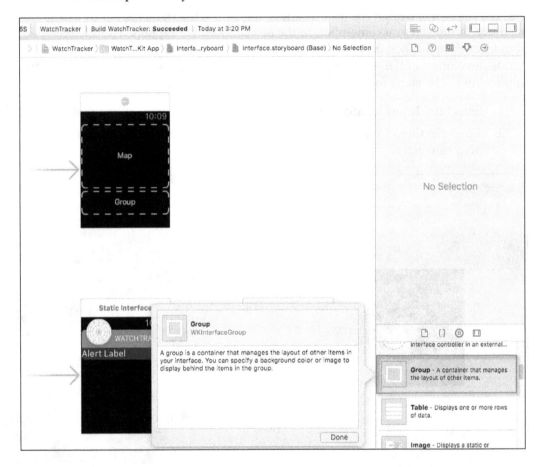

4. Then, from the Object Library, drag a `WKInterfaceLabel` control to the watch area canvas, and place this within the `WKInterfaceGroup` control that we added previously.

5. Next, in the Attributes Inspector section, in the **Text** property, enter `Adjust map zooming`:

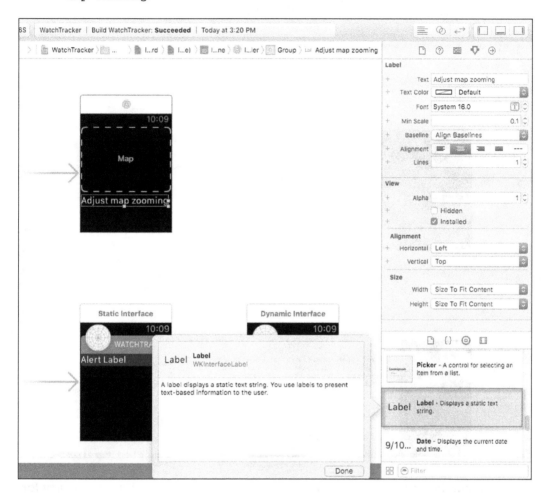

6. From the Object Library, drag a `WkInterfaceSlider` control to the watch area canvas, and place this under the **Adjust map zooming** (`WKInterfaceLabel`) control that we added previously:

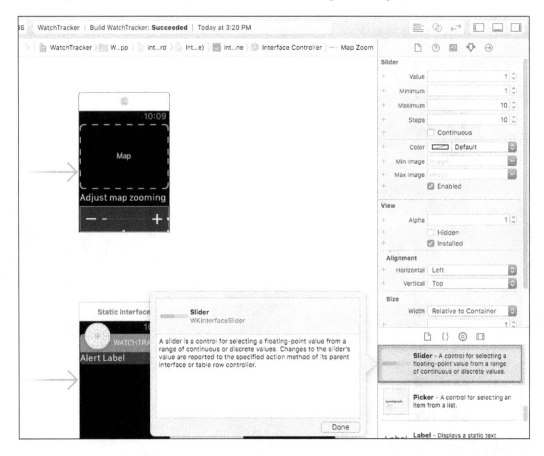

7. From the Attributes Inspector section, change the starting **Value** property for our slider control to **1**.

8. Next, we need to set the **Minimum** property of our slider control to **1** so that it doesn't exceed the minimum set amount.

9. Then, we need to change the **Maximum** value property for our slider control to **10** so that we don't exceed the limit.

10. Lastly, we need to set the **Steps** property for our slider control to **10** increments (as dashes) when we press the **+** and **–** buttons.

Creating the Outlets for our Interface Builder objects

In the previous section, we looked at how to add controls to our `Interface.storyboard` canvas for constructing the user interface for our *Watch Tracker* app, and set some properties for each of our controls.

Our next step is to create the necessary Outlets for each of our controls — we will need to access these, through our code, to handle the displaying of information within our `WKInterfaceMap` control, as well as to provide the ability to handle zooming in and out of our map by using the `WKInterfaceSlider` control:

1. Open the Assistant Editor window by selecting **Navigate | Open in Assistant Editor**, or by pressing *Option + Command + ,.*

2. Select the `WKInterfaceMap` control, then hold down the *Control* key, and drag it into the `InterfaceController.swift` file within the body of the `InterfaceController: WKInterfaceController` class.

3. Choose **Outlet** from the **Connection** drop-down menu for the type of connection to be created, and enter `mapView` for the name of the Outlet property.

4. Next, choose **Weak** from the **Storage** drop-down menu, and click on the **Connect** button:

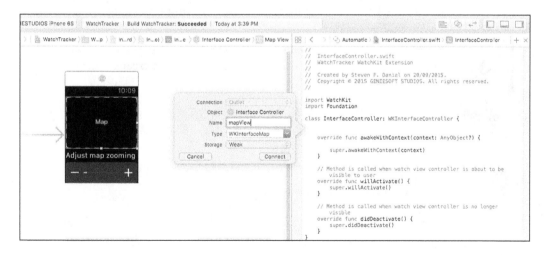

5. Next, select the `WKInterfaceSlider` control, then hold down the *Control* key and drag it into the `InterfaceController.swift` file, as we did for our `mapView` Outlet.

6. Then, choose **Outlet** from the **Connection** drop-down menu for the type of connection to be created, and enter `mapZoom` for the name of the Outlet property.

7. Now select **Weak** from the **Storage** drop-down menu, and click on the **Connect** button:

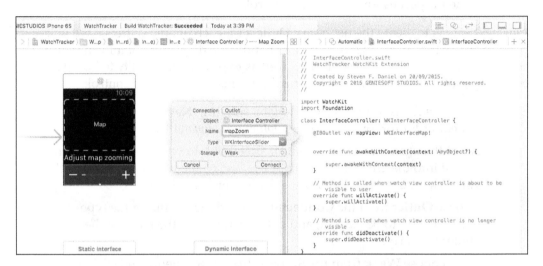

8. Once you have created the necessary Outlets, you should save your project by selecting **File | Save**, or alternatively, by pressing *Command + S*.

 Whenever you create an Outlet, you must remember to create it within the `InterfaceController` class, as these cannot be created outside this class body.

The following code snippet shows the complete implementation of the Outlets that we created in the previous steps:

```
//
//  InterfaceController.swift
//  WatchTracker WatchKit Extension
//
//  Created by Steven F. Daniel on 20/09/2015.
//  Copyright © 2015 GENIESOFT STUDIOS. All rights reserved.
//
```

```
import WatchKit
import Foundation

class InterfaceController: WKInterfaceController {

    @IBOutlet var mapView: WKInterfaceMap!
    @IBOutlet var mapZoom: WKInterfaceSlider!
```

As you can see from the preceding code snippet, Interface Builder has created each of our control objects, as well as the associated type of control that we have used. In our next section, we will create an Action event that will respond when we change the value of our WKInterfaceSlider control.

Creating an Action event to handle our map zooming

In the previous section, you learned how to add controls to our Interface. storyboard canvas to construct our user interface for the *Watch Tracker* app, and to connect each of the necessary Outlets for our controls.

In this section, we will look at how to communicate with the mapZoom Outlet when the slider values change:

1. Open the Assistant Editor window by selecting **Navigate | Open in Assistant Editor**, or by pressing *Option + Command + ,*.

2. Ensure that the InterfaceController.swift file is displayed within the Assistant Editor window.

3. Then, select the WKInterfaceSlider control, hold down the *Control* key, and drag it into the InterfaceController.swift file, below the didDeactivate method.

4. Choose **Action** from the **Connection** drop-down menu for the type of connection to be created, and enter `handleMapZooming` as the name of the Action:

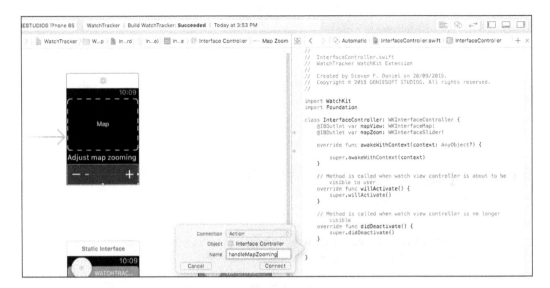

Now that we have added the zoom slider to our WatchKit application, we need to implement the ability to zoom in and out of our map. This zooming effect will be applied to the map by enlarging and reducing the currently displayed region.

Open the `InterfaceController.swift` file located within the **WatchTracker WatchKit Extension** group in the project navigation window, and locate the `handleMapZooming:` method; now enter the following code snippet:

```
// Method is called when the slider value changes.
@IBAction func handleMapZooming(value: Float) {
    let degrees  : CLLocationDegrees = CLLocationDegrees(value) / 10
    let span = MKCoordinateSpanMake(degrees, degrees)
    let region =
    MKCoordinateRegionMake((lastFoundLocation?.coordinate)!, span)
    mapView.setRegion(region)
}
```

In the preceding code snippet, we declare a variable called `degrees` that will be responsible for holding the value chosen from our `WKInterfaceSlider` control. We then divide this by the number of steps that we defined within the Attributes Inspector designer for the `WKInterfaceSlider` control. Finally, we apply the calculated region to our `WKInterfaceMap` using the `setRegion` method of the `mapView` control.

Using Core Location with the WatchKit extension

In this section, we will hook up the `WatchTracker` WatchKit extension to the Core Location framework just like we did in the *Watch Tracker* iPhone app, so that we can begin receiving location update information that is based on the user's current location.

We will also need to use the Core Location delegate callback methods for receiving the user's latitude and longitude coordinates in order to represent this information on the map, using the MapKit framework:

1. Open the `InterfaceController.swift` file located within the **WatchTracker WatchKit Extension** group in the project navigation window, and enter the following highlighted code snippet:

```
import CoreLocation

class InterfaceController: WKInterfaceController,
CLLocationManagerDelegate {

    @IBOutlet var mapView: WKInterfaceMap!
    @IBOutlet var mapZoom: WKInterfaceSlider!

    // Instantiate our location Manager class
    private let locationManager = CLLocationManager()
    private var lastFoundLocation: CLLocation?

    override func awakeWithContext(context: AnyObject?) {
        super.awakeWithContext(context)

        // Remove all annotations on our mapview
        self.mapView.removeAllAnnotations()

        // Initialize our location Manager class
        locationManager.desiredAccuracy =
kCLLocationAccuracyKilometer
        locationManager.delegate = self
    }
```

The preceding code snippet begins by importing our Core Location framework so that our WatchKit extension can start receiving location updates. Next, we extend our class to include the class protocol for our `CLLocationManagerDelegate` in order to access the protocol's respective methods. We then declare the class variables for our `locationManager`, and begin creating an instance of it that will inherit from the `CLLocationManager` class. Afterwards, we create a variable, `lastFoundLocation`, just as we did previously for our iPhone app, to hold the user's last found coordinates.

Next, we set the `desiredAccuracy` property of the `locationManager` as we did for our iPhone app. This is required for specifying the location and heading information provided by the `locationManager` class. Finally, we set the delegate for the `locationManager` object, and tell it that our current class will be responsible for handling the callback methods.

2. Next, open the `InterfaceController.swift` file located within the **WatchTracker WatchKit Extension** group in the project navigation window, locate the `willActivate:` method, and enter the following highlighted code snippet:

```
// Method is called when watch view controller is about
// to be visible to user
override func willActivate() {
    super.willActivate()

    // Then ask location manager to give you an updated location.
    // If the new location is significantly different,
    // you'll dispatch another request.
    let authorizationStatus = CLLocationManager.
authorizationStatus()
    handleLocationServicesAuthorizationStatus(authorizationStatus)

    // Query to see if we have a valid last known location which
    // we set by the session (_:, didReceiveApplicationContext:)
    // method in our iPhone section of the WCSessionDelegate
    if let lastUpdatedLocation = lastFoundLocation {
        queryWatchTrackerForLocation(lastUpdatedLocation)
    }
}
```

In the preceding code snippet, we perform a check to determine if our location manager has authorized our Watch app to perform location updates, and assign the status code to our `authorizationStatus` variable.

Next, we make a call to our `handleLocationServicesAuthorizationStatus` method, passing in the authorization code to determine if our WatchKit extension has already requested access to location services with the paired iPhone. We then perform a check to see if our location has changed since the last time we queried our location, prior to calling the `queryWatchTrackerForLocation` method.

3. Open the `InterfaceController.swift` file located within the **WatchTracker WatchKit Extension** group in the project navigation window, and enter the following code snippet:

```
// Method is called to check if we can access our
// location services
func handleLocationServicesAuthorizationStatus
    (status:CLAuthorizationStatus)
{
    switch status {
        case .NotDetermined:
            locationManager.requestAlwaysAuthorization()
        case .Restricted, .Denied:
            print("Locations Disabled\n\nEnable locations for this
            app via the Settings in your iPhone.")
        case .AuthorizedAlways, .AuthorizedWhenInUse:
            locationManager.requestLocation()
    }
}
```

The `locationManager` object will try to make a request to get the user's location whenever the `CLLocationManager` delegate detects a change in the authorization status, or if the user has turned off location-based services (to avoid your application from crashing). If any issues are detected, the `.Restricted` or `.Denied` case statements will be executed, which will prevent your application from crashing.

4. Next, open the `InterfaceController.swift` file located within the **WatchTracker WatchKit Extension** group in the project navigation window, and enter the following code snippet:

```
// Method is called to check if our location has changed
// since last time.
func didLocationDistanceChange(updatedLocation: CLLocation) ->
Bool {
    guard let lastUpdatedLocation = lastFoundLocation else { return
        true }
    let distance =
    lastUpdatedLocation.distanceFromLocation(updatedLocation)
    return distance > 400
}
```

In the preceding code snippet, the `didLocationDistanceChange` method performs a comparison to check if the location that was queried last time is the same as the current location, that is, to see if we have actually moved. If we haven't, it will exit this method. Alternatively, we use the `distanceFromLocation` method of the `CLLocation` class to calculate the distance in meters to determine if the new location is more than 400 meters from the previous location, and then return `true`.

5. Open the `InterfaceController.swift` file located within the **WatchTracker WatchKit Extension** group in the project navigation window, and enter the following code snippet:

```
// Method is called to check if our location has changed
// since last time.
private func queryWatchTrackerForLocation(location: CLLocation) {
    // Check to see if our distance has changed
    if didLocationDistanceChange(location) == false { return }

    // Store our current location for next time round.
    print("WatchKit: Current location has been changed.")
    lastFoundLocation = location

    // Get our Coordinate for the location
    let coordinate = location.coordinate
    mapView.addAnnotation(coordinate, withPinColor:
    WKInterfaceMapPinColor.Red)
}
```

In the preceding code snippet, we call the `didLocationDistanceChange` method to see if our current location has changed significantly since the last one that was queried. If our method has determined that our location has changed, it will return `true`. We store the new determined location to our `lastFoundLocation` variable, create a pin placeholder based on the geographic latitude and longitude values, and then add this to our `mapView` control.

6. Open the `InterfaceController.swift` file located within the **WatchTracker WatchKit Extension** group in the project navigation window, and enter the following code snippet:

```
// CLLocationManagerDelegate method: invoked when a new
// location arrives
func locationManager(manager: CLLocationManager,
didUpdateLocations locations: [CLLocation]) {
    // Get our current location that has been determined
```

```
print("Did update Locations: \(locations)")
guard let mostRecentLocation = locations.last else { return }
queryWatchTrackerForLocation(mostRecentLocation)
}
```

In the preceding code snippet, the `CLLocationManager` delegate calls the `didUpdateLocations` method whenever the location manager generates location event information to determine if the user's location has changed. Upon receiving these new geographical coordinates, we assign this to our `mostRecentLocation` variable, call the `queryWatchTrackerForLocation` method, and pass the new coordinates.

7. Next, open the `InterfaceController.swift` file located within the **WatchTracker WatchKit Extension** group in the project navigation window, and enter the following code snippet:

```
func locationManager(manager: CLLocationManager, didFailWithError
error: NSError) {
    if error.code == CLError.LocationUnknown.rawValue { return }
    print("Failed to get a valid location: \(error)")
}
```

The `didFailWithError` method will always be called if it has determined that the use of location services is unavailable, or if, for any reason whatsoever, it is unable to retrieve a location straight away. We use the `error` property to determine the type of error that occurred, and if this is rendered as `LocationUnknown`, we exit from the method. Alternatively, if any other error occurs, it will be printed out to the console.

Communicating between the iPhone app and the WatchTracker WatchKit extension

In order to make communication between the WatchKit extension and the iPhone app effective, we need to leverage and make use of the Watch Connectivity framework so that we can send messages between them using the `WCSession` class. Once a session has been established successfully on both devices, only then will you be able to pass information back and forth.

Integrating the Watch Connectivity framework – iPhone app

In this section, we will take a look at what is required for successful communication between the paired iOS device and the WatchKit extension for sending geographical location-based updates from the Core Location manager in the background:

1. Open the `ViewController.swift` file located within the **WatchTracker** group in the project navigation window, and enter the following highlighted code sections:

```
import CoreLocation
import WatchConnectivity

class ViewController: UIViewController, MKMapViewDelegate,
WCSessionDelegate, CLLocationManagerDelegate {

    var mapView: MKMapView!
    var locationManager: CLLocationManager!
    var session: WCSession?
    var lastFoundLocation: CLLocation?

    override func viewDidLoad() {
        super.viewDidLoad()

        // Start our WatchConnectivity Session
        startWatchKitSession()
```

In the preceding modified code snippet, we start by importing our Watch Connectivity framework, and then include the `WCSessionDelegate` class protocol method to begin accessing the protocol's respective method callbacks.

In our next step, we declare a session object that conforms to the `WCSession` class, which is used to facilitate communication between our iOS app and our WatchKit extension. Finally, we call the `startWatchKitSession` method, which will be used to instantiate the `session` object to begin the communication between our iOS app and the WatchKit extension.

2. Open the `ViewController.swift` file located within the **WatchTracker** group in the project navigation window, and enter the following code snippet:

```
// ****************************************************
// WCSessionDelegate
// ****************************************************
```

```
private func startWatchKitSession() {
    if (WCSession.isSupported()) {
        session = WCSession.defaultSession()
        session?.delegate = self
        session?.activateSession()
    }
}
```

In the `startWatchKitSession` method, we perform a check to see if our iOS device can support the Watch Connectivity framework session objects in order to facilitate communication between the WatchKit extension and our iOS app. Next, we create and configure an instance of the `WCSession` class, and set the Watch Connectivity `delegate` object to conform to our class. We then activate the `session` object on our iOS device to immediately send messages back and forth between the iOS device and the WatchKit extension. When only one session is active, the active session may still send updates and transfer files, but those transfers will end up happening within the background.

3. Open the `ViewController.swift` file located within the **WatchTracker** group in the project navigation window, and enter the following code snippet:

```
func updateSessionLocationDetails(location: CLLocation) {
    guard let session = session else { return }
    print("iPhone: Set application context: (applicationContext)")
    let data = NSKeyedArchiver.archivedDataWithRootObject(location)
    let context = ["lastFoundLocation": data]
    do {
        try session.updateApplicationContext(context)
    } catch {
        print("Update application context failed.")
    }
}
```

The `updateSessionLocationDetails` method accepts a `CLLocation` object containing the current location coordinates, and then performs a check to ensure that we have a valid `session` object before proceeding. Next, we use the `NSKeyedArchiver` subclass to encode our location coordinates, using the `archivedDataWithRootObject` method, to create a `data` object. We declare a `context` dictionary object, which will store our location data. Then we update the `session` object's application context to send the dictionary `context` value to the WatchKit extension.

For more information on the NSKeyedArchiver class, refer to the Apple Developer documentation at https://developer.apple.com/library/prerelease/ios/documentation/Cocoa/Reference/Foundation/Classes/NSKeyedArchiver_Class/index.html#//apple_ref/occ/clm/NSKeyedArchiver/archivedDataWithRootObject.

4. Open the ViewController.swift file located within the **WatchTracker** group from the project navigation window, and enter the following highlighted code sections:

```
// Method is called when we have received an updated user location
func locationManager(manager: CLLocationManager,
didUpdateLocations locations: [CLLocation]) {
    guard let mostRecentLocation = locations.last else { return }
    updateSessionLocationDetails(mostRecentLocation)
    updateWatchTrackerLocation(mostRecentLocation)
}
```

The didUpdateLocations method will be called whenever the CLLocationManager determines that the user's location has changed since the last time. We need to modify this method and include an additional line, updateSessionLocationDetails, which will pass the location coordinates for our session object, and pass this onto our WatchKit extension so that this is reflected on the WatchKit extension's mapView control.

Integrating the Watch Connectivity framework – WatchKit extension

Now that we have successfully integrated the Watch Connectivity framework into our *Watch Tracker* iOS app, we need to apply the same logic to our WatchKit extension so that it is able to receive the location information for displaying it within our WKInterfaceMap mapView object.

1. Open the InterfaceController.swift file located within the **WatchTracker WatchKit Extension** group from the project navigation window, and enter the following highlighted code sections:

```
import CoreLocation
import WatchConnectivity

class InterfaceController: WKInterfaceController,
WCSessionDelegate, CLLocationManagerDelegate {
```

```
@IBOutlet var mapView: WKInterfaceMap!
@IBOutlet var mapZoom: WKInterfaceSlider!

// Instantiate our location Manager class
private let locationManager = CLLocationManager()
private var session: WCSession?
private var lastFoundLocation: CLLocation?

override func awakeWithContext(context: AnyObject?) {

    super.awakeWithContext(context)

    // Start the WatchKit Connectivity Session
    startWatchKitSession()

    // Remove all annotations on our mapview
    self.mapView.removeAllAnnotations()

    // Initialize our location Manager class
    locationManager.desiredAccuracy =
kCLLocationAccuracyKilometer
    locationManager.delegate = self
}
```

In the preceding modified code snippet, we start by importing the Watch Connectivity framework. We then include the `WCSessionDelegate` class protocol method to begin accessing the protocol's respective method callbacks. Next we declare a `session` object that conforms to the `WCSession` class so that we are able to receive communication between our WatchKit extension and our iOS app.

In our next step, we make a call to the `startWatchKitSession` method, which will be used to instantiate the `session` object to begin accepting communication requests between our WatchKit extension and the iOS app.

2. Open the `InterfaceController.swift` file located within the **WatchTracker WatchKit Extension** group in the project navigation window, and enter the following code snippet:

```
// ****************************************************
// WCSessionDelegate
// ****************************************************
private func startWatchKitSession() {
    if (WCSession.isSupported()) {
        session = WCSession.defaultSession()
        session?.delegate = self
        session?.activateSession()
    }
}
```

As you can see, within our `startWatchKitSession` method, we begin by checking to see if our WatchKit extension is capable of accepting sessions; this is determined by the `WCSession` class. Next, we create and configure an instance of our `WCSession` class, and set the `delegate` object for our current session before activating the `session` object for our WatchKit extension to begin receiving message information from our iOS device.

3. Open the `InterfaceController.swift` file located within the **WatchTracker WatchKit Extension** group in the project navigation window, and enter the following code snippet:

```
func session(session: WCSession, didReceiveApplicationContext
    applicationContext: [String : AnyObject]) {
    print("WatchKit: Received application context:
    (applicationContext)")
    guard let data = applicationContext["lastFoundLocation"] as?
    NSData else { return }
    guard let location =
    NSKeyedUnarchiver.unarchiveObjectWithData(data) as?
CLLocation
    else { return }
    queryWatchTrackerForLocation(location)
}
```

The `didReceiveApplicationContext` method accepts an object which is sent from the iOS app to the WatchKit extension. Once messages have been received from the paired iOS device, we then proceed to retrieve the location data for the active session from the application context dictionary.

In order to retrieve this, we need to use the `NSKeyedArchiver` subclass to decode our location coordinates using the `unarchiveObjectWithData` method, and then convert this into a `CLLocation` object that will contain the coordinates for the current location.

 For more information on the `NSKeyedUnArchiver` class, refer to the Apple Developer documentation at `https://developer.apple.com/library/ios/documentation/Cocoa/Reference/Foundation/Classes/NSKeyedUnarchiver_Class/`.

Building and running the Watch Tracker application

In this section, we will look at how to compile and run our application. You have the option of choosing to run your application on the watchOS device, or within the simulators for Apple Watch:

1. To run the app, select the **WatchTracker WatchKit App** scheme and choose your preferred device, as shown in the following screenshot:

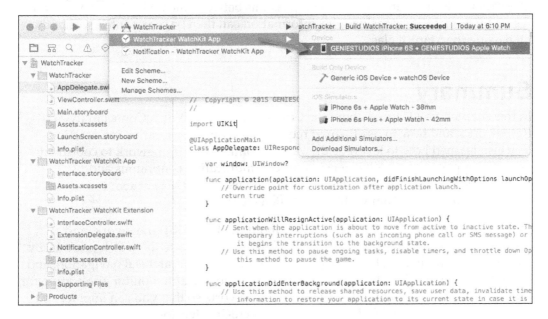

2. Next, build and run the application by selecting **Product | Run** from the **Product** menu, or alternatively, by pressing *Command + R*:

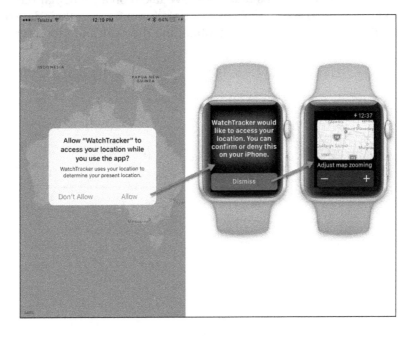

As you can see from the previous screenshot, by using the Core Location framework and leveraging the Watch Connectivity framework, it becomes very easy to access geographical location information and pass this between the iOS paired device and the Apple WatchKit extension. This information can then be represented within the map using the MapKit class.

Summary

In this chapter, you learned about the Core Location and Watch Connectivity frameworks, and how to use them to request and authorize location information. You also learned how to leverage the Watch Connectivity framework to coordinate your iOS app and WatchKit extension for communicating continuous and background updates. We also discussed how to use the `WKInterfaceSlider` control to adjust and zoom within our WatchKit map.

In the next chapter, we will explore more about the WatchKit framework, and introduce you to some of the ways in which you can navigate the watch face's UI by learning the difference between page-based, modal and hierarchical navigation, and when to use them. We will also explain how to build a health monitor application for the Apple Watch leveraging the HealthKit framework, so that you can interact and share data between the iOS device and the WatchKit extension.

In the next chapter, you'll learn how to access health data to read a person's heart-rate and the number of steps that they have taken on a particular day. You will also learn how to access their profile data for extracting their date of birth and calculating their age along with obtaining their sex and blood type.

5
Navigating Around in WatchKit

We will begin this chapter by building a *Health Monitor* application for the Apple Watch, leveraging the HealthKit framework so that you can interact and share data between the iOS device and the WatchKit extension. You will also learn about the various modes of navigation that are available within the WatchKit platform when interacting between interface controllers. We will explain how to use the HealthKit framework to access health data in order to do the following:

- Read a person's heart rate
- Count the number of steps that the person takes on a particular day
- Access the user's profile data to extract their date of birth for calculating their age as well as their sex and blood type

To end the chapter, we will compile, build, and run the *Health Monitor* application and install this on the Apple Watch so that you can test the app and ensure that everything is working correctly.

This chapter includes the following topics:

- Building a *Health Monitor* WatchKit extension application
- Provisioning your app so that it can use HealthKit
- Integrating with and using the HealthKit framework
- Creating page-based navigation controllers
- Creating modal navigation controllers
- Creating hierarchical navigation controllers

We have an exciting project ahead of us, so let's get started.

Building the Health Monitor application

In this section, we will look at designing our user interface for our *Health Monitor* application. We will begin by developing the WatchKit portion of our application.

Before proceeding, we need to create our `HealthMonitor` project using Xcode. Simply follow the steps listed next:

1. Launch Xcode from the `/Applications` folder.
2. Choose **Create a new Xcode project**, or go to **File | New Project**.

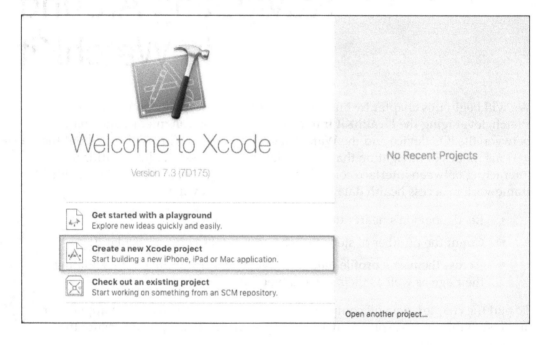

3. Select the **iOS App with WatchKit App** option from the list of available templates under the **watchOS** section, as shown in the following screenshot:

4. Click on the **Next** button to proceed to the next step in the wizard.
5. Next, enter `HealthMonitor` as the name for your project.
6. Select **Swift** from the **Language** drop-down menu.
7. Select **iPhone** from the **Devices** drop-down menu.
8. Ensure that the **Include Notification Scene** checkbox has been selected.

9. Click on the **Next** button to proceed to the next step in the wizard:

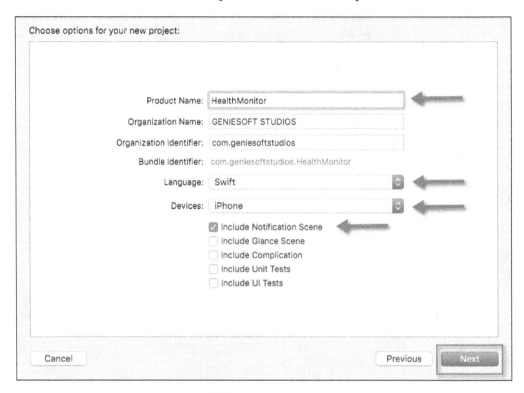

The **Organization Identifier** for your app needs to be unique. Apple recommends that you use the reverse domain style (for example, `com.domainName.appName`).

10. Specify the location where you would like to save your project.

11. Then click on the **Create** button to save your project at the specified location.

Once your project has been created, you will be presented with the Xcode development environment along with the project files that the template created for you.

Understanding page-based interfaces and navigation

Page-based interfaces are similar to the page-view controller, `UIPageViewController`, within iOS apps. These allow you to show multiple pages of information in a specific order.

These types of interfaces are best suited for scenarios where your application needs to display multiple screens of information that are related to each other.

Page-based navigations are created using the *next page Relationship Segue option* between the interface controllers that you want to link. A link is created by holding down the *Control* key, dragging it to the interface controller that you would like to link, and then choosing the **next page** segue from the popup, as shown in the following screenshot:

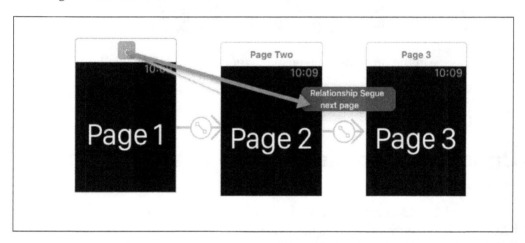

To link other interface controllers, you apply the same linkage between each of the interface controllers. The order in which you create the segue linkages between the interface controllers is the order in which they will appear when the user moves between them.

Understanding modal interfaces and navigation

Modal interfaces are similar to hierarchical interfaces. However, instead of pushing the currently displayed view to another controller, modal interfaces are designed to display information on top of the existing view as opposed to transitioning to them:

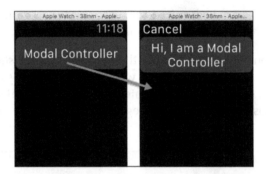

As you can see in the preceding screenshot, when the **Modal Controller** button is pressed, it transitions to another interface controller, and this takes focus. Clicking on the **Cancel** button will dismiss the interface controller, and return to the previous interface controller.

Understanding hierarchical interfaces and navigation

Hierarchical interfaces are similar to the UINavigationController class within iOS, and are called by using the pushControllerWithName method and specifying the storyboard identifier. The pushed view controller will contain the < icon which allows the user to move back to the previous screen:

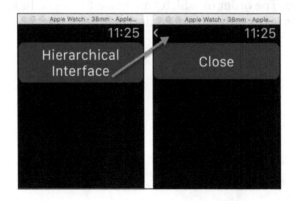

As you can see in the preceding screenshot, when the **Hierarchical Interface** button is pressed, it transitions to another interface controller, and this takes focus until the user taps on the **<** icon, or alternatively, clicks on the **Close** button to transition back to the previous interface controller.

Integrating the HealthKit framework to handle updates

When working with the HealthKit framework, you need to provision your WatchKit application target with the HealthKit entitlement. This needs to be coordinated between the iPhone app and the WatchKit extension, which is specifically due to watchOS 2 not supporting this functionality.

Our next step is to provide our app with the ability to monitor HealthKit-related updates in the background:

1. Click and select the **HealthMonitor** project from the project navigation window.
2. Then select and click on the **Capabilities** tab within the project settings.
3. Next, choose **HealthMonitor WatchKit Extension** in the **TARGETS** section.
4. Then, enable HealthKit by selecting the switch in the **HealthKit** section so that Xcode can provision your app to monitor continuous updates:

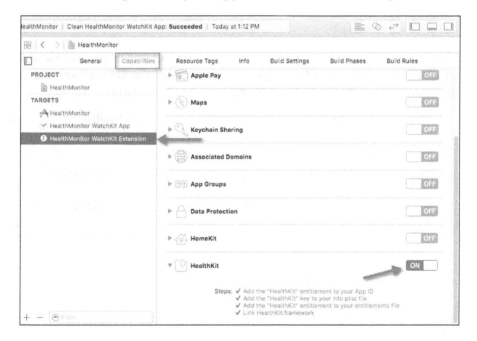

Now that we have successfully configured our project to use HealthKit, in our next section, we will need to make some changes to the applications file `AppDelegate. swift` so that it can communicate between the iOS app and the WatchKit extension to request and authorize access.

Integrating the HealthKit framework – iPhone app

In this section, we will look at what is required for successful communication between the WatchKit extension and the Apple Watch in order to access heart rate information, characteristics-related information from the iOS device's *Health* app, as well as the number of steps that the user has taken during the day:

1. Open the `AppDelegate.swift` file located within the **HealthMonitor** group in the project navigation window, and enter the following highlighted code sections:

```
//   HealthMonitor
//   AppDelegate.swift
//
//   Created by Steven F. Daniel on 25/11/2015.
//   Copyright © 2015 GENIESOFT STUDIOS. All rights reserved.
//

import UIKit
import HealthKit
```

In the preceding code snippet, we import our HealthKit framework so that we can begin accessing the respective callback methods to allow successful communication between the iOS app and the WatchKit extension.

2. Next, within the `AppDelegate.swift` file, enter the following code snippet underneath the `func applicationWillTerminate(application: UIApplication)` method:

```
// Handle a request to authorize HealthKit from the Watch
Extension
func applicationShouldRequestHealthAuthorization(application:
UIApplication) {
    // Create our HKHealthStore object to handle reading and saving
    let healthStore: HKHealthStore? = {
        if HKHealthStore.isHealthDataAvailable() {
            return HKHealthStore()
        }
        else { return nil }
```

```
    } ()

    healthStore!.handleAuthorizationForExtensionWithCompletion {
        success, error in
        print(success == true ? "WatchKit Extension allowed
access." :
        "WatchKit Extension didn't allow access")
    }
}
```

The `applicationShouldRequestHealthAuthorization` method is responsible for authorizing and allowing our WatchKit extension to access all health-related information.

We declare a `HKHealthStore` object, `healthStore`, which provides us with an interface and a means for accessing and storing the user's health data. When we proceed to make a call to `handleAuthorizationForExtensionWithCompletion`, we are simply making a request to ask the iPhone app to handle the authorization for us.

When the user authorizes this, the completion block is immediately called. It is worth mentioning that since the `HealthStore` class is not available on all devices, such as iPad, it is best to use the `isHealthDataAvailable` property to check when you instantiate your `healthStore` object.

For more information on the `HKHealthStore` class, refer to the Apple Developer documentation at `https://developer.apple.com/library/prerelease/ios/documentation/HealthKit/Reference/HKHealthStore_Class/index.html`.

Now that we have provided our iOS app application delegate to handle the authorization of our HealthKit store, our next step is to proceed with designing the user interface for our Apple Watch *Health Monitor* app.

Building the Health Monitor application – WatchKit

In this section, we will begin building the user interface for our *Health Monitor* application using the Interface Builder, as well as the associated code for the `HealthMonitor` WatchKit extension portion of our *Health Monitor* application:

1. Select the **Interface.storyboard** file from the project navigation window.

2. From the Object Library, drag a `WKInterfaceGroup` control to the watch area canvas:

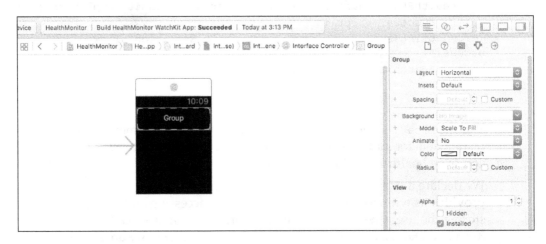

3. Next, drag a `WKInterfaceLabel` control from the Object Library to the watch area canvas, and place this within the `WKInterfaceGroup` control that we added previously. Then, modify the **Text** property to read **Health Data** in the Attributes Inspector section:

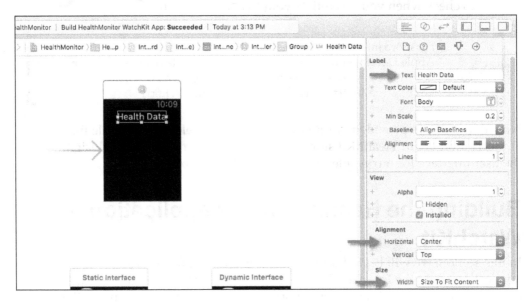

4. From the Object Library, drag a `WKInterfaceLabel` control to the watch area canvas, and place this under the `WKInterfaceSlider` control that we added previously:

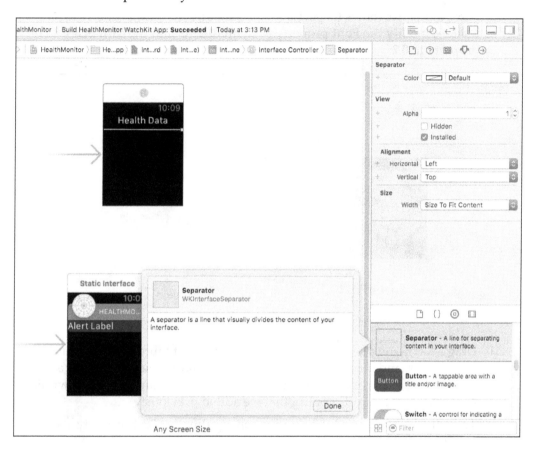

5. Now, drag a `WkInterfaceSeparator` control from the Object Library to the watch area canvas, and place this under the `WKInterfaceGroup` control that we added previously.

6. Then, from the Object Library, drag a `WKInterfaceGroup` control to the watch area canvas; then drag a `WKInterfaceLabel` control to the watch area canvas, and place this within the `WKInterfaceGroup` control that we added previously.

7. In the Attributes Inspector section, modify the **Text** property to read **Heart (bpm):**.

8. Drag a `WKInterfaceLabel` control from the Object Library to the watch area canvas, and place this to the right of the **Heart (bpm):** (`WKInterfaceLabel`) control, within the `WKInterfaceGroup` control that we added previously.

9. Next, in the Attributes Inspector section, modify the **Text** property to read **---**; modify the **Font** property to **Symbol 23.0**, and the **Min Scale** property to **0.2**:

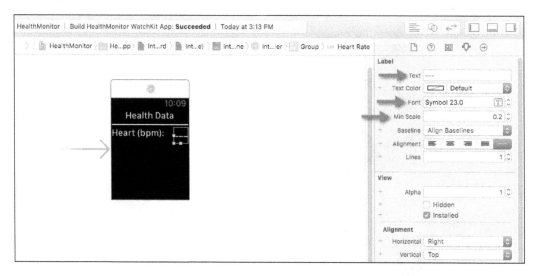

10. Drag a `WKInterfaceGroup` control from the Object Library to the watch area canvas, and place this below the **Heart (bpm):** group; then drag a `WKInterfaceLabel` control to the watch area canvas, and place this within the `WKInterfaceGroup` control that we added previously.

11. Then, in the Attributes Inspector section, modify the **Text** property to read **Steps:**.

12. Drag a `WKInterfaceLabel` control from the Object Library to the watch area canvas, and place this to the right of the **Steps:** (`WKInterfaceLabel`) control within the `WKInterfaceGroup` control that we added previously.

13. Next, in the Attributes Inspector section, modify the **Text** property to read **---**; modify the **Font** property to **Symbol 23.0**, and the **Min Scale** property to **0.2**:

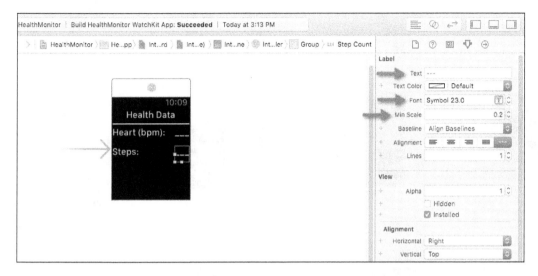

14. Then, from the Object Library, drag a `WKInterfaceButton` control to the watch area canvas, and place this underneath the **Steps:** (`WKInterfaceGroup`) control.

15. Next, in the Attributes Inspector section, modify the **Text** property to read **Start Monitoring**, and modify the **Font** property to **System 15.0**:

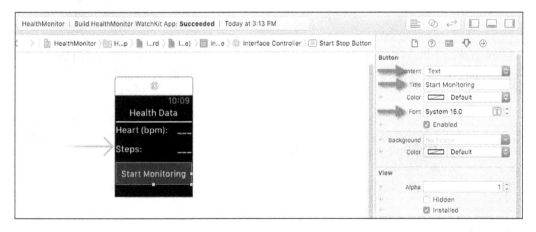

16. Our next step is to add a new interface controller to our storyboard. This will be responsible for displaying the user's characteristic information.

17. From the Object Library, drag a `WKInterfaceController` control to the watch area canvas:

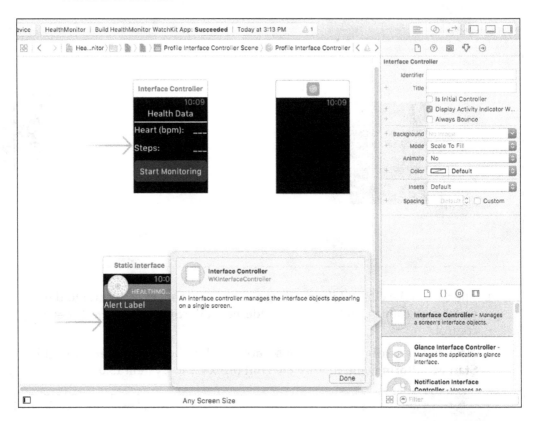

The next step is to create a connection to this interface controller, which will be a page-based navigation and will allow the user to swipe to the right to see the information contained within this view:

1. Ensure that the **Health Data** (`WKInterfaceController`) control is selected, then hold down the *Control* key, and drag it to the `WKInterfaceController` control that we just added in the previous step:

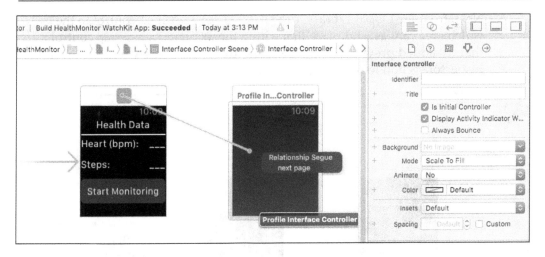

2. Next, choose the **next page** option from the **Relationship Segue** menu.

   Now that we have added our interface controller, we can start building the user interface as we did for our health data controller.

3. From the Object Library, drag a `WKInterfaceGroup` control to the watch area canvas for our new interface controller, as shown in following screenshot:

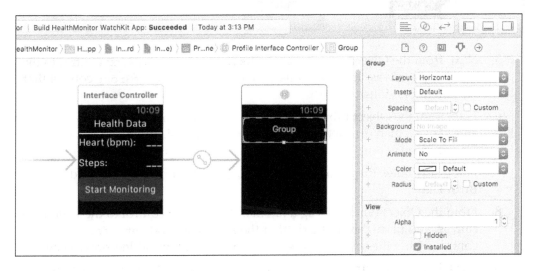

4. Next, from the Object Library, drag a `WKInterfaceLabel` control to the watch area canvas, and place this within the `WKInterfaceGroup` control that we added previously. Then, modify the **Text** property in the Attributes Inspector section to read **Profile Details**:

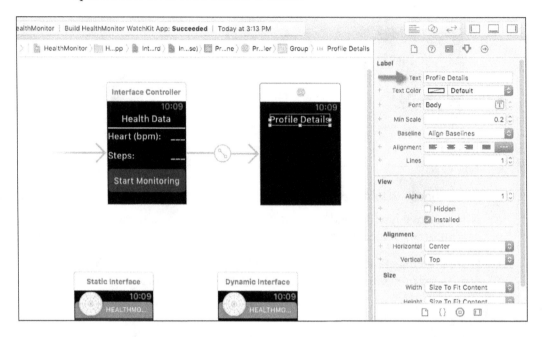

5. Next, from the Object Library, drag a `WkInterfaceSeparator` control to the watch area canvas, and place this under the `WKInterfaceGroup` control that we added previously.

6. Then from the Object Library, drag a `WKInterfaceGroup` control to the watch area canvas; then drag a `WKInterfaceLabel` control, and place this within the `WKInterfaceGroup` control that we added previously.

7. In the Attributes Inspector section, modify the **Text** property to read **Birth Date:**.

8. From the Object Library, drag a `WKInterfaceLabel` control to the watch area canvas, and place this to the right of the **Birth Date:** (`WKInterfaceLabel`) control within the `WKInterfaceGroup` control that we added previously.

9. Next, in the Attributes Inspector section, modify the **Text** property to read **---**; modify the **Font** property to **Symbol 15.0**, and the **Min Scale** property to **0.2**:

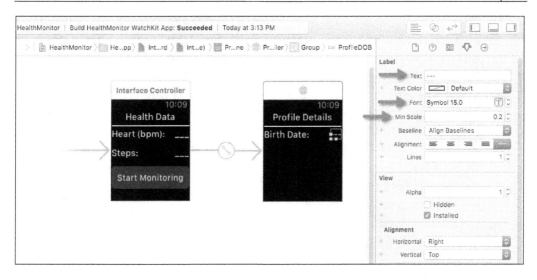

10. From the Object Library, drag a `WKInterfaceGroup` control to the watch area canvas and place this underneath the **Birth Date:** group. Then drag a `WKInterfaceLabel` control to the watch area canvas, and place this within the `WKInterfaceGroup` control that we added previously.

11. In the Attributes Inspector section, modify the **Text** property to read **Age:**. Then drag a `WKInterfaceLabel` control to the watch area canvas, and place this to the right of the **Age:** (`WKInterfaceLabel`) control within the `WKInterfaceGroup` control that we added previously.

12. Next, in the Attributes Inspector section, modify the **Text** property to read **---**; modify the **Font** property to **Symbol 15.0**, and the **Min Scale** property to **0.2**.

13. Now drag a `WKInterfaceGroup` control from the Object Library to the watch area canvas, and place this underneath the **Age:** group. Then drag a `WKInterfaceLabel` control to the watch area canvas, and place this within the `WKInterfaceGroup` control that we added previously.

14. In the Attributes Inspector section, modify the **Text** property to read **Sex Type:**; drag a `WKInterfaceLabel` control to the watch area canvas, and place this to the right of the **Sex Type:** (`WKInterfaceLabel`) control, within the `WKInterfaceGroup` control that we added previously.

15. Again, in the Attributes Inspector section, modify the **Text** property to read **---**; modify the **Font** property to **Symbol 15.0** and the **Min Scale** property to **0.2**.

16. Then, drag a WKInterfaceGroup control from the Object Library to the watch area canvas, and place this underneath the **Sex Type:** group. Then drag a WKInterfaceLabel control to the watch area canvas, and place this within the WKInterfaceGroup control that we added previously.

17. In the Attributes Inspector section, modify the **Text** property to read **Blood Type:**. Now drag a WKInterfaceLabel control to the watch area canvas, and place this to the right of the **Blood Type:** (WKInterfaceLabel) control within the WKInterfaceGroup control that we added previously.

18. In the Attributes Inspector section, modify the **Text** property to read **---**; modify the **Font** property to **Symbol 15.0**, and the **Min Scale** property to **0.2**:

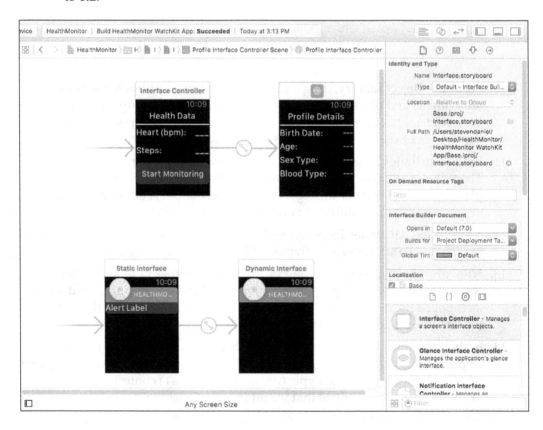

The preceding screenshot shows the complete user interface for our profile details interface view controller. In the next section, we will create a new WatchKit class for our profile details controller.

Creating the profile details interface controller's WatchKit class

Now that we have created the user interface for our profile details controller, we can now create a class that will inherit from the WatchKit `InterfaceController` class:

1. In the project navigation window, select the **HealthMonitor WatchKit App** group, and choose **File | New…**, or right-click and choose **New File…** from the list of options, as shown in the following screenshot:

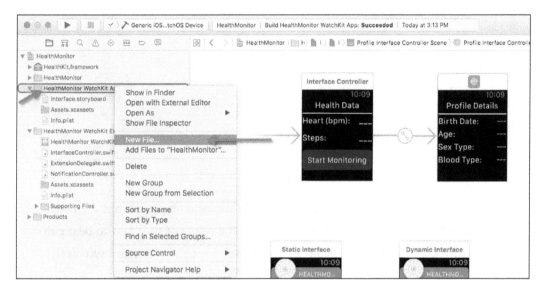

2. Next, choose the **watchOS** group. Under the **Source** section, select **WatchKit Class** from the list of available templates:

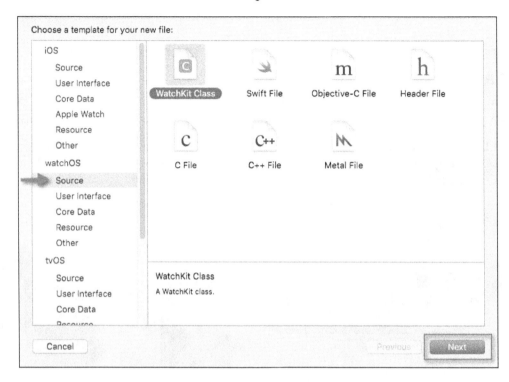

3. Click on the **Next** button to proceed with the next step within the wizard.

4. Enter `ProfileInterfaceController` as the name of the class to be created.

5. Ensure that you have selected `WKInterfaceController` (from which the subclass is to be created) from the **Subclass of** drop-down list.

6. Ensure that you have selected **Swift** as the language to use from the **Language** drop-down list:

7. Click on the **Next** button to proceed with the next step of the wizard.

8. Then click on the **Create** button to save the file to the specified folder location.

Our next step is to set our profile details interface controller to use this newly created class which we will use later on to set up the Outlets within this class:

1. Select the **Interface.storyboard** file from the project navigation window.

2. Next, choose the profile details interface controller, and click on the Identity Inspector button.

3. Then, from the **Class** dropdown, select the **ProfileInterfaceController** class that we just created to use as our main class:

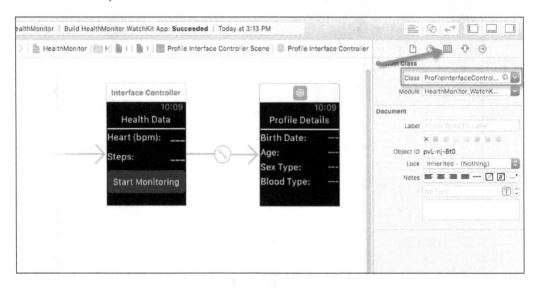

In this section, we successfully created a new WatchKit class to be used for our profile details controller, to which we will begin adding the necessary code later on. In the next section, we will start connecting the Outlets for each of our Interface Builder objects.

Creating the Outlets for our Interface Builder objects

In the previous section, you learned how to add controls to the Interface. storyboard canvas for the construction of a user interface for our *Health Monitor* app, as well as setting some properties for each of our controls.

Our next step is to create the necessary Outlets for each of our Interface Builder controls, as we will need to access these through our code to handle the display of health-related information within each of our controllers:

1. Open the Assistant Editor window by selecting **Navigate | Open in Assistant Editor**, or by pressing *Option + Command + ,.*

2.   Ensure that the `InterfaceController.swift` file is displayed within the Assistant Editor window, as shown in the following screenshot:

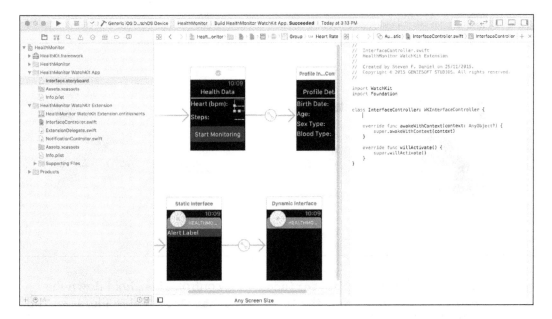

3.   Next, select the **Heart (bpm):** (`WKInterfaceLabel`) control. Then hold down the *Control* key, and drag it into the `InterfaceController.swift` file, within the body of `class InterfaceController: WKInterfaceController`.

4.   Choose **Outlet** from the **Connection** drop-down menu for the type of connection, and enter `heartRate` for the name of the Outlet property to be created.

5. Next, choose **Weak** from the **Storage** drop-down menu, and click on the **Connect** button:

6. Next, select the **Steps:** (`WKInterfaceLabel`) control. Then, hold down the *Control* key and drag it into the `InterfaceController.swift` file, as we did for the **heartRate** Outlet.

7. Choose **Outlet** from the **Connection** drop-down menu for the type of connection to be created, and enter `stepCount` for the name of the Outlet property. Then, choose **Weak** from the **Storage** drop-down menu, and click on the **Connect** button:

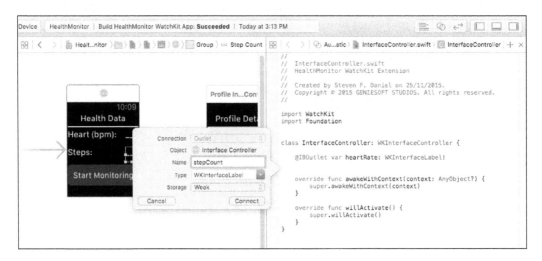

8. Now, select the **Start Monitoring** (`WKInterfaceButton`) control, then hold down the *Control* key and drag it into the `InterfaceController.swift` file, as we did for our **stepCount** Outlet.

9. Choose **Outlet** from the **Connection** drop-down menu for the type of connection to be created, and enter `startStopButton` for the name of the Outlet property. Select **Weak** from the **Storage** drop-down menu, and click on the **Connect** button:

10. Once you have created the necessary Outlets, save your project by selecting **File** | **Save**, or alternatively, by pressing *Command + S*.

> Whenever you create an Outlet, you must remember to create it within the `InterfaceController` class, as these cannot be created outside this class body.

The following code snippet shows the complete implementation of the Outlets that we created in the previous steps:

```
//   InterfaceController.swift
//   HealthMonitor WatchKit Extension
//
//   Created by Steven F. Daniel on 25/11/2015.
//   Copyright © 2015 GENIESOFT STUDIOS. All rights reserved.
//

import WatchKit
import Foundation
```

```
import HealthKit

class InterfaceController: WKInterfaceController {

    @IBOutlet var heartRate:    WKInterfaceLabel!
    @IBOutlet var stepCount:    WKInterfaceLabel!
    @IBOutlet var startStopButton: WKInterfaceButton!
```

As you can see from the preceding code snippet, the Interface Builder has created each of our control objects as well as the associated type of control that we have used. In our next section, we will create the Outlets for our `ProfileInterfaceController` so that we can display the profile details information to those controls later on:

1. Open the Assistant Editor window by selecting **Navigate | Open in Assistant Editor**, or by pressing *Option + Command + ,*.

2. Ensure that the `ProfileInterfaceController.swift` file is displayed within the Assistant Editor window, as shown in the following screenshot:

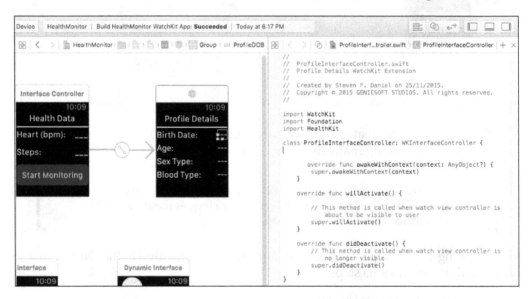

3. Next, select the **Birth Date:** (WKInterfaceLabel) control; then hold down the *Control* key, and drag it into the ProfileInterfaceController. swift file, within the body of class ProfileInterfaceController: WKInterfaceController.

4. Choose **Outlet** from the **Connection** drop-down menu for the type of connection to be created, and enter profileDOB as the name of the Outlet property.

5. Next, choose **Weak** from the **Storage** drop-down menu, and click on the **Connect** button:

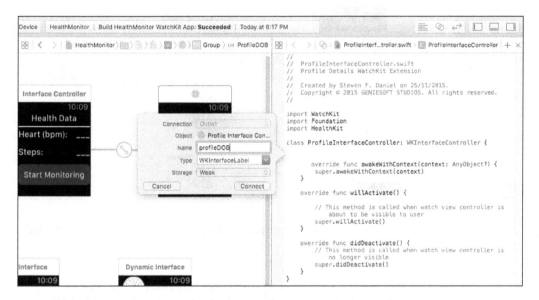

6. Select the **Age:** (WKInterfaceLabel) control; then hold down the *Control* key, and drag it into the ProfileInterfaceController.swift file as we did for our **profileDOB** Outlet.

7. Choose **Outlet** from the **Connection** drop-down menu for the type of connection to be created, and enter `profileAge` for the name of the Outlet property. Then, choose **Weak** from the **Storage** drop-down menu, and click on the **Connect** button:

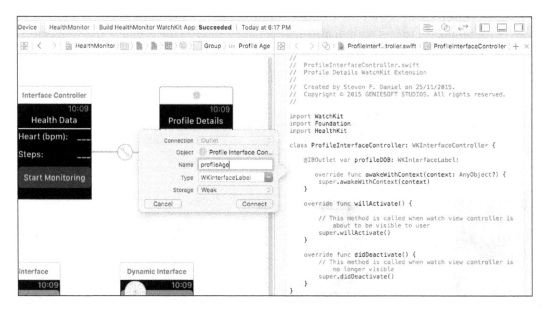

8. Next, select the **Sex Type:** (`WKInterfaceLabel`) control; then hold down the *Control* key, and drag it into the `ProfileInterfaceController.swift` file as we did for our **profileAge** Outlet.

9. Choose **Outlet** from the **Connection** drop-down menu for the type of connection to be created, and enter `profileSexType` for the name of the Outlet property. Select **Weak** from the **Storage** drop-down menu, and click on the **Connect** button.

10. Next, select the **Blood Type:** (`WKInterfaceLabel`) control; then hold down the *Control* key, and drag it into the `ProfileInterfaceController.swift` file as we did for our **profileSexType** Outlet.

11. Select **Outlet** from the **Connection** drop-down menu for the type of connection to be created, and type `profileBloodType` for the name of the Outlet property. Then choose **Weak** from the **Storage** drop-down menu, and click on the **Connect** button.

12. Once you have created the necessary Outlets, save your project by selecting **File** | **Save**, or alternatively, by pressing *Command + S*.

Whenever you create an Outlet, you must remember to create them within the `ProfileInterfaceController` class, as these cannot be created outside this class body.

The following code snippet shows the complete implementation of the Outlets that we created in the preceding steps:

```
//  ProfileInterfaceController.swift
//  Profile Details WatchKit Extension
//
//  Created by Steven F. Daniel on 25/11/2015.
//  Copyright © 2015 GENIESOFT STUDIOS. All rights reserved.
//

import WatchKit
import Foundation
import HealthKit

class ProfileInterfaceController: WKInterfaceController {

    @IBOutlet var ProfileDOB:        WKInterfaceLabel!
    @IBOutlet var profileAge:        WKInterfaceLabel!
    @IBOutlet var profileSexType:    WKInterfaceLabel!
    @IBOutlet var profileBloodType:  WKInterfaceLabel!
```

As you can see from the preceding code snippet, the Interface Builder has created each of our control objects as well as the associated type of control that we have used. In our next section, we will create an Action event that will respond when we press the **Start Monitoring** (`WKInterfaceButton`) control.

Creating an Action event to handle our Start Monitoring button

In the previous section, we looked at how to add controls to our `Interface.storyboard` canvas for the construction of a user interface for the *Health Monitor* app. You also learned how to connect each of the necessary Outlets for our controls apart from creating a new WatchKit class interface for our profile details interface controller.

In this section, we will look at how to create the Action event for our **Start Monitoring** button, to which we will add the necessary code later:

1. Open the Assistant Editor window by selecting **Navigate | Open in Assistant Editor**, or by pressing *Option + Command + ,*.

2. Ensure that the `InterfaceController.swift` file is displayed within the Assistant Editor window, as shown in the screenshot that follows.

3. Next, select the `WKInterfaceButton` control. Hold down the *Control* key, and drag it into the `InterfaceController.swift` file, below the `willActivate` method.

4. Choose **Action** from the **Connection** drop-down menu for the type of connection to be created, and enter `startStopButtonPressed` for the name of the Action:

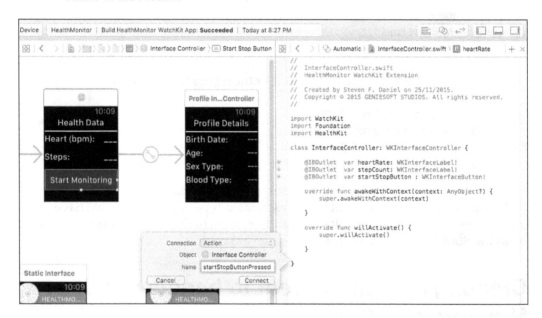

Now that we have added the Action event for our **Start Monitoring** button, we need to add the necessary HealthKit code within our interface controller, for retrieving the heart rate and pedometer information.

Using HealthKit to obtain heart rate and pedometer information

In this section, we will need to hook up our interface controller to use the HealthKit framework so that we can start receiving health-related information. You will learn how to use certain method calls, so that we can query the Apple Watch and return the heart rate (bpm) information. We will also query the pedometer to return the total number of steps that the user has made:

1. Open the `InterfaceController.swift` file located within the **HealthMonitor WatchKit Extension** group in the project navigation window, and enter the following highlighted code snippet:

```swift
import WatchKit
import Foundation
import HealthKit

class InterfaceController: WKInterfaceController {

    @IBOutlet  var heartRate: WKInterfaceLabel!
    @IBOutlet  var stepCount: WKInterfaceLabel!
    @IBOutlet  var startStopButton : WKInterfaceButton!

    // Is the current session active
    var isSessionActive = false

    // Define our HealthKit Store for loading and saving object
data
    let healthKitStore = HKHealthStore()

    var anchor = HKQueryAnchor(fromValue:
Int(HKAnchoredObjectQueryNoAnchor))

    override func awakeWithContext(context: AnyObject?) {
        super.awakeWithContext(context)

        self.heartRate.setText("---")
        self.heartRate.setTextColor(UIColor(red: 255, green:0,
                                    blue: 0, alpha: 1))
        self.stepCount.setText("---")
        self.stepCount.setTextColor(UIColor.greenColor())
    }
```

The preceding code snippet begins by importing our HealthKit framework so that our WatchKit extension can start receiving health-related information. Next, we declare our class variables for `isSessionActive`, which determines if we are monitoring an active session, and the `healthKitStore` object, which allows us to access and store the user's health data.

We then declare an anchor object, which is responsible for querying and returning all of the matching samples currently in the HealthKit store. Next, within the `awakeWithContext` method, we initialize each of our control objects within the interface, setting the initial text and colors.

2. Now, with the `InterfaceController.swift` file still open, locate the `willActivate` method, and enter the following highlighted code snippet:

```swift
override func willActivate() {
    super.willActivate()

    guard HKHealthStore.isHealthDataAvailable() == true else {
        self.showDialog("HealthKit",
        message: "HealthKit not supported", buttonText: "OK")
        return
    }
    // Specify our HealthKit object types to read
    let healthKitTypesToRead = NSSet(
        objects: HKObjectType.characteristicTypeForIdentifier
                    (HKCharacteristicTypeIdentifierDateOfBirth)!,
                 HKObjectType.characteristicTypeForIdentifier
                    (HKCharacteristicTypeIdentifierBloodType)!,
                 HKObjectType.characteristicTypeForIdentifier
                    (HKCharacteristicTypeIdentifierBiologicalSex)!,
                 HKQuantityType.quantityTypeForIdentifier
                    (HKQuantityTypeIdentifierHeartRate)!,
                 HKQuantityType.quantityTypeForIdentifier
                    (HKQuantityTypeIdentifierStepCount)!) as!
                 Set<HKObjectType>

    healthKitStore.requestAuthorizationToShareTypes(nil,
    readTypes: healthKitTypesToRead) {
        (success, error) -> Void in
        if success == false {
            self.showDialog("HealthKit", message: "HealthKit is
            not allowed", buttonText: "OK")
        }
    }
}
```

In the preceding code snippet, we begin by checking to see if HealthKit is available for the device using the `isHealthDataAvailable` property of the `HKHealthStore` class, and display a dialog box to the user if HealthKit is not supported on their device.

We then set up our HealthKit object type variable, `healthKitTypesToRead`, which specifies the set of types that we wish to read from the HealthKit database. Thereafter we call the `requestAuthorizationToShareTypes` method to request permission for reading the specified data types. If authorization is not allowed for a particular HealthKit type, an error is raised, and a dialog is displayed to the user, using the `showDialog` method.

3. Next, with the `InterfaceController.swift` file still open, type the following code snippet after the `willActivate` method:

```
// method to display a popup dialog if HealthKit is unavailable
func showDialog(title: String, message: String, buttonText:
String)-> Void
{
    let buttonAction = WKAlertAction(title: buttonText,
    style: WKAlertActionStyle.Cancel) { () -> Void in
    }
    presentAlertControllerWithTitle(title, message: message,
    preferredStyle: .ActionSheet, actions: [buttonAction])
    return
}
```

In the preceding code snippet, the `showDialog` method is used to display useful information within the Apple Watch dialog. The `WKAlertAction` object creates an alert action; you then specify the title and visual style to be applied to the button and a block to be executed whenever the button is tapped. The `presentAlertControllerWithTitle` method presents an alert over the current interface controller.

4. With the `InterfaceController.swift` file still open, create the following `heartRateStreamingQuery` code snippet after the `showDialog` method:

```
// Create our Heart Rate Query
func heartRateStreamingQuery(workoutStartDate: NSDate) -> HKQuery?
{
    guard let heartRateSample =
        HKObjectType.quantityTypeForIdentifier
        (HKQuantityTypeIdentifierHeartRate) else { return nil }

    let heartRateQuery = HKAnchoredObjectQuery(type:
    heartRateSample, predicate: nil, anchor: anchor, limit:
    Int(HKObjectQueryNoLimit)) { (query, sampleObjects,
```

```
    deletedObjects, newAnchor, error) -> Void in
        guard let newAnchor = newAnchor else {return}
        self.anchor = newAnchor
    }
}
heartRateQuery.updateHandler = {(query, samples, deleteObjects,
newAnchor, error) -> Void in
        self.anchor = newAnchor!
        guard let heartRateSamples = samples as? [HKQuantitySample]
        else { return }

        dispatch_async(dispatch_get_main_queue()) {
            guard let sample = heartRateSamples.first else { return
}

            let value =
            sample.quantity.doubleValueForUnit(HKUnit(fromString:
            "count/min"))
            self.heartRate.setText(String(UInt16(value)))
        }
        self.heartRate.setTextColor(UIColor(red: 255, green:0, blue:
0,
        alpha: 1))
        }
        return heartRateQuery
}
```

In the preceding code snippet, we begin by setting up a `heartRateSample` variable, and specify that we are interested in reading the heart rate sample information from the HealthKit database. Next, we create an anchored query, `heartRateQuery`, that will be used to continually return the heart rate information as it becomes available.

We then create an anchor variable called `newAnchor`, which returns a cursor to the last data returned by the query, and then assign our anchor to be used to get only new data since the last anchor was updated.

The `updateHandler` runs continuously whenever a change in the user's heart rate is detected, and returns a `samples` object containing a collection of the heart rate readings, which we assign to our `heartRateSamples` variable. Thereafter, as part of the main queue, we grab the first heart rate reading returned by our WatchKit extension, and display this to our heart rate interface controller before finally returning the heart rate query.

5. Next, with the `InterfaceController.swift` file still open, create
   the following `dailyStepsStreamingQuery` code snippet after the
   `heartRateStreamingQuery` method:

```
// Query the HealthKit store to return the total number of
// steps attempted for a given day
func dailyStepsStreamingQuery(workoutStartDate: NSDate) ->
HKQuery?
{
    // Call our Sample type for our HealthKit class to return
    guard let dailyStepsSample =
    HKSampleType.quantityTypeForIdentifier
    (HKQuantityTypeIdentifierStepCount) else { return nil }

    let calendar = NSCalendar.currentCalendar()
    let startDate = calendar.dateByAddingUnit(NSCalendarUnit.Day,
                value: -1, toDate: workoutStartDate, options:
                NSCalendarOptions.WrapComponents)

    let predicate = HKQuery.predicateForSamplesWithStartDate
                (startDate, endDate: workoutStartDate,
                options: HKQueryOptions.StrictEndDate)
    let dailyStepsQuery = HKSampleQuery(sampleType:
dailyStepsSample,
        predicate: predicate, limit: 0, sortDescriptors: nil) {
            [unowned self] (query, results, error) in
            guard let dailyStepsSamples = results as?
                [HKQuantitySample] else { return }
            guard dailyStepsSamples.count > 0 else { return }

            dispatch_async(dispatch_get_main_queue()) {
                var dailySteps : Double = 0
                for steps in dailyStepsSamples {
                    dailySteps +=
                    steps.quantity.doubleValueForUnit(
                    HKUnit.countUnit())
                }
                self.stepCount.setText(String(UInt16(dailySteps)))
                self.stepCount.setTextColor(UIColor.greenColor())
            }
        }

    // Return our Query string back to the calling method
    return dailyStepsQuery
}
```

In the preceding code snippet, we begin by setting up a `dailyStepsSample` variable, and specify that we are interested in reading the step count sample information from the HealthKit database. Next, we create a `calendar` variable to return a calendar based on the settings for the current user's chosen system locale. We then create a `startDate` variable, and use the `dataByAddingUnit` method of the `calendar` object to calculate the starting date from our ending date, as specified by the `workoutStartDate` variable.

You will have noticed that we subtract one day from the current date. This is because Apple Watch skips one day ahead from the current day. In our next step, we create a `predicate` object, and use the `predicateForSamplesWithStartDate` method to return a predicate of the step count samples where the starting and ending dates fall within those specified.

Next, we perform a check to see if we have returned the step count sample data by using the `count` property. If we haven't, we return from the method. Otherwise, we proceed, and sum up the total number of steps achieved for the given day that are returned by the `predicate` object, and display this within our health data interface controller before finally returning the `dailyStepsQuery`.

6. With the `InterfaceController.swift` file still open, create the following `didSessionStart` code snippet after the `dailyStepsStreamingQuery` method:

```swift
// Start a workout
func didSessionStart(date : NSDate) {

    // Start a Step Counter WorkOut
    if let dailyStepsQuery = dailyStepsStreamingQuery(date) {
        healthKitStore.executeQuery(dailyStepsQuery)
    }

    // Start a Heart Rate WorkOut
    if let heartRateQuery = heartRateStreamingQuery(date) {
        healthKitStore.executeQuery(heartRateQuery)
    }
}
```

In the preceding code snippet, the `didSessionStart` method is called when the **Start Monitoring** button is pressed, and starts off by creating two query objects: `dailyStepsQuery` and `heartRateQuery`. These object variables call the `dailyStepsStreamingQuery` and `heartRateStreamingQuery` methods which in turn pass in a `date` object. As we saw in the previous code snippets, the `dailyStepsStreamingQuery` as well as the `heartRateStreamingQuery` begin setting up the `HKQuery` object based on the information that has been sent to it. They then set up the update handler, which will begin executing the query returned by the method.

7. Next, with the `InterfaceController.swift` file still open, create the following `didSessionEnd` code snippet after the `didSessionStart` method:

```
func didSessionEnd(date : NSDate) {

    // Stop Heart Rate Query from Running
    if let heartRateQuery = heartRateStreamingQuery(date) {
        healthKitStore.stopQuery(heartRateQuery)
        self.heartRate.setText("---")
    }
    if let dailyStepsQuery = dailyStepsStreamingQuery(date) {
        healthKitStore.stopQuery(dailyStepsQuery)
        self.stepCount.setText("---")
    }
}
```

In the preceding code snippet, the `didSessionEnd` method is called when the **Start Monitoring** button is pressed. It creates a `heartRateQuery` object, which checks to see if the `heartRateStreamingQuery` method is currently running prior to stopping the query and before initializing the `heartRate` display field. The same applies to the `dailyStepsQuery` method, which checks to see if the `dailyStepsStreamingQuery` method is currently running prior to stopping the query and before initializing the `stepCount` display field.

```
// MARK: - Action event to handling starting and stopping
@IBAction func startStopButtonPressed()
{
    if (self.isSessionActive)
    {
        // Finish the current session
        self.isSessionActive = false
        self.startStopButton.setTitle("Start Monitoring")
        self.didSessionEnd(NSDate())
    } else {
```

```
        // Start a new session
        self.isSessionActive = true
        self.startStopButton.setTitle("Stop Monitoring")
        self.didSessionStart(NSDate())
    }
}
```

In the preceding code snippet, the `startStopButtonPressed` method is called when the **Start Monitoring** button is pressed. We declare a variable, `isSessionActive`, which is responsible for determining if we are already monitoring. If we are already monitoring, we initialize the `isSessionActive` variable to `false`, and update the button's title. We then call our `didSessionEnd` method, passing in the current date so that any existing queries which are currently running will be suspended. Alternatively, if no session is running, we initialize the `isSessionActive` variable to `true`, and update the button's title. Next, we proceed to call the `didSessionStart` method and pass in the current date so that we can begin monitoring and checking for updates in the heart rate, as well as receive the total number of steps that our user has achieved.

Using HealthKit to obtain biological personal information

In this section, we will need to hook up our `ProfileInterfaceController` to use the HealthKit framework so that we can start receiving health-related biological characteristic information from the *Health* app on the iOS device:

1. Open the `ProfileInterfaceController.swift` file located within the **HealthMonitor WatchKit Extension** group in the project navigation window, and enter the following highlighted code snippet:

```
import WatchKit
import Foundation
import HealthKit

class ProfileInterfaceController: WKInterfaceController {

    @IBOutlet  var profileDOB: WKInterfaceLabel!
    @IBOutlet  var profileAge: WKInterfaceLabel!
    @IBOutlet  var profileSexType: WKInterfaceLabel!
    @IBOutlet  var profileBloodType: WKInterfaceLabel!

    // Define our HealthKit Store for loading and saving object
data
```

```
let healthKitStore = HKHealthStore()

override func awakeWithContext(context: AnyObject?) {
    super.awakeWithContext(context)

    // Configure interface objects here.
    self.profileDOB.setText("---")
    self.profileAge.setText("---")
    self.profileSexType.setText("---")
    self.profileBloodType.setText("---")
}
}
```

The preceding code snippet begins by importing our HealthKit framework so that the WatchKit extension can start receiving health-related information. Next we declare our class variables for our `healthKitStore` object, which is responsible for allowing us to access and store the user's health data. Finally, within the `awakeWithContext` method, we initialize each of our label control objects within the interface.

2. With the `ProfileInterfaceController.swift` file still open, locate the `willActivate` method, and enter the following highlighted code snippet:

```
override func willActivate() {
    super.willActivate()

    // Set up our Profile Characteristics
    let dateOfBirth = getProfileDOB()!
    let calculatedAge = calculateAgeOfPersion(dateOfBirth)
    let SexType = getProfileSexType()!
    let BloodType = getProfileBloodType()!

    self.profileDOB.setText(dateOfBirth)
    self.profileAge.setText(String(UInt16(calculatedAge!)))
    self.profileSexType.setText(SexType)
    self.profileBloodType.setText(BloodType)
}
```

In the preceding code snippet, we begin by declaring our variables `dateOfBirth`, `SexType`, and `BloodType`. Once the user is granted permission to get user characteristic data, these variables will query the HealthKit database, and return the user's date of birth (formatted as an `NSDate` object), their gender (male/female), as well as their blood type (formatted as a string object). The `calculatedAge` variable makes a call to the `calculateAgeOfPerson` method, passes in the user's date of birth which has been obtained by the `dateOfBirth` variable, and returns their age.

3. With the `profileInterfaceController.swift` file still open, create the following code snippet after the `willActivate` method:

```
// Calculate the Age based on the Date Of Birth
func calculateAgeOfPersion(birthDate: String) -> Int?
{
    // Request the user's Birthday and calculate the age
    let dateFormatter = NSDateFormatter()
    dateFormatter.dateStyle = .ShortStyle

    let today = NSDate()
    let calendar = NSCalendar.currentCalendar()
    let dateComponents = calendar.components(NSCalendarUnit.Year,
    fromDate: dateFormatter.dateFromString(birthDate)!,
    toDate: today, options: NSCalendarOptions.WrapComponents)

    // Calculate the Age and return
    return dateComponents.year
}
```

In the preceding code snippet, the `calculatedAgeOfPerson` method is responsible for calculating the user's age, based on their date of birth. This method accepts a birth date, which is passed in from the `willActivate` method. We create a variable `dateFormatter`, which specifies our date to be in the dd/mm/yyyy format, which is based on the user's locale.

Next we declare a variable, `today`, which is assigned the current date, as defined by the `NSDate` class. We then use the `NSCalendar` class to work out the user's age, by subtracting their birth date from the current date, and return their calculated age, which is stored within the `year` portion.

4. With the `ProfileInterfaceController.swift` file still open, create the following `getProfileDOB` code snippet after the `calculateAgeOfPersion` method:

```
// Get the Date Of Birth Information
func getProfileDOB() -> String?
{
    var dateOfBirth: String?

    do {
        // Request the user's Birthday and calculate the age
        let birthdate = try healthKitStore.dateOfBirth()

        // Get the Date of Birth and format it
        let dateFormatter = NSDateFormatter()
```

```
        dateFormatter.dateStyle = .ShortStyle
        dateOfBirth = dateFormatter.stringFromDate(birthdate)
    }
    catch { return nil }

    // Return our Date Of Birth Information
    return dateOfBirth
}
```

In the preceding code snippet, we begin by extracting the user's date of birth from the HealthKit database, and assign this to our variable, `birthdate`. We then proceed to use the `NSDateFormatter` class and the `stringFromDate` method to format our date using the `ShortStyle` date style. Finally, we return the formatted date so that it can be displayed within the profile details interface controller.

5. Again, with the `ProfileInterfaceController.swift` file still open, create the following `getProfileSexType` code snippet after the `getProfileDOB` method:

```
// Get the Biological Sex Information
func getProfileSexType()-> String? {

    var biologicalSexType: String?

    do {
        let biologicalSex = try healthKitStore.biologicalSex()
        switch biologicalSex.biologicalSex {
        case .Female:
            biologicalSexType = "Female"
        case .Male:
            biologicalSexType = "Male"
        case .NotSet:
            biologicalSexType = ""
        default:
            biologicalSexType = ""
        }
    }
    catch { return nil }

    // Return our information back
    return biologicalSexType
}
}
```

In the preceding code snippet, we begin by extracting the user's biological sex type from the HealthKit database, and assign this to our variable, `biologicalSex`. We then proceed to use a `switch` statement that determines the user's sex type which is returned as `HKBiologicalSexObject` from the HealthKit database. Based on the type returned, we assign their sex type as a string to our variable `biologicalSexType`, and return this so that it can be displayed within the profile details interface controller.

For more information on the `HKBiologicalSexObject` class, refer to the Apple Developer documentation at `https://developer.apple.com/library/prerelease/ios/documentation/HealthKit/Reference/HKBiologicalSexObject_Class/index.html#//apple_ref/swift/cl/c:objc(cs)HKBiologicalSexObject`.

6. Next, with the `InterfaceController.swift` file still open, create the following `getProfileBloodType` code snippet after the `getProfileSexType` method:

```
// Get the Biological Blood Type Information
func getProfileBloodType() -> String? {

    var biologicalBloodType: String?

    do {
        let bloodType = try healthKitStore.bloodType()

        switch bloodType.bloodType {
        case .APositive:
            biologicalBloodType = "A+"
        case .ANegative:
            biologicalBloodType = "A-"
        case .BPositive:
            biologicalBloodType = "B+"
        case .BNegative:
```

```
            biologicalBloodType = "B-"
        case .ABPositive:
            biologicalBloodType = "AB+"
        case .ABNegative:
            biologicalBloodType = "AB-"
        case .OPositive:
            biologicalBloodType = "O+"
        case .ONegative:
            biologicalBloodType = "O-"
        case .NotSet:
            biologicalBloodType = ""
        }
    }
    catch { return nil }

    return biologicalBloodType
}
```

In the preceding code snippet, we begin by extracting the user's biological blood type from the HealthKit database, and assign this to our variable `biologicalSex`. We then proceed to use a `switch` statement that determines the user's blood type which is returned as `HKBloodTypeObject` from the HealthKit database. Based on the type returned, we assign their blood type as a string to our variable `biologicalBloodType`, and return this so that it can be displayed within the profile details interface controller.

For more information on the `HKBloodTypeObject` class, refer to the Apple Developer documentation at `https://developer.apple.com/library/prerelease/ios/help/HKBloodTypeObject_Class/index.html#//apple_ref/doc/c_ref/HKBloodTypeObject`.

Building and running the Health Monitor application

In this section, we will take a look at how to compile and run our *Health Monitor* application. You have the option of choosing to run your application on the watchOS device, or within the simulators for Apple Watch:

1. To run the app, select the **HealthMonitor WatchKit App** scheme and choose your preferred device, as shown in the following screenshot:

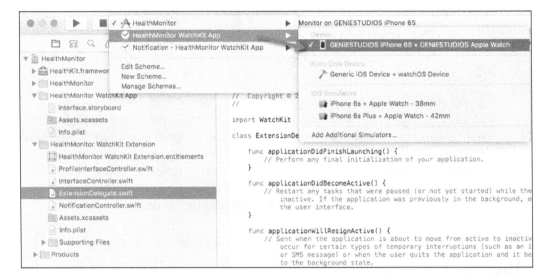

2. Next, build and run the application by selecting **Product | Run** from the **Product** menu, or alternatively, by pressing *Command + R*.

When the compilation completes, the *Health Monitor* app will be displayed. If you haven't previously allowed access to HealthKit, you will receive a dialog popup on both, Apple Watch and the iOS device.

In order to proceed, you will need to allow access to HealthKit so that you can retrieve the allowable characteristics that we specified within our app. You have the ability to turn on and off certain features so that they don't appear within the app. Tapping on the **Open "HealthMonitor"** button will display the **Health Access** screen, as seen in the following screenshot:

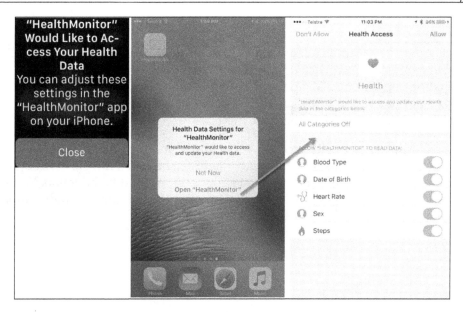

The preceding screenshot shows you the iterations that take place when you begin tapping on the **Start Monitoring** button. On this screen, you will notice two dots appearing at the bottom of the screen. If you swipe right, you will see the profile details screen; swiping left will take you back to the **Health Data** screen:

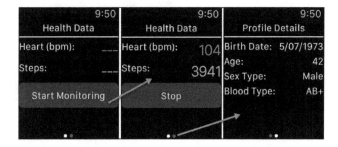

As you can see in the preceding screenshot, it is very easy to access health related information by using the HealthKit framework. The HealthKit framework includes a variety of other characteristics that you can access. For example, you can access the height and weight of an individual and work out their BMI.

Summary

In this chapter, you learned about the HealthKit framework, and how you can leverage this framework to request and authorize health information, by coordinating between the iOS app and the WatchKit extension. You also learned how to create a new WatchKit class for our profile details controller, and how to update the interface controller to utilize this class.

In the next chapter, you will learn how to use the table controller within the WatchKit platform, how to set it up and configure it, how to populate it through code, determine when a user has selected a row, and respond to the action. You will also learn how to integrate with the PassKit framework, and how to handle Apple Pay payments.

6

Implementing Tables within Your App

With the release of iPhone 6 and Apple Pay, Apple took a big step into the world of mobile payments, which will help users when purchasing items using their mobile devices. Purchasing items using Apple Pay can be achieved in two ways: by using **Near Field Communication** (**NFC**), or directly within the iOS app itself.

In this chapter, we will start developing a *Shopping List* application for Apple Watch and the iOS application, leveraging the PassKit framework so that our app is able to handle Apple Pay payments, and pass information between the iOS device and the WatchKit extension. You will learn how to use the WKInterfaceTable controller within the WatchKit platform, how to set them up and configure them, determine when a row has been selected by the user, and how to respond to that action.

You will also learn to populate your table, using the information stored within a dictionary dataset. To end the chapter, we will compile, build, and run the *Shopping List* application, and install it on the Apple Watch so that you can test the app and ensure that everything is working correctly.

This chapter includes the following topics:

- Provisioning, integrating, and using the PassKit framework for Apple Pay
- Building a *Shopping List* iOS and WatchKit extension application
- Adding a WKInterfaceTable table to the WatchKit extension
- Creating and configuring row controllers for your table content
- Populating a table, and determining when a row has been selected

We have an exciting project ahead of us, so let's get started.

Building the Shopping List application

In this section, we will design the user interface for our *Shopping List* application. Let's begin by developing the WatchKit portion of our application.

Before we proceed, we need to create our `ShoppingList` project; it is very simple to create using Xcode. Simply follow the steps listed next:

1. Launch Xcode from the `/Applications` folder.

2. Choose **Create a new Xcode project**, or go to **File | New Project**:

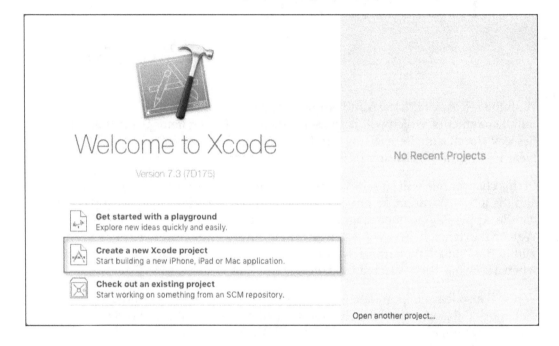

3. Select **iOS App with WatchKit App** from the list of available templates under the **watchOS** section, as shown in the following screenshot:

4. Click on the **Next** button to proceed to the next step in the wizard.
5. Next, enter in ShoppingList as the name for your project.
6. Select **Swift** from the **Language** drop-down menu.
7. Select **iPhone** from the **Devices** drop-down menu.
8. Ensure that the **Include Notification Scene** checkbox has been checked.

9. Click on the **Next** button to proceed to the next step in the wizard:

Choose options for your new project:

Product Name: ShoppingList

Organization Name: GENIESOFT STUDIOS

Organization Identifier: com.geniesoftstudios

Bundle Identifier: com.geniesoftstudios.ShoppingList

Language: Swift

Devices: iPhone

☑ Include Notification Scene
☐ Include Glance Scene
☐ Include Complication
☐ Include Unit Tests
☐ Include UI Tests

Cancel   Previous   Next

 The **Organization Identifier** for your app needs to be unique. Apple recommends that you use the reverse domain style (for example, `com.domainName.appName`).

10. Specify the location where you would like to save your project.

11. Then click on the **Create** button to save your project at the specified location.

Once your project has been created, you will be presented with the Xcode development environment along with the project files that the template created for you.

Setting up and provisioning your app for Apple Pay

Before you can begin accepting Apple Pay payments, you need to provision your iOS development profile to support this. In this section, we will look at the steps involved in providing your apps with the ability to accept and handle the processing of transactions that will be used outside of your app.

We have a lot to cover in this section, so let's get started:

1. First, log in to the iOS Developer portal at `http://developer.apple.com/`.

2. Click on the **Member Center** link that is located at the top of the screen.

3. Sign in to your account using your Apple ID and password. This will display the **Developer Program Resources** page from where you can download the SDKs and latest beta software, as well as manage your apps that are published on the App Store and the Mac App Store. This is seen in the following screenshot:

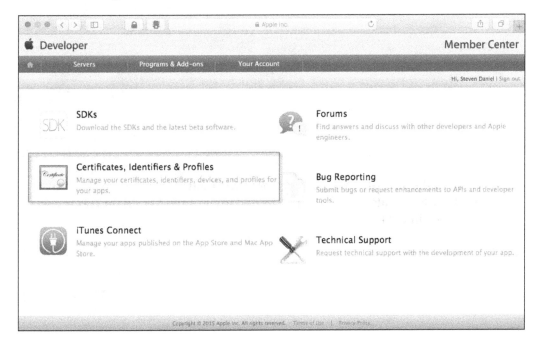

4. Next, click on the **Certificates, Identifiers & Profiles** button, as highlighted in the preceding screenshot. This is where you can manage your certificates and devices, and provision profiles for your apps.

5. On the **Certificates, Identifiers & Profiles** screen, click on the **Identifiers** button, as shown in the following screenshot:

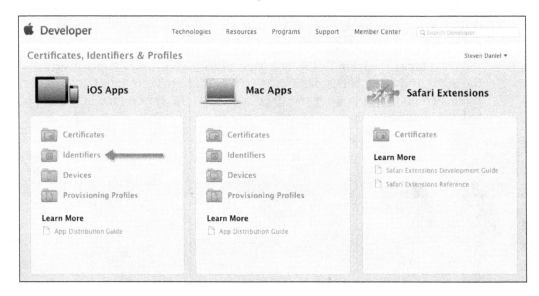

6. Next, in the **Identifiers** section, choose **Merchant IDs**, and then click on the **+** button located on the upper-right corner of the **Merchant IDs** screen, as shown in the following screenshot:

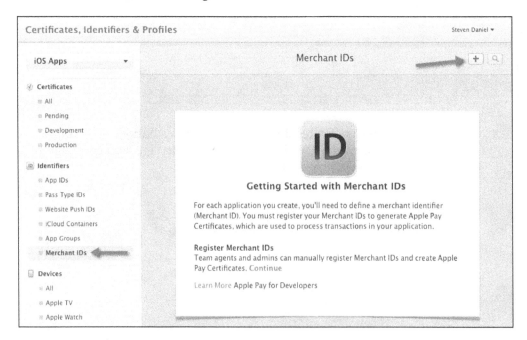

7. Provide a suitable name in the merchant **Description** field, or type in `WatchKit Shopping List` as the description.

8. Next, provide a suitable name in the merchant **ID** field, or enter `merchant.com.geniesoftstudios.ShoppingList` as the merchant ID:

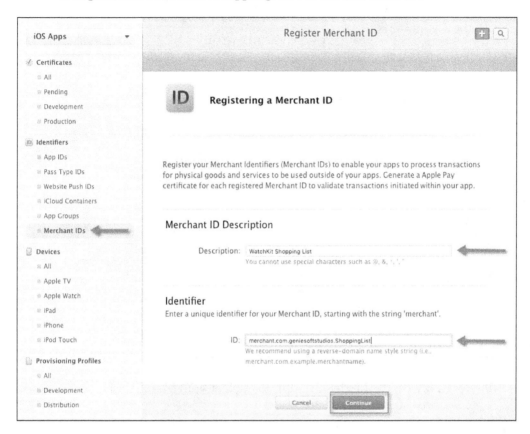

When you register your merchant identifiers, your apps are provided with the ability to handle processing of transactions that will be used outside of your app.

The identifier for your merchant ID needs to be unique, and must start with the string, `merchant`. Apple recommends that you use the reverse domain style (for example, `merchant.com.domainname.appName`).

9. Click on the **Continue** button to proceed to the next step in the wizard:

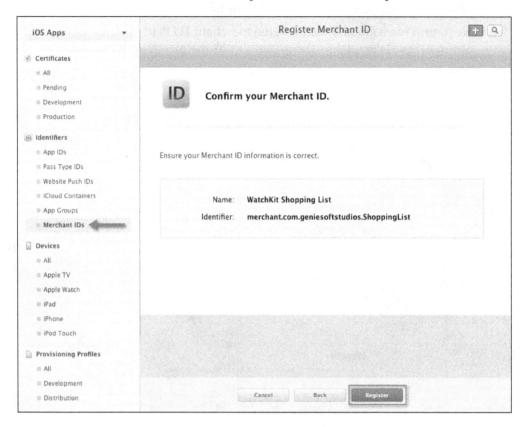

10. Next, click on the **Register** button to register your merchant ID, and proceed to the final step in the wizard:

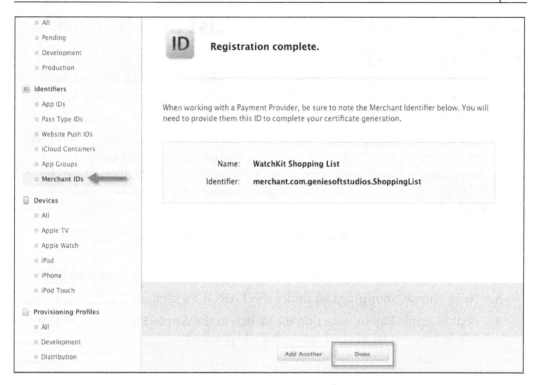

11. Click on the **Done** button to finalize the registration of your merchant ID.

 You will need to keep a copy of the identifier field, as you will need to enter this within your Xcode project's entitlements file which we will be covering in the next section.

Now that your App ID and merchant ID are both set up, our next step is to configure our `ShoppingList` Xcode project to support Apple Pay.

Configuring our Shopping List app to work with Apple Pay

When working with the PassKit framework, you need to provision the WatchKit application target with the PassKit entitlement so that the iPhone app is able to support Apple Pay payments.

In our next step, we need to enable the functionality for our `ShoppingList` iPhone target application. This will allow the app to communicate with the merchant ID that we set up in our developer portal. This will enable our application to handle any Apple Pay-related payment requests, and display the payment summary sheet when invoked:

1. Click and select the **ShoppingList** project from the project navigation window.

2. Then, select and click on the **Capabilities** tab within the project settings.

3. Next, choose **ShoppingList** under the **TARGETS** section.

4. Enable Apple Pay by selecting the switch in the **Apple Pay** section so that Xcode can provision your app to handle payments:

If you have any merchant IDs that you have previously set up within your Apple Developer account, Xcode will automatically download these for you, and display them within the **Merchant IDs** list box, as shown in the preceding screenshot.

5. Next, select and tick the **merchant.com.geniesoftstudios.ShoppingList** merchant ID that we created previously.

Now that we have successfully configured our project to use Apple Pay, our next step is to design the user interface for our *Shopping List* WatchKit extension counterpart, and integrate it with the Watch Connectivity framework that will handle the communication between the iPhone app and the WatchKit extension for passing product information.

Understanding the WatchKit table object

The WatchKit table (`WKInterfaceTable`) is similar to the `UITableView` class, which is used to manage and display a collection of data within an iPhone app.

However, the `WKInterfaceTable` class is not as flexible as the `UITableView` class, and now with the release of watchOS 2, the `WKInterfaceTable` class can only display a single dimension of data with no sections.

As with all the other classes that come with the WatchKit framework, that is, `WKInterfaceController`, `WKInterfaceObject`, and `WKInterfaceButton`, the `WKInterfaceTable` object works extremely well if you insist on using it within your storyboards. It is also very easy to set up and configure.

All you have to do is connect `WKInterfaceTable` to an `IBOutlet` from your storyboard, and set the number of rows to display and the row type, as follows:

```
tableName.setNumberOfRows(50, withRowType: "ShoppingRow")
```

The preceding code snippet initializes and sets up your table object with 50 rows. The great thing with using the `WKInterfaceTable` object, as compared to the `UITableView` class in iOS, is that there is no need to implement any data source, delegate a protocol, or to override any methods.

 The row type identifier used in the code snippet given previously is an identifier that behaves in the same way as the `UITableViewCell` reuse identifier.

Now that we have got all the theory behind WatchKit's `WKInterfaceTable` out of the way, we can move on to building our user interface for our *Shopping List* app.

Building the Shopping List application – WatchKit

In this section, we will begin building the user interface for our *Shopping List* application using Interface Builder, as well as all of the associated code for our ShoppingList WatchKit extension portion of our *Shopping List* application:

1. Select the **Interface.storyboard** file from the project navigation window.

2. From the Object Library, drag a WKInterfaceTable control to the watch area canvas:

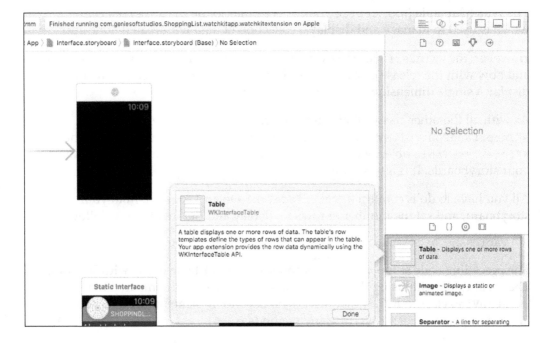

3. Next, select the WKInterfaceTable control that we added in the previous step.

4. In the **Table** section under Attributes Inspector, modify the **Prototype Rows** property to read **1**:

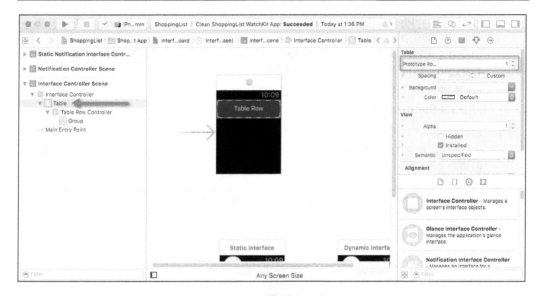

5. Select the **Table Row Controller** object as shown in the following screenshot. In the Attributes Inspector section, modify the **Identifier** property to read **ProductRow** and ensure that the **Selectable** checkbox is ticked:

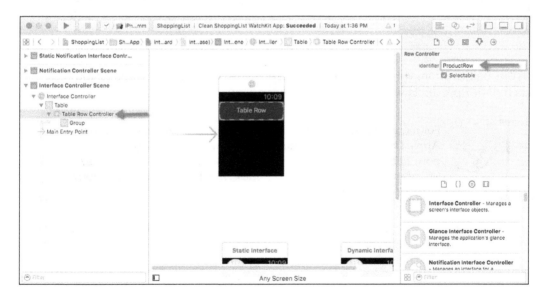

6. From the Object Library, drag a `WKInterfaceLabel` control to the watch area canvas, and place this within the `WKInterfaceGroup` control that we added in our previous step. Then, in the Attributes Inspector section, modify the **Text** property to read **Product Title**.

7. Next, modify the **Font** property to **Title 1**, the **Min Scale** property to **0.5**, and set the **Lines** property to **2**.

8. Ensure that both the **Width** and **Height** properties under the **Size** section are set to **Relative to Container**; this ensures that the label takes up the full size of the group:

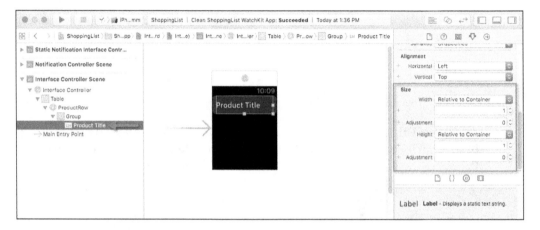

In our next section, we will create a new table row controller class for displaying each of our products within the table for each row.

For more information on the `WKInterfaceTable` class, refer to the Apple Developer documentation at `https://developer.apple.com/library/ios/documentation/WatchKit/Reference/WKInterfaceTable_class/index.html#//apple_ref/doc/uid/TP40014965`.

Creating the table row interface controller's WatchKit class

Now that we have created the user interface for our products, we can create a table row controller class that will inherit from the NSObject class. This class will be used to represent each row, and is wired up to each row within the ProductRow controller, which is responsible for setting up and configuring your row controllers:

1. From the project navigation window, select the **ShoppingList WatchKit App** group, and choose **File | New...**, or right-click and choose **New File...** from the list of options.

2. Next, choose the **watchOS** group; then, from the **Source** section, select the **WatchKit Class** from the list of available templates:

3. Click on the **Next** button to proceed to the next step within the wizard.

4. Enter ProductTableRow as the name of the class to be created.

5. Ensure that you have selected **NSObject** (from which the subclass is to be created) in the **Subclass of** drop-down list. Also, select **Swift** as the language to use from the **Language** drop-down list:

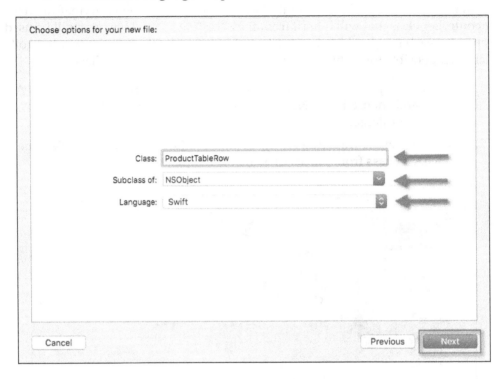

Choose options for your new file:

Class: ProductTableRow

Subclass of: NSObject

Language: Swift

Cancel   Previous   Next

6. Click on the **Next** button to proceed to the next step of the wizard.
7. Click on the **Create** button to save the file to the folder location specified.

The next step is to set the table row controller to use our `ProductTableRow` class — this will be used to display product-related information, and used later on to set up the Outlets within this class:

1. Select the **Interface.storyboard** file from the project navigation window.
2. Next, choose the interface controller, and select the **ProductRow** control; then click on the Identity Inspector button.

3. From the **Class** drop-down list, select the **ProductTableRow** class that we just created to use as our main class:

In this section, we successfully created a new `ProductTableRow` object class to use for our table row controller — we will add the necessary code later on. In the next section, we will connect the Outlets for each of our Interface Builder objects.

Configuring our product table row controller class

In the previous section, we added controls to our `Interface.storyboard` canvas to form the user interface for our *Shopping List* watch app, and set some properties for each of our controls as well.

Our next step is to create the Outlet for our table row controller class, which will be used to display our product information:

1. Open the Assistant Editor window by selecting **Navigate | Open in Assistant Editor**, or by pressing *Option + Command + ,*.

2. Ensure that the `ProductTableRow.swift` file is displayed within the Assistant Editor window, as shown in the following screenshot:

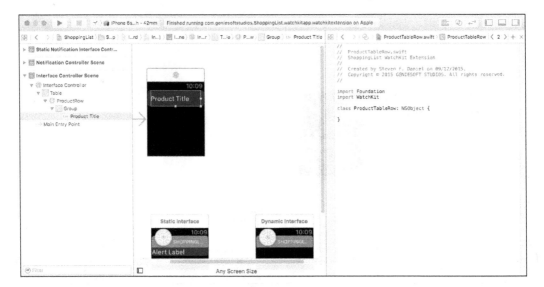

3. Next, select the **Product Title** (`WKInterfaceLabel`) control, then hold down the *Control* key, and drag it into the `ProductTableRow.swift` file within the body of `class ProductTableRow: NSObject`.

4. Choose **Outlet** from the **Connection** drop-down menu for the type of connection to create, and enter `productTitle` as the name of the Outlet property.

5. Next, choose **Weak** from the **Storage** drop-down menu, and click on the **Connect** button:

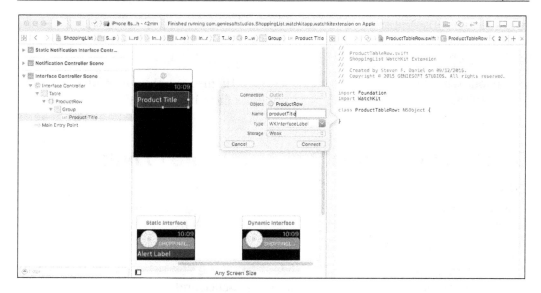

6. Once you have created the Outlet for our **Product Title**, save your project by selecting **File | Save**, or alternatively, pressing *Command + S*.

> Whenever you create an Outlet, you must remember to create it within the `InterfaceController` class, as it cannot be created outside this class body.

The following code snippet shows the complete implementation of the Outlets that we created in the preceding steps:

```
//    ProductTableRow.swift
//    ShoppingList WatchKit Extension
//
//    Created by Steven F. Daniel on 09/12/2015.
//    Copyright © 2015 GENIESOFT STUDIOS. All rights reserved.
//

import Foundation
import WatchKit

class ProductTableRow: NSObject {
    @IBOutlet var productTitle:  WKInterfaceLabel!
}
```

This was a pretty exhaustive section, but I am sure that you can really see and appreciate that using tables within the WatchKit platform is not too different from using them within your iPhone apps.

In the following sections, we will create a class structure to hold our product information. You will also learn how to populate the table row with information from a property list file.

Creating the product class structure to hold product items

Now that we have created the user interface for our table controller and product row controller, we will create a structure class, which will be used to hold information relating to each product:

1. From the project navigation window, select the **ShoppingList WatchKit App** group, and choose **File | New...**, or right-click and choose **New File...** from the list of options.

2. Next, choose the **iOS** group. From the **Source** section, select **Swift File** from the list of available templates, as shown in the following screenshot:

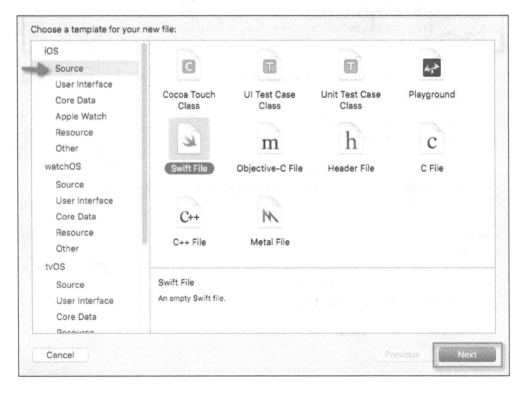

3. Click on the **Next** button to proceed to the next step within the wizard.

4. Type in Product as the name of the file to be created.

5. Ensure that you have selected **ShoppingList** as the name of the location for saving the file from the **Where** drop-down list.

6. Next, since we want to use the Product class for both our iPhone app and WatchKit extension classes, we need to ensure that both the **ShoppingList and ShoppingList WatchKit Extension** options have been ticked in the **Targets** section:

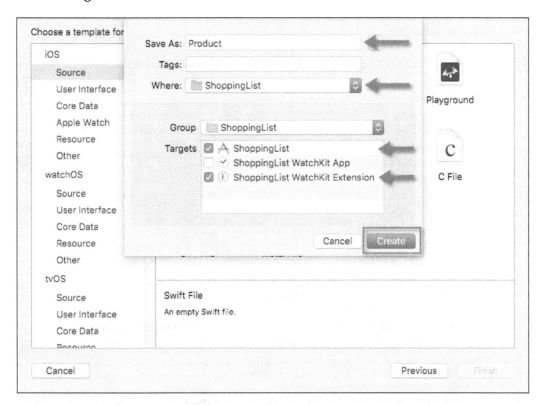

7. Finally, click on the **Create** button to save the file to the folder location specified.

Our next step is to add the code to our product file so that it can be shared between both our iOS and its WatchKit counterpart.

Open the `Product.swift` file located within the **ShoppingList** group from the project navigation window, and enter the following code snippet:

```
//
//  Product.swift
//  ShoppingList
//
//  Created by Steven F. Daniel on 09/12/2015.
//  Copyright © 2015 GENIESOFT STUDIOS. All rights reserved.
//

import Foundation

// A struct that maps to the products contained inside
// the ProductsList.plist file.
struct Product {

    // Allowable keys for a 'Products' dictionary representation.
    enum DictionaryKey: String {
        case Name  = "name"
        case Price = "price"
    }

    // Declare our class Properties
    var name: String
    var price: String

    // Initialization our structure class dictionary
    init(dictionary: [String: AnyObject]) {
     self.name = dictionary[DictionaryKey.Name.rawValue] as! String
     self.price = dictionary[DictionaryKey.Price.rawValue] as! String
    }
}
```

The preceding code snippet begins by importing our `Foundation` framework, which is a base layer for all Objective-C classes. This class provides useful object classes, which represent basic data types for handling strings, byte arrays, and all related classes based on the `NSObject` class. Next, we define an object, `struct`, for our product. This object groups all our objects within one object, making them easily accessible.

We then declare an enum object, `DictionaryKey`, which contains the allowable keys for each of our products. In our final step, we proceed to declare our class properties that will be used to store each value of name and price when items are added to our dictionary in the `init (dictionary: [String: AnyObject])` method call.

In this section, we successfully created a new struct class object. Structs are one of the named types that come with the Swift programming language. They allow you to encapsulate a collection of properties and the related behavior methods that you can use within your code. We will be using this struct class object to display product-related information details within our WatchKit extension and pass this information from the WatchKit extension controller to the iOS app counterpart to which we will begin adding the necessary code later on.

In the next section, we will populate our `WKInterfaceTable` object using the information stored within a property list—this is just a text file containing product information.

> For more information on the `Foundation` framework class, refer to the Apple Developer documentation at `https://developer.apple.com/library/ios/documentation/Cocoa/Reference/Foundation/ObjC_classic/`.

Creating the ProductsList property list

In our last section, we created the product structure, which will be used to store the information to be displayed within the WatchKit `WKInterfaceTable` control. It will also be used to send information when the user taps on a row within the table control.

In this section, we will look at how to create a property list file for storing product-related static information:

1. In the project navigation window, select the **ShoppingList WatchKit App** group, and choose **File | New...**, or right-click and choose **New File...** from the list of options.

2. Next, choose the **watchOS** group. Under the **Resource** section, select **Property List** from the list of available templates, as shown in the following screenshot:

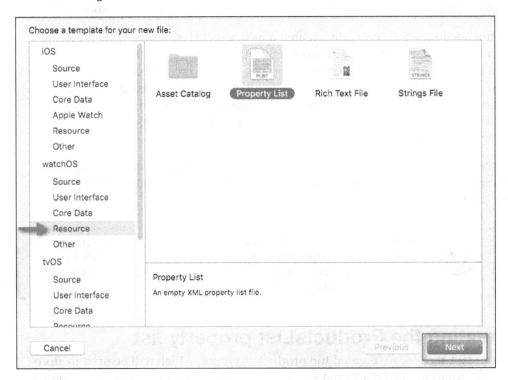

3. Click on the **Next** button to proceed to the next step within the wizard.

4. Enter ProductsList as the name of the file to be created.

5. Ensure that you have selected **ShoppingList WatchKit Extension** as the name of the location for saving the file from the **Where** drop-down list.

6. Next, ensure that the **ShoppingList WatchKit Extension** option has been ticked in the **Targets** section:

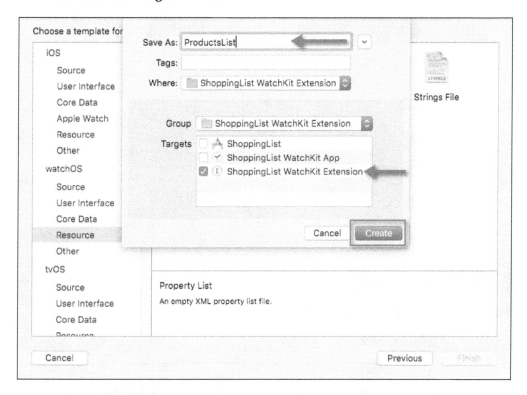

7. Finally, click on the **Create** button to save the file to the folder location specified.

Our next step is to add the code to our ProductsList.plist file so that we can display information within our WatchKit table controller:

1. Open the ProductsList.plist file located within the **ShoppingList WatchKit Extension** group in the project navigation window.

2. Next, right-click on the **ProductsList.plist** file, and choose **Open As | Source Code**, as shown in the following screenshot:

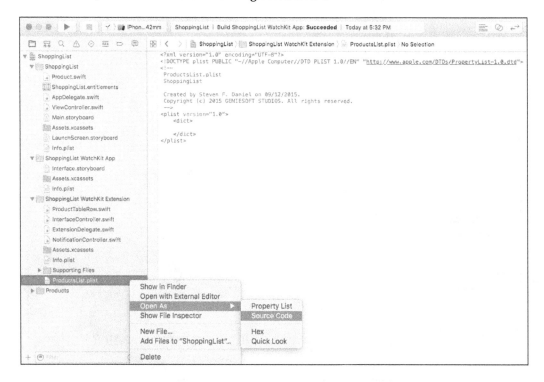

3. This will display the skeleton contents of our property list that we just created. Next, with the `ProductsList.plist` file displayed, enter the following highlighted code sections:

```
<plist version="1.0">
    <array>
        <dict>
            <key>name</key>
            <string>XBOX One 1TB</string>
            <key>price</key>
            <string>499.00</string>
        </dict>
        <dict>
            <key>name</key>
            <string>Apple Watch Sports Model</string>
            <key>price</key>
```

```
            <string>579.00</string>
        </dict>
        <dict>
            <key>name</key>
            <string>Samsung Galaxy Tab S (10.5, Wi-Fi)</string>
            <key>price</key>
            <string>759.00</string>
        </dict>
        <dict>
            <key>name</key>
            <string>LG 55UF850T 55&quot; 4K Ultra HD LED-LCD Smart
TV</string>
            <key>price</key>
            <string>1796.00</string>
        </dict>
    </array>
</plist>
```

What we have modified in our property list is to set up an array of dictionary items by specifying the `<array>` tag at the beginning. We subsequently created each dictionary object as well as the associated key-values for each item. This is so that we can easily access these objects from our `Product` class object, which we created previously.

Whilst property lists are great for handling small amounts of information, the following points explain when you should not use them in your application:

- Since the entire property list gets loaded into memory, you should avoid using them if you are dealing with huge amounts of data.

- If you need to set up and use relationships, such as database joins and query searches between table objects, or if you need to update, edit data, or remove items often, it is better to use Core Data or SQL.

- If your data doesn't consist of string or numbers, you should invest in looking for an alternative method.

For more information about property lists, refer to the Apple Developer documentation at https://developer.apple.com/library/mac/documentation/Cocoa/Conceptual/PropertyLists/AboutPropertyLists/AboutPropertyLists.html.

Populating our WatchKit table controller with row information

In the last section, we created the product structure that will be used to store the information to be displayed within the WatchKit `WKInterfaceTable` control, and which will be used to send information when the user taps on a row within the table control.

In this section, we will look at how we can use a property list file to read product-related static information, and populate each row of `WKInterfaceTable` using the `ProductTableRow` class:

1. Open the `InterfaceController.swift` file located within the **ShoppingList WatchKit Extension** group in the project navigation window, and enter the following code snippet:

```
//  InterfaceController.swift
//  ShoppingList WatchKit Extension
//
//  Created by Steven F. Daniel on 09/12/2015.
//  Copyright © 2015 GENIESOFT STUDIOS. All rights reserved.
//

import WatchKit
import Foundation
import WatchConnectivity

class InterfaceController: WKInterfaceController,
WCSessionDelegate {

    @IBOutlet weak var table: WKInterfaceTable!

    // Populate the products array from a plist and store
    // into an Array.
    lazy var ProductsList: [Product] = {
        let productsURL =
            NSBundle.mainBundle().URLForResource("ProductsList",
            withExtension: "plist")!
        let unarchivedProducts = NSArray(contentsOfURL:
productsURL)
        as! [[String: AnyObject]]
        return unarchivedProducts.map { Product(dictionary: $0) }
    }()
```

In the preceding code snippet, we begin by importing our Watch Connectivity framework. We then include the `WCSessionDelegate` class protocol method so that we can begin accessing the protocol's respective method callbacks.

Next we declare an `IBOutlet` property to our `WKInterfaceTable` object so that we can populate our list of product titles. We then declare a `ProductsList` object, that conforms to our products class object, and then proceed to read the contents of the `ProductsList.plist` file into an `NSArray` object. Finally, we use the `map` property of our `unarchivedProducts` variable to return an array of product titles from the `Product` dictionary.

2. With the `InterfaceController.swift` file still open, locate the `awakeWithContext` method, and enter the following highlighted code snippet:

```
override func awakeWithContext(context: AnyObject?) {
    super.awakeWithContext(context)

    // Perform any final initialization of your application.
    if WCSession.isSupported() {
        let session = WCSession.defaultSession()
        session.delegate = self
        session.activateSession()
    }
}
```

In the preceding code snippet, we check to see if our WatchKit extension is capable of accepting sessions, which is determined by the `WCSession` class. Next, we create and configure an instance of our `WCSession` class. We also set the delegate object for our current session before activating the `session` object for our WatchKit extension so that we can begin sending and receiving messages from our iOS device.

3. With the `InterfaceController.swift` file still open, locate the `willActivate` method, and enter the following highlighted code snippet:

```
// This method is called when watch view controller is about
// to be visible to user
override func willActivate() {

    super.willActivate()

    // Determine the total number of items within our array
    let rows = Array(count: ProductsList.count,
```

```
                          repeatedValue: "ProductRow")

      table.setRowTypes(rows)

      // Iterate through our collection and populate each
      // row within our WKInterfaceTable
      for i in 0 ..< ProductsList.count {
          let object = ProductsList[i];
          if let row = table.rowControllerAtIndex(i) as?
              ProductTableRow {
              row.productTitle.setText(object.name)
          }
      }
}
```

In the preceding code snippet, we begin by determining the number of rows that we have read from our `ProductList.plist` file, and the total number to our `rows` variable. Next, we use the `setRowTypes` method, which removes any existing rows from the table and configures a new set of rows based on the number of rows passed in.

In our next step, we iterate through the `ProductsList` array collection, create a new row that corresponds to the name of our row controller `ProductTableRow` that we defined within our storyboard file, and display the name of the product title.

Responding when a row has been selected within our table

In this section, we will look at how to determine when the user has tapped on a specific row within our `WKInterfaceTable` controller:

1. With the `InterfaceController.swift` file still open, enter the following code snippet to create the `didSelectRowAtIndex` method:

    ```
    // MARK: WKInterfaceTable Delegate Callbacks

    // Handle when a row has been selected within our table
    override func table(table: WKInterfaceTable, didSelectRowAtIndex
    rowIndex: Int) {

        // Send the product to be charged by sending the product as
        // a dictionary object,
        // and then converting it to a 'Product' type value in our
        // application delegate.
    ```

```
        // We will then have our iOS app immediately display the
        // payment sheet when it is invoked.
        let purchasedItem = [
            "product": [
              Product.DictionaryKey.Name.rawValue:
                      ProductsList[rowIndex].name,
              Product.DictionaryKey.Price.rawValue:
                      ProductsList[rowIndex].price
            ]
        ]
        // The paired iPhone has to be connected via Bluetooth so that
        // we can display the Apple Pay payment controller on the
phone.
        if WCSession.defaultSession().reachable {
            WCSession.defaultSession().sendMessage(purchasedItem,
            replyHandler: {
                    replyData in
                    },
                    errorHandler: { error in
                        // catch any errors here
                        print("Error occurred: \(error)")
            })
        }
    }
```

In the preceding code snippet, we start by creating a dictionary object, purchasedItem. We then grab the selected product from the ProductsList dictionary object for the row chosen by the user, which is returned in the rowIndex variable. Next, we check to see if our WCSession object for the current session is reachable on the iPhone counterpart, and then use the sendMessage method to notify the iOS application's didReceiveMessage method, which is located within the iOS app's view controller. The sendMessage method also declares the replyHandler and errorHandler closures, which will be called and passed back by the iOS application once the message request has been handled.

2. With the InterfaceController.swift file still open, type in the following code snippet to create the didReceiveMessage method:

```
// Handle the received message from the iOS app after
// successfully processing the payment
func session(session: WCSession, didReceiveMessage message:
[String : AnyObject], replyHandler: ([String : AnyObject]) ->
Void) {
        let cancel = WKAlertAction(title: "Cancel", style:
            WKAlertActionStyle.Cancel, handler: { () -> Void in
            })
        let action = WKAlertAction(title: "OK", style:
```

```
        WKAlertActionStyle.Default, handler: { () -> Void in
        })

        // Extract the Confirmation message sent by the iOS
        // app Confirmation screen
        let transactionDetails = message["confirmation"] as! String?
        presentAlertControllerWithTitle("Order Confirmation",
message:
        transactionDetails, preferredStyle:
        WKAlertControllerStyle.SideBySideButtonsAlert,
        actions: [cancel, action])
}
```

In the preceding code snippet, the `didReceiveMessage` method declares a `replyHandler` closure, which will be called when information has been sent by the iOS application. In this method, once we have successfully processed an Apple Pay payment, the order confirmation receipt message sent from the iOS app will be displayed.

Running the Shopping List application – WatchKit

In this section, we will compile and run our *Shopping List* application. Since Apple Pay supports only non-bank issued American Express cards, we will be running this within the WatchKit simulator:

1. To run the app, select the **ShoppingList WatchKit App** scheme and choose your preferred device from the **iOS Simulators** section, as shown in the following screenshot:

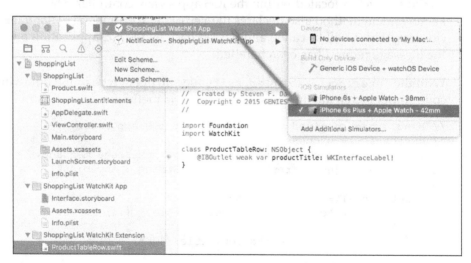

2. Next, build and run the application by selecting **Product | Run** from the
   Product menu, or alternatively, by pressing *Command + R*.

When the compilation completes, the *Shopping List* app will be installed on the
watchOS Simulator, and you will see something like the following screenshot
when the WatchKit extension is launched:

The preceding screenshot shows you the list of all the products, which have been
read and populated from the ProductsList.plist file, and displayed within our
WKInterfaceTable control. In the next section, we will build the iOS application
counterpart so that it can receive the product detail information.

You will also see how easy it is to use the PassKit framework for accepting payment
transactions for Apple Pay. We will then use the PassKit delegate callback methods
to determine if the transaction was successful, and present this to the user.

Handling payment requests with the PassKit framework

1. Open the ViewController.swift file located within the **ShoppingList**
   group from the project navigation window, and enter the following
   highlighted code snippet:

```
//  ViewController.swift
//  ShoppingList
//
//  Created by Steven F. Daniel on 09/12/2015.
//  Copyright © 2015 GENIESOFT STUDIOS. All rights reserved.
```

```
import UIKit
import PassKit
import Contacts
import WatchConnectivity

class ViewController: UIViewController,
PKPaymentAuthorizationViewControllerDelegate, WCSessionDelegate {

    // Declare our Apple Pay Merchant ID
    static let ApplePayMerchantID =
            "merchant.com.geniesoftstudios.ShoppingList"

    // Our app will support all available networks in Apple Pay.
    static let supportedPaymentNetworks = [
        PKPaymentNetworkAmex,
        PKPaymentNetworkMasterCard,
        PKPaymentNetworkVisa ]

    var product: Product!
    var paymentToken: PKPaymentToken!
```

In the preceding code snippet, we begin by importing the PassKit and `Contacts` frameworks, and include their `PKPaymentAuthorizationViewControllerDelegate` and `WCSessionDelegate` class protocol methods so that we can begin accessing each of the protocol's respective method callbacks. Next, we declare the Apple Pay merchant ID that we specified in the Apple Developer portal and the **Capabilities** tab, and then declare the `supportedPaymentNetworks`, which defines an array of payment networks that you are able to accept. Finally, we declare our `product` and `paymentToken` variables—the `product` variable will store the product passed from the WatchKit extension, while `paymentToken` will contain the token generated by the payment processor upon a successful transaction.

2. Next, with the `ViewController.swift` file still open, locate the `viewDidLoad` method, and enter the following highlighted code snippet:

```
override func viewDidLoad() {
    super.viewDidLoad()

    // Override point for customization after application launch.
    if WCSession.isSupported() {
        let session = WCSession.defaultSession()
        session.delegate = self
        session.activateSession()
    }
}
```

In the preceding code snippet, we begin by checking if our iPhone app is capable of accepting sessions, which is determined by the `WCSession` class. Next, we create and configure an instance of our `WCSession` class. We also set the delegate object for our current session before activating the `session` object for our iOS app, so that we can begin sending and receiving messages from our WatchKit extension.

3. With the `ViewController.swift` file still open, create the following `applePayButtonPressed` code snippet after the `didReceiveMemoryWarning` method:

```
// Method to handle when the Apple Pay button has been pressed
func applePayButtonPressed()
{
  // Check to see if we are authorized to make Apple Pay payments,
  // this will avoid crashes from our WatchKit Extension.
  if PKPaymentAuthorizationViewController.
canMakePaymentsUsingNetworks
    (ViewController.supportedPaymentNetworks) == true {
      // Set up our payment request.
      let paymentRequest = PKPaymentRequest()

      // Our merchant identifier needs to match what we
      // previously set up in the Capabilities window (or the
      // developer portal).
      paymentRequest.merchantIdentifier =
      ViewController.ApplePayMerchantID

      // Both country code and currency code are standard
      // ISO formats. Country should be the region you will
      // process the payment in. Currency should be the
      // currency you would like to charge in.
      paymentRequest.countryCode = "AU"
      paymentRequest.currencyCode = "AUD"

      // The networks we are able to accept.
      paymentRequest.supportedNetworks =
      ViewController.supportedPaymentNetworks

      // Specify the payment processing protocols that you
      // will be supporting. Default is .Capability3DS
      paymentRequest.merchantCapabilities = .Capability3DS

      // An array of Payment Summary Items that we'd like to
      // display on the payment sheet, which is declared in the
```

```
    // createSummaryItems function.
    paymentRequest.paymentSummaryItems = createSummaryItems(
    requiresInternationalSurcharge: false)

    // Request shipping information, in this case just
    // postal address.
    paymentRequest.requiredShippingAddressFields =
.PostalAddress

    // Display the view controller.
    let viewController = PKPaymentAuthorizationViewController(
    paymentRequest: paymentRequest)
     viewController.delegate = self
     presentViewController(viewController, animated: true,
     completion: nil)
  }
}
```

In the preceding code snippet, we begin by checking the
canMakePaymentsUsingNetworks property to see if the user can make
payments. Next, we create and instantiate a PKPaymentRequest object that
will be used to represent a single Apple Pay payment, and then assign
the capabilities for our transaction. The merchantIdentifier property
is a merchant ID, which we set up in the Apple Developer portal, and is
used to decrypt the data on the backend. The countryCode property is a
two-character country code where your transaction is taking place. The
currencyCode property is the currency that you want to set your transaction
to be processed in.

The supportedNetworks property tells the payment request about
the payment networks that will be supported within your app. The
merchantCapabilities property is the security standard that you want to
use — the default standard recommended by Apple Pay is 3DS. In our next
step, we make a call to the createSummaryItems method that provides
the user with a breakdown of the items in their purchase order. Here we
pass in false to let the payment sheet know that we don't want to charge
for international orders. Using the requiredShippingAddressFields, we
specify that we are requesting the user for their postal address for the order,
which will also incur a shipping fee.

Finally, we make a call to the PKPaymentAuthorizationViewController
method, and pass in our paymentRequest object, which contains all items
required to be purchased. We then call the presentViewController method
to present and display our Apple Pay payment sheet to the user. Our next
step is to create a list of summary items for the items chosen, including any
shipping or international charges on those items.

4. With the `ViewController.swift` file still open, create the following `createSummaryItems` code snippet after the `applePayButtonPressed` method:

```swift
// This function is used primarily to handle generation
// of our payment summary items, as well as applying
// international surcharges if required.
func createSummaryItems(requiresInternationalSurcharge
requiresInternationalSurcharge: Bool) -> [PKPaymentSummaryItem] {

    // Create our Product Summary Item object
    var items = [PKPaymentSummaryItem]()

    let productSummaryName = PKPaymentSummaryItem(label:
        String(product.name), amount:  NSDecimalNumber(string:
        ((product) != nil ? product.price : "0.00")))

    let productSummaryItem = PKPaymentSummaryItem(label: "Sub-
total",
        amount: NSDecimalNumber(string: ((product) != nil ?
        product.price : "0.00")))

    // For each item added, we need to apply this to our items
object
    items += [productSummaryName, productSummaryItem]
    let totalSummaryItem = PKPaymentSummaryItem(label: "GENIESOFT
        STUDIOS", amount: productSummaryItem.amount)

    // Apply an international surcharge, if needed.
    if requiresInternationalSurcharge {
        let handlingSummaryItem = PKPaymentSummaryItem(label:
        "International Handling", amount: NSDecimalNumber(string:
        "20.00"))

        // Calculate the total items in our shopping cart
        totalSummaryItem.amount =
        productSummaryItem.amount.decimalNumberByAdding
        (handlingSummaryItem.amount)
        items += [handlingSummaryItem]
    }

    items += [totalSummaryItem]
    return items
}
```

In the preceding code snippet, we create and instantiate a `PKPaymentSummaryItem` object, which will be used to provide the user with a breakdown of the items that they are purchasing. We then create a `productSummaryName` variable that creates a `PKPaymentSummaryItem` summary item, and we pass in the name and price of the chosen product, as sent by the WatchKit extension, to the iPhone app. The `productSummaryItem` variable creates a sub-total header for our order before adding these variable objects to our `items` object. Next, we create a `totalSummaryItem` header that will display **PAY GENIESOFT STUDIOS** in our payment summary sheet when invoked, along with the total amount payable.

In our next step, we check to see if we need to apply any international surcharges to our order. In the previous code snippet, we had passed in `false`, so our `requiresInternationalSurcharge` variable won't proceed to be executed. If we pass in `true`, we would have a new summary item added — **International Handling** — with a fee amount of $20.00. In our final steps, we calculate the total number of items for our shopping cart order, and return the items in our order to the `applePayButtonPressed` method. The `paymentSummaryItems` for our `PaymentRequest` object will contain our generated order details. Our next step is to create the `didSelectShippingContact` method, which will be responsible for any changes made by the user in their shipping information.

5. With the `ViewController.swift` file still open, create the following `didSelectShippingContact` code snippet after the `createSummaryItems` method:

```
func paymentAuthorizationViewController(controller:
PKPaymentAuthorizationViewController, didSelectShippingContact
contact: PKContact, completion: (PKPaymentAuthorizationStatus,
[PKShippingMethod], [PKPaymentSummaryItem]) -> Void) {
    // Create a shipping method
    let shipping = PKShippingMethod(label: "Standard Shipping",
    amount: NSDecimalNumber.zero())
    shipping.detail = "Delivers within two working days"

    // Obtain the postal address and check that it is correct,
    // we also check to see if country is not equal to Australia and
    // therefore don't apply the International Surcharge.
    let address = contact.postalAddress
    let requiresInternationalSurcharge = address!.country !=
        "Australia"
    let summaryItems =
        createSummaryItems(requiresInternationalSurcharge:
        requiresInternationalSurcharge)
        completion(.Success, [shipping], summaryItems)
}
```

Since we are using the `Contacts` framework in the preceding code snippet, the user has the ability to choose a shipping contact from their iOS device's address book. Upon selecting a contact, the `didSelectShippingContact` method is called, and a standard shipping method is created. However, if the postal address for the chosen contact is not in Australia, then an international surcharge is applied to the order (if `requiresInternationalSurcharge` has been set to `true`).

6. With the `ViewController.swift` file still open, enter the following `didAuthorizePayment` code snippet after the `didSelectShippingContact` method:

```
// This method handles the payment that is being processed, and
// presents a confirmation screen. If for any reason the payment
// processing of the payment fails, you would return
// 'completion(.Failure)' instead.
func paymentAuthorizationViewController(controller:
PKPaymentAuthorizationViewController, didAuthorizePayment payment:
PKPayment, completion: PKPaymentAuthorizationStatus -> Void) {
        paymentToken = payment.token
        completion(PKPaymentAuthorizationStatus.Success)
}
```

In the last code snippet, the `didAuthorizePayment` method is called when a payment has been sent for processing on the Apple Pay payment server. If a successful payment transaction has taken place, a `paymentToken` will be generated, and the `paymentAuthorizationViewControllerDidFinish` method is called to dismiss the payment summary sheet.

7. Next, with the `ViewController.swift` file still open, create the following `paymentAuthorizationViewControllerDidFinish` code snippet after the `didAuthorizePayment` method:

```
// This method tells the delegate that the payment
// authorization has completed.
func paymentAuthorizationViewControllerDidFinish(controller:
PKPaymentAuthorizationViewController) {
    // We always need to dismiss our payment view
    // controller when done.
    dismissViewControllerAnimated(true, completion: nil)

    // Use this to update the UI instantaneously (otherwise, takes a
    // little while)
    dispatch_async(dispatch_get_main_queue()) {
```

```
    // Send the payment transaction identifier to
    // the WatchKit Extension.
    if (self.paymentToken!.transactionIdentifier != "") {
        self.orderCompleted(self.paymentToken!.
transactionIdentifier)
        }
    }
}
```

In the preceding code snippet, the
paymentAuthorizationViewControllerDidFinish method is called
whenever the didAuthorizePayment method returns a status code of
PKPaymentAuthorizationStatus.Success from the Apple Pay processing
server. We then dismiss the payment view controller, and send the
transaction payment identifier to our orderCompleted method, which
will send the details to the WatchKit extension.

8. With the ViewController.swift file still open, create
    the following orderCompleted code snippet after the
    paymentAuthorizationViewControllerDidFinish method:

```
// This method is responsible for displaying the order
// receipt popup dialog on the Apple Watch
func orderCompleted(paymentIdentifier : String) {

    // Create our confirmation message which will be send
    // to the Watch.
    let confirmationMessage = [
        "confirmation": "Order successfully Processed, your
receipt#:
        \(paymentIdentifier)"
    ]
    // Send our order completed message to the paired Apple Watch.
    if WCSession.defaultSession().reachable {
        WCSession.defaultSession().sendMessage(confirmationMessage,
        replyHandler: {
            replyData in
        },
        errorHandler: { error in
            // If an error occurred, we need to handle it here.
            print("Error occurred: \(error)")
        })
    }
}
```

In the preceding code snippet, we begin by declaring the `confirmationMessage` object variable, which will contain the payment identifier once the order has successfully been processed by the `PKPaymentAuthorizationViewControllerDelegate` protocol methods. In our next step, we check to see if our paired Apple Watch is reachable and is capable of accepting sessions from the iPhone app, which is determined by the `WCSession` class.

Next, we create and configure an instance of our `WCSession` class. We also set the delegate object for our current session before activating the `session` object for our iOS app so that we can begin sending and receiving messages from the app. Any errors that occur during communication between the iOS app and the paired Apple Watch will be handled by the `errorHandler` closure.

9. Next, with the `ViewController.swift` file still open, create the following `sendMessage` code snippet after the `orderCompleted` method:

```
// This method is called when a response message is sent
// from the Apple Watch to a message sent by the counterpart
// process using the sendMessage:replyHandler:errorHandler:
method.
func session(session: WCSession, didReceiveMessage message:
[String : AnyObject], replyHandler: ([String : AnyObject]) ->
Void)
    {
    // Use this to update the UI instantaneously (otherwise,
    // takes a little while)
    dispatch_async(dispatch_get_main_queue()) {
        // Create a new product dictionary using the
        // supplied product.
        if let productDictionary = message["product"] as?
           [String: AnyObject] {
            let product = Product(dictionary: productDictionary)
            // Manually set the product we want to display, and
            // display the payment summary sheet.
            self.product = product
            self.applePayButtonPressed()
        }
    }
    }
}
```

In the preceding code snippet, we start by creating a dictionary object, `product`, and then grab the selected product from the `productDictionary` dictionary object for the chosen product from our WatchKit extension. We then manually set the product that we want to display within our payment summary sheet before making a call to our `applePayButtonPressed` method. The `didReceiveMessage` method also declares a `replyHandler` closure that can be used to communicate to the WatchKit extension to let the watch know that the message was received and handled.

For more information on Apple Pay, and to get a better understanding of the technology behind it, refer to the Apple Developer documentation at `https://developer.apple.com/library/ios/ApplePay_Guide/#//apple_ref/doc/uid/TP40014764-CH1-SW1`.

Building and running the Shopping List application

In this section, we will look at compiling and running our *Shopping List* application. Since Apple Pay supports only non-bank issued American Express cards, we will be running this within the WatchKit Simulator:

To run the app, select the **ShoppingList WatchKit App** scheme and choose your preferred device from the **iOS Simulators** section, as shown in the following screenshot:

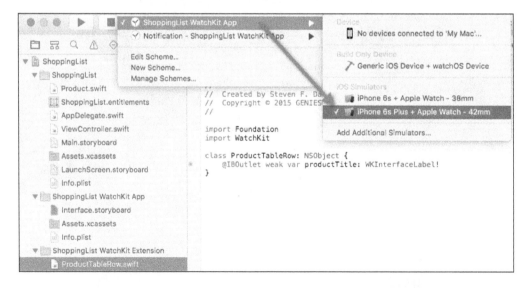

The preceding screenshot shows you the process when a product has been selected from the WatchKit extension and communicated with the iOS device. Since we have requested to have a shipping address as a requirement, you will notice that the **SHIPPING ADDRESS REQUIRED** text appears in red. The **Shipping Address** info with an exclamation mark prevents the user from progressing further, until they have provided this information:

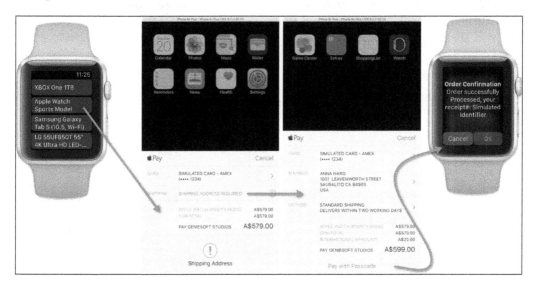

As you can see from the preceding screenshot, using the PassKit and the Watch Connectivity frameworks, you can allow your users to make purchases directly within your app, and then have this information coordinated between the iOS app and the WatchKit extension.

Summary

In this chapter, you learned how to set up and provision your app for use with Apple Pay and the PassKit framework. You learned how to manually set up a merchant ID for your development certificate in the Apple Developer portal, and add this to the **Capabilities** section of your iOS app. We then moved on to explaining how to use the WatchKit WKInterfaceTable, how to set it up, and configure it.

You learned how to create a table row controller that inherits from the NSObject class to store our product information. You now know how to use this class to populate product related information from our ProductsList property list file, and determine when a user has selected a row, and respond to the action.

In the final sections, you learned how to integrate with the PassKit framework, how to handle Apple Pay payments using the `PKPaymentAuthorizationViewControllerDelegate` protocol methods, and how to communicate between the WatchKit extension and the iOS app.

In the next chapter, you will learn how to incorporate menus within the WatchKit platform, and how you can allow your users to respond to actions. You'll learn how to create actions, and how to respond to them based on what the user has chosen. You will also learn how to integrate haptic feedback within your application.

7
Adding Menus to Your App

Apple introduced a new, easy-to-use API to create context menus on the WatchKit platform. This simple API doesn't require you to include any delegate callbacks within your code, and these menu items can be easily created using Interface Builder; all you have to do is connect them to each of the Action methods, similar to what you would do with buttons or other Interface Builder objects.

The Apple Watch retina display includes a new touch-based technology known as **Force Touch**, which is nothing more than a long press gesture on iOS devices or **3D Touch** on newer devices and is detected when the user applies slightly more pressure than performing a tap gesture. Whenever Apple Watch detects that a Force Touch gesture has been applied, the WatchKit app that is running displays the context menu, if one is configured.

In this chapter, we will begin by providing an overview of context menus before working through an application that builds upon our *Shopping List* application, which we built in the previous chapter, involving the use of incorporating WatchKit context menus and using the `WKInterfaceMenu` class.

We will also cover a section on how to use Taptic Engine to integrate haptic feedback within our application to respond to the actions chosen by the user.

This chapter includes the following topics:

- WatchKit menus using the `WKInterfaceMenu` class
- Gestures and how to handle these within the menu interface
- Adding `WKInterfaceMenu` to our *Shopping List* application
- Working with menus and responding to actions when selected
- Learning about the Apple Watch device's Taptic Engine and how to integrate haptic feedback that responds to actions

We have an exciting project ahead of us, so let's get started!

Introduction to gestures and the menu interface

Before we can begin creating a menu for our *Shopping List* application, we need to get an understanding of how WatchKit context menus work within the WatchKit framework and how you can go about creating them.

Understanding WatchKit context menu gestures

Under the iOS platform, you will be familiar with a gesture called long press, which you can define in your code using the `UILongPressGestureRecognizer` gesture, whereas under the WatchKit platform, the only gesture that is available to you is the Force Touch gesture.

So, what happens when a user initiates a Force Touch gesture? The Apple Watch hardware determines the difference between a hard force touch to bring up a menu and a tap to handle when a tap happens. All of the user swipe gestures to navigate forward and backward through your view controllers and scrolling through views within the WatchKit layout are automatically handled for you, and there is no need to add any additional code or gesture configurations. All that is required is to define the segues and layout of the objects in Interface Builder, and the watchOS takes care of the rest.

 Currently, within watchOS, there is no way of changing the behavior of the Force Touch gesture; this will always bring up the context menu should one exist within the current scene. The Apple Watch hardware, in its current state, doesn't provide support for multifinger gestures, such as pinches.

Let's take a look at how we would implement the `UILongPressGestureRecognizer` gesture recognizer within an iOS application to display different colored circles within the main view when the user presses down for a certain period of time. Execute the following code:

```
class ViewController: UIViewController, UIGestureRecognizerDelegate
{
    override func viewDidLoad() {
        super.viewDidLoad()

        let longPressGesture = UILongPressGestureRecognizer(target:
```

```
                                        self, action:
#selector(handleLongPress(_:)))

        longPress.minimumPressDuration = 1.0
        longPress.delegate = self
        self.view.addGestureRecognizer(longPressGesture)
    }
```

In the preceding code snippet, we began by creating `longPressGesture` using the
`UILongPressGestureRecognizer` class. This class accepts two parameters: the
`target` property, which will accept the long press gesture, and an `action` property
that will be triggered when the amount of time crosses the `minimumPressDuration`
property's value, which specifies the minimum period that a finger must be pressed
upon the view for the gesture to be recognized. Next, we will specify and set up our
delegate for our current view controller so that it can begin receiving gesture-level
events when the user presses within the view. Execute the following code:

```
func handleLongPress(gestureReconizer: UILongPressGestureRecognizer) {
    // Check to see if we have began our long-press gesture
    if gestureReconizer.state != UIGestureRecognizerState.Ended {
        return
    }

    // find touch/long press location
    let touchLocation = gestureReconizer.locationInView(self.view)

    // create a custom frame having touched point as the center
    // of the given frame.
    let myCustomView = UIView(frame: CGRectMake(touchLocation.x - 25,
                    touchLocation.y - 25, 50, 50))

    // set corner radius and border thickness
    myCustomView.layer.cornerRadius = myCustomView.layer.frame.width/2
    myCustomView.layer.borderWidth = 1.0

    // set view background color randomly
    let Red = CGFloat( (arc4random_uniform(255) + 50)  / 255)
    let Green = CGFloat( (arc4random_uniform(255) + 50) / 255)
    let Blue = CGFloat( (arc4random_uniform(255) + 50) / 255)

    // Set the background color for our custom view
    myCustomView.backgroundColor = UIColor(red: Red, green: Green,
                                    blue: Blue, alpha: 1.0)

    // add custom view in to main view
    self.view.addSubview(myCustomView)
    }
}
```

In the preceding code snippet, we began by checking whether our gesture began using the `.state` property of our `gestureRecognizer` parameter. If we lifted our finger from the view, we would exit from this method; otherwise, we would proceed to determine the location where the touch was made by the user using the `locationInView` method and passing in our current view.

This method will return the coordinate locations, representing the x and y positions within the view where the user placed their finger. Next, we will create a custom frame containing the touched area to be the center point within our given frame and then apply the radius and border thickness. In our next step, we will set the background colors randomly for red, green, and blue using the `arc4random_uniform` method to randomize a value between 50 and 255, and change each color by dividing it by 255. Finally, will we set the background color for our custom view and then add the custom view to the main view at the touched location within the view.

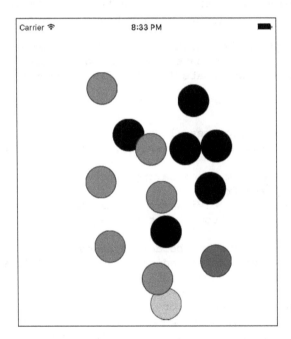

The preceding screenshot shows you the various touch locations within the current view, each containing different colored circles as generated by our `arc4random_uniform` method.

You can create some interesting apps using gestures, and the iOS framework contains a number of different gesture recognizers; the `UILongPressGestureRecognizer` is only one of them.

 For more information on the `UILongPressGestureRecognizer` class, you can refer to the Apple Developer documentation at `https://developer.apple.com/library/ios/documentation/UIKit/Reference/UILongPressGestureRecognizer_Class/`.

Understanding the WatchKit context menu interface

Whenever you need to incorporate a WatchKit context menu to your current interface, you need to first set up each of the menu items using Interface Builder.

Each of these menu items comprises a title that will be displayed as text in the context menu interface as well as an image. The following screenshot showcases the standard menu icons that come as part of the WatchKit context menu interface, which you can use within your own applications, as follows:

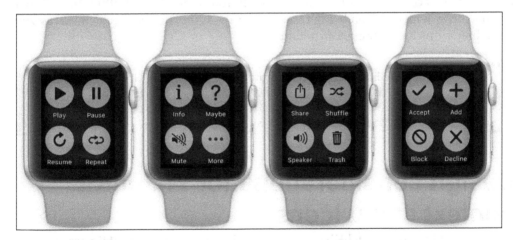

As Apple Watch comes in two different sizes, 38 mm and 42 mm, you will need to handle these differently if you are planning on creating your own custom icons as you will need to create differently sized icons for each device.

WatchKit context menus don't provide you with the ability to scroll within the interface or allow you to add any interface objects. If you decide to add more than four objects, the WatchKit framework will only show the first four and then discard the rest.

Apple Watch Human Interface Guidelines include best practices and recommendations for designing your own customized icons, some of which are as follows:

- When designing custom icons for the 38 mm Apple Watch device, you'll want to make your icon canvas size 70 pixels and the content size 46 pixels

- When designing custom icons for the 42 mm Apple Watch device, you'll want to make your icon canvas size 80 pixels and the content size 54 pixels

 The canvas size of an icon is the entire size that it occupies. The content size defines the actual bounds of the icon: its height and width. When creating WatchKit icons, you can simply fit your icons into the content size, and the system will scale the images appropriately.

With WatchKit context menus, you can only fit four menu icons within the screen at any one time, with one icon being reserved for the **Cancel** button, which leaves you with three icons for your custom actions.

 For more information on designing your own WatchKit context menu icons, you can refer to the Apple Watch Human Interface Guidelines at https://developer.apple.com/watch/human-interface-guidelines/icons-and-images/.

Design considerations for WatchKit context menu icons

When designing your WatchKit context menu icons, they must contain actions that users can perform, and each action must contain a label and icon. Text labels associated with the menu can contain up to two lines of text, and menu icons are template images, which use the image's alpha value to define their shape.

The following table explains the different menu icon sizes for each of the associated asset image types:

Asset image types	Apple Watch (38 mm)	Apple Watch (42 mm)
The notification center icon	48 pixels	55 pixels
The long-look notification icon	80 pixels	88 pixels
The home screen icon	80 pixels	80 pixels
The short look icon	172 pixels	196 pixels

The following screenshot highlights the required design considerations that you must adhere to when creating your customized menu icons. You need to consider using line weights that are appropriate for your device size, and the complexity of the icon by setting the line thickness to four pixels or greater to ensure that they remain legible.

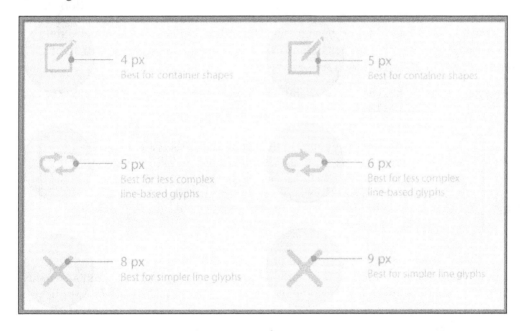

Now that we have all of the theory behind WatchKit menus and the considerations behind them when creating customized icons, we can move on to discussing how to call WatchKit context menu actions using the WatchKit context menu methods.

Understanding the default WatchKit context menu actions

Unlike `UIActionSheet` or `UIAlertView`, you don't need to conform to any protocols or delegate objects to get WatchKit menus working. All you have to do is simply create your menu items in Interface Builder or within the code and then connect the items to actions in `WKInterfaceController`.

By default, all the menu items that you add to the `WKInterfaceMenu` object are set up as **Cancel** button actions. If you don't decide to connect your menu item to an action either through Interface Builder or through code, simply tapping on a menu item will dismiss the context menu.

You also have the ability to dynamically create your own menu items within code by making a call to the `addMenuItemWithIcon` method by referencing the WatchKit context menu icon options defined within the `WKMenuItemIcon` enumeration class.

To take a look at how this can be achieved, the following code adds a menu item to a context menu using the Trash template icon that is configured to call an action method named `clearAllMenuItems`:

```
addMenuItemWithItemIcon(WKMenuItemIcon.Trash, title: "Clear List",
action: "clearAllMenuItems")
```

> For more information on the `WKMenuItemIcon` enumeration class, you can refer to the `WKInterfaceController` class for information on its methods at `https://developer.apple.com/library/ios/documentation/WatchKit/Reference/WKInterfaceController_class/#//apple_ref/c/tdef/WKMenuItemIcon`.

Now that you have a better understanding of how to programmatically add WatchKit menu items and use the methods associated with the `WKInterfaceMenu` class, we can move on to building the user interface for our *Shopping List* application.

Adding a menu to our Shopping List application – WatchKit

In this section, you will learn how to add a menu to our existing *Shopping List* application from the previous chapter. Perform the following steps:

1. Select the **ShoppingList.xcodeproj** file from the Chapter 06 folder in the accompanying code bundle, as shown in the following screenshot:

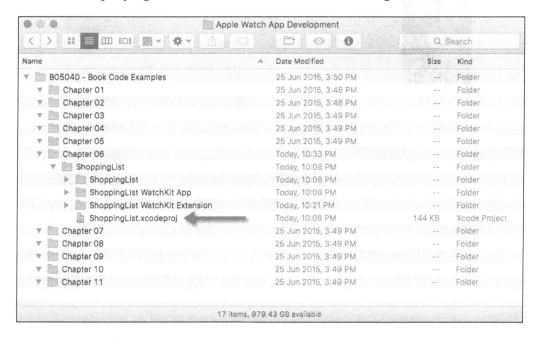

2. Next, ensure that the ShoppingList Xcode project file is open within the Xcode development IDE.

3. Now, select the **Interface.storyboard** file located within the **ShoppingList WatchKit Extension** group in the project navigation window.

4. Then, from Object Library, drag a `WKInterfaceMenu` control to the watch area canvas.

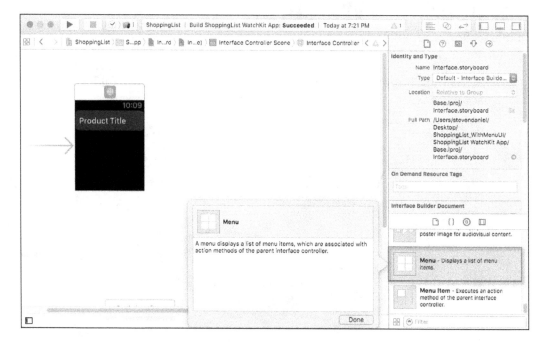

5. Next, select the **Menu** (`WKInterfaceMenu`) control that we added previously.

6. Then, from the Attributes Inspector section in the **Menu** section, change the **Items** property to **4**.

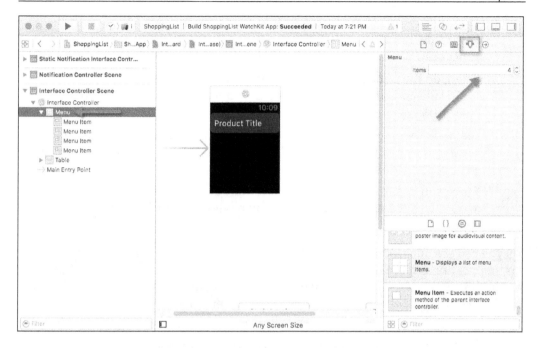

7. Now, select the first **Menu Item** (`WKInterfaceMenuItem`) object under **Menu** on the left-hand side and modify the **Title** property to **Clear List** and the **Image** property to **Trash**.

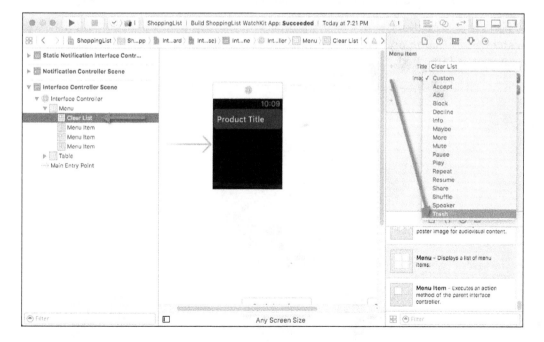

8. Repeat the same for the second **Menu Item** object under **Menu** on the left-hand side, but change its **Title** property to **Refresh List** and **Image** property to **Repeat**.

9. Then, do the same for the third **Menu Item** object under **Menu** on the left-hand side and change its **Title** property to **Scroll to Top** and **Image** property to **Shuffle**.

10. Next, do the same for the fourth **Menu Item** object under **Menu** on the left-hand side and change its **Title** property to **Scroll to Bottom** and **Image** property to **Shuffle**.

11. Once you create all of the menu items for our WatchKit context menu, it would be good to save your project by navigating to **File | Save** or pressing *Command + S*.

As you can see, incorporating WatchKit context menus within our *Shopping List* application is a breeze. Next, we need to compile and run our *Shopping List* application to watch our menu in action. Selecting menu items won't do anything until we connect them to their associated action event methods. So, perform the following steps:

1. To run the app, select the **ShoppingList WatchKit App** scheme and choose your preferred device from under the **iOS Simulators** section.

2. Next, build and run the application by going to **Product | Run** from the **Product** menu or by pressing *Command + R*.

When the compilation is complete, the *Shopping List* app will be installed on the watchOS simulator, and you will see the following image when the WatchKit extension is launched:

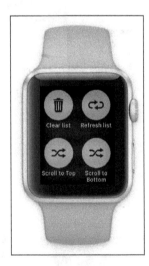

If you run this within the Apple Watch simulator, you will need to navigate to the **Hardware | Force Touch Pressure | Deep Press** menu option or press *Command + Shift + 2* and then click on the screen before switching back to the **Shallow Press** mode by pressing *Command + Shift + 1*.

In the next section, we will take a look at how we can create the WatchKit context menu items programmatically through code using the `addMenuItemWithItemIcon` method.

Establishing the WatchKit context menu connections

There are two ways in which we can go about creating WatchKit context menu items. In the previous section, we discussed how we can drag and drop a `WKInterfaceMenu` control in `InterfaceController` within the storyboard that will contain the menu.

You can also create them programmatically using the `WKInterfaceController` method and provide an image, a title, and the associated action method that will get executed when the menu item is tapped by the user. Simply perform the following steps:

1. Open the `InterfaceController.swift` file located within the **ShoppingList WatchKit Extension** group from the project navigation window.

2. Next, locate the `awakeWithContext` method and enter the following highlighted code snippet:

```
override func awakeWithContext(context: AnyObject?) {
    super.awakeWithContext(context)

    // Perform any final initialization of your application.
    if WCSession.isSupported() {
        let session = WCSession.defaultSession()
        session.delegate = self
        session.activateSession()
    }
    // Call our instance method to create our Menu Items
    createMenuButtons()
}
```

In the preceding code snippet, we checked whether our WatchKit extension is capable of accepting sessions by calling the `isSupported` method using the `WCSession` class. Next, we created and configured an instance of our `WCSession` class and set the `delegate` object for our current session before calling the `activateSession` property to activate our current session for our WatchKit extension so that we can begin sending and receiving messages from our iOS device, before finally calling our `createMenuButtons` instance method to create our menu items.

3. Next, with the `InterfaceController.swift` file still open, create the following `createMenuButtons` method and enter the following code snippet:

```
// Instance method to handle creating of our WKInterfaceMenu
// menu items
func createMenuButtons() {

    // Create and add our menu item for our Clear List button
    addMenuItemWithItemIcon(WKMenuItemIcon.Trash, title: "Clear
list",

                            action: "menuClearList")

    // Create and add our menu item for our Refresh List button
    addMenuItemWithItemIcon(WKMenuItemIcon.Repeat, title: "Refresh
        List", action: "menuRefreshList")

    // Create and add our menu item for our Clear List button
    addMenuItemWithItemIcon(WKMenuItemIcon.Shuffle, title: "Scroll
to
        Top", action: "menuScrollToTop")

    // Create and add our menu item for our Clear List button
    addMenuItemWithItemIcon(WKMenuItemIcon.Shuffle, title: "Scroll
to
        Bottom", action: "menuScrollToBottom")
}
```

In the preceding code snippet, we began by creating our `createMenuButtons` method and then used the `addMenuItemWithItemIcon` method to create each of our menu items. The `addMenuItemWithItemIcon` method accepts an image using one of the defined types as mentioned in the *Understanding the default WatchKit context menu actions* section of this chapter. We then specified a title for our menu item using the `title` property and an `action` property to call the associated method when the button is pressed.

4. Next, with the `InterfaceController.swift` file still open, create the following `menuClearList` method and enter the following code snippet:

```
// Handle clearing all items within our list when the user
// presses the Clear List button
@IBAction func menuClearList() {
    print("Clear List Pressed")

    // Quick way to remove all rows from our table
    table.setNumberOfRows(0, withRowType: "ProductRow")
}
```

In the preceding code snippet, we checked whether our WatchKit extension is capable of accepting sessions, which is determined by the `WCSession` class. Next, we created and configured an instance of our `WCSession` class and set the `delegate` object for our current session before activating the `session` object for our WatchKit extension so that we can begin sending and receiving messages from our iOS device.

5. Next, with the `InterfaceController.swift` file still open, create the following `menuRefreshList` method and enter the following code snippet:

```
// Handle refreshing our list when the user presses the
// Refresh List button
@IBAction func menuRefreshList() {
    print("Refresh List")

    // Specify the number of rows that our table will contain
    table.setNumberOfRows(ProductsList.count, withRowType:
    "ProductRow")

    // Iterate through our collection and populate each
    // row within our WKInterfaceTable
    for i in 0 ..< ProductsList.count {
        let object = ProductsList[i]
        if let row = table.rowControllerAtIndex(i) as?
ProductTableRow {
            row.productTitle.setText(object.name)
        }
    }
}
```

In the preceding code snippet, we began by determining how many rows we read from our `ProductList.plist` file and the total number of our row variables. Next, we used the `setNumberOfRows` method to configure a new set of rows based on the number of rows passed in. In our next step, we iterated through our `ProductsList` array collection and created a new row corresponding to the name of our `ProductTableRow` row controller, which we defined within our storyboard file, and displayed the name of the product title.

6. Next, with the `InterfaceController.swift` file still open, create the following `menuScrollToTop` method and enter the following code snippet:

```
// Handle scrolling to the top of the list when the user presses
// the Scroll to Top button
@IBAction func menuScrollToTop() {
    // Scroll to the first item within our table
    table.scrollToRowAtIndex(0)
}
```

In the preceding code snippet, we began by calling the `scrollToRowAtIndex` method of our WatchKit extension's `table` instance to scroll to a specific row programmatically. This method accepts an integer parameter value that represents the index position of the destination row. In this example, as we wanted to scroll to the first item within our `table` object instance, we passed in a value of `0` so as to position us at the top of our list.

7. Next, with the `InterfaceController.swift` file still open, create the following `menuScrollToBottom` method and enter the following code snippet:

```
// Handle scrolling to the bottom of the list when the user
presses
// the Scroll to Bottom button
@IBAction func menuScrollToBottom() {
    // Scroll to the last row item within our table
    table.scrollToRowAtIndex(table.numberOfRows - 1)
}
```

In the preceding code snippet, we began by calling the `scrollToRowAtIndex` method of our WatchKit extension's `table` instance to scroll to a specific row programmatically. In this method, we passed in the total number of rows that our `table` instance contains using the `numberOfRows` property on our `table` instance and then subtracted one to represent the index position of the last item within our table.

Design considerations when using Taptic Engine

According to Apple, Taptic Engine is an electromagnetic linear actuator, which is basically a small electronic motor that controls a magnetic field to produce haptic feedback.

Haptic feedback is basically a series of small taps that notifies you in response to different actions. An example of this would be if you were iterating through items within an array and wanted to be notified once you scrolled to the end of the list, you could send a `.Click` haptic for the `table` instance within the WatchKit extension.

Whenever you design your apps to include support for playing haptics using Apple Watch Taptic Engine, there is no ability to play more than one haptic at the same time, and there is a delay between each one that can be played.

For more information on Apple Watch Design Guidelines, refer to the Apple Developer documentation at `https://developer.apple.com/watch/human-interface-guidelines/watch-technologies/`.

In the next section, we will look at how easy it is to integrate the use of Apple Watch haptics within your applications.

Learning how to integrate Apple Watch haptics within an app

The integration of haptics within your applications is an important way of getting a user's attention and displaying important information within Apple Watch. Each haptic that is generated by Taptic Engine is combined with an audible tone, with both the elements working together to handle the same information in a consistent manner.

Apple Watch defines haptics for each specific purpose, and each haptic type conveys a specific meaning and should be used infrequently by your app. When using haptics, Taptic Engine prevents any two haptics from playing at the same time.

In this section, we will take a look at how we can incorporate the use of haptics within our application. The following table explains the purpose of haptics and when you should use them in your applications:

Apple Watch haptic purposes	Haptic purpose description
Exercise restraint when using haptics	You should use haptics to draw attention only to important events, and an overuse of haptic feedback can confuse the user as well as reduce the usefulness of this feedback.
Use each haptic only for its intended purpose	Each haptic and audible tone was designed for a specific purpose, and using haptics for different purposes will confuse the meaning for the user.
Provide visual cues to correspond with haptics	Updating the visual appearance or content of your interface reinforces the meaning of a triggered haptic. Providing visual and haptic feedback together creates a deeper connection between the user's action and the result.
Initiate the playback of haptics at the appropriate time	There is usually some time involved in playing haptics, and it is better to initiate the playback of a haptic sooner than later. If you initiate playback as the final step of a task, the haptic feedback might happen too late and present a disconnected feeling between the haptic and the current task at hand.

The notification property of the haptic tells the user that something significant or out of the ordinary has happened and requires the user's attention. This same haptic is played by the system when a local or remote notification arrives.

Playing haptics is really simple using the API; just make a call to the `playHaptic()` method as shown in the following code snippet:

```
WKInterfaceDevice.currentDevice().playHaptic(.Click)
```

Unfortunately, there is no ability to allow developers to define their own custom haptic events, so if you want to include the ability to incorporate haptic feedback within your app, you will have to do it with one of the haptic feedbacks explained in the following table:

Haptic type (WKHapticType)	Description
`.Notification`	The `.Notification` type is the normal notification haptic that is used to alert the user when something requires their attention
`.DirectionUp`	The `.DirectionUp` type is used to alert the user when a significant increase in value has happened above the set threshold, such as when moving up through a list

Haptic type (WKHapticType)	Description
.DirectionDown	The .DirectionDown type is used to alert the user when a significant decrease in value has happened below the set threshold, such as when moving down through a list
.Success	The .Success type is used to indicate when an action is completed successfully
.Failure	The .Failure type is used to indicate when an action fails
.Retry	The .Retry type is used to indicate when an action fails, but it provides the user with an opportunity to try again
.Start	The .Start type is used to indicate that a process is about to begin, such as when you want to use a timer to count down
.End	The .End type is used to indicate when a process is about to end, such as when your countdown timer reaches zero
.Click	The .Click type is used to indicate a subtle tap sound, such as when clicking on a button

In the preceding table, we covered each of the various haptic type events and provided an explanation of what each one does as well as when each of these haptic types should be used.

> For more information on the PlayHaptic class, refer to the Apple Developer documentation at https://developer.apple.com/ library/watchos/documentation/WatchKit/Reference/ WKInterfaceDevice_class/index.html/navigation/#// apple_ref/doc/uid/TP40014996-CH1-SW16.

Now that you have a good understanding of Taptic Engine and the design considerations surrounding how to properly use it, we need to incorporate haptic feedback when we successfully process our shopping list order or, alternatively, if we receive an error due to something going wrong with the payment server. Perform the following steps:

1. Open the InterfaceController.swift file located within the **ShoppingList WatchKit Extension** group in the project navigation window.

2. Next, locate the didSelectRowAtIndex method and enter the following highlighted code snippet:

```
// MARK: WKInterfaceTable Delegate Callbacks

// Handle when a row has been selected within our table
```

```
    override func table(table: WKInterfaceTable, didSelectRowAtIndex
    rowIndex: Int) {

        // Send the product to be charged by sending the product
        // as a dictionary object, and then converting it to a 'Product'
        // type value in our application delegate.

        // We will then have our iOS app immediately display the
        // payment sheet when it is invoked.
        let purchasedItem = [
            "product": [
                    Product.DictionaryKey.Name.rawValue:
                    ProductsList[rowIndex].name,
                    Product.DictionaryKey.Price.rawValue:
                    ProductsList[rowIndex].price
                ]
            ]

        // The paired iPhone has to be connected via Bluetooth so that
        // we can display the Apple Pay payment controller on the phone.
        if WCSession.defaultSession().reachable {
            WCSession.defaultSession().sendMessage(purchasedItem,
            replyHandler: { replyData in
            },
            errorHandler: { error in
             // Catch any errors here

            // Engage the haptic engine within the Apple Watch
            // to provide haptic feedback to the user, when an
            // error has occurred sending product details.
            WKInterfaceDevice.currentDevice().playHaptic(.Failure)
             print("Error occurred: \(error)")
            })
        }
    }
```

In the preceding code snippet, we started by creating a purchasedItem dictionary object and then grab the selected product from the ProductsList dictionary object for the chosen row by the user, which is returned in the rowIndex variable.

Next, we checked whether our `WCSession` object for the current session is reachable on the iPhone counterpart and then used the `sendMessage` method to notify the iOS application's `didReceiveMessage` method, which is located within the iOS app's view controller. The `sendMessage` method also declared `replyHandler` and `errorHandler` closures that will be called and passed back by the iOS application once the message request is handled.

If any errors occur during the processing of our order, we will engage the Apple Watch Taptic Engine by calling the `playHaptic` API method, passing in the `.Failure` property to notify the user that an error has occurred.

3. Next, with the `InterfaceController.swift` file still open, locate the `didReceiveMessage` method and enter the following highlighted code snippet:

```
// Handle the received message from the iOS app after successfully
// processing the payment
func session(session: WCSession, didReceiveMessage message:
[String : AnyObject], replyHandler: ([String : AnyObject]) ->
Void) {
    let cancel = WKAlertAction(title: "Cancel", style:
        WKAlertActionStyle.Cancel, handler: { () -> Void in
        })
    let action = WKAlertAction(title: "OK", style:
        WKAlertActionStyle.Default, handler: { () -> Void in
    })

    // Engages the haptic engine within the Apple Watch to
    // provide haptic feedback to the user, to let them know
    // that the order has successfully processed.
    WKInterfaceDevice.currentDevice().playHaptic(.Success)

    // Extract the Confirmation message sent by the iOS app
    // Confirmation screen.
    let transactionDetails = message["confirmation"] as! String?
        presentAlertControllerWithTitle("Order Confirmation",
message:
        transactionDetails, preferredStyle:
        WKAlertControllerStyle.SideBySideButtonsAlert, actions:
        [cancel, action])
    }
```

In the preceding code snippet, the `didReceiveMessage` method declared a `replyHandler` closure that will be called when information is sent by the iOS application. In this method, once we successfully process an Apple Pay payment, we will call the `playHaptic` API method to engage Apple Watch Taptic Engine and pass in the `.Success` haptic feedback type to play.

This will notify the user that the order is successfully processed before displaying an order confirmation receipt message that is sent from the iOS app.

When using the `playHaptic` method, it is advisable to use the defined haptic types for their intended purposes by referencing `WKHapticType`, which is defined in the Apple Developer documentation at `https://developer.apple.com/library/watchos/documentation/WatchKit/Reference/WKInterfaceDevice_class/index.html/navigation/#//apple_ref/c/tdef/WKHapticType`.

Running the Shopping List application – WatchKit

In this section, we will look at how to compile and run our *Shopping List* application to display our Force Touch WatchKit context menu. Perform the following steps:

1. To run the app, select the **ShoppingList WatchKit App** scheme and choose your preferred device from the **iOS Simulators** section, as shown in the following screenshot:

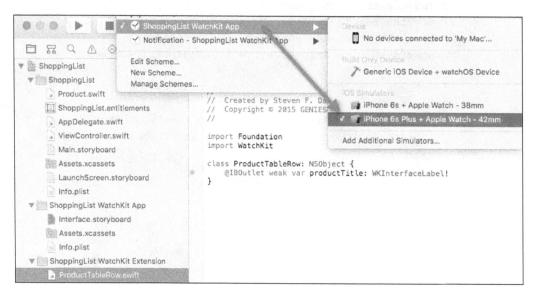

2. Next, build and run the application by navigating to **Product** | **Run** from the **Product** menu or by pressing *Command + R*.

When the compilation is complete, the *Shopping List* app will be installed on the watchOS simulator, and you will see the following image when the WatchKit extension is launched:

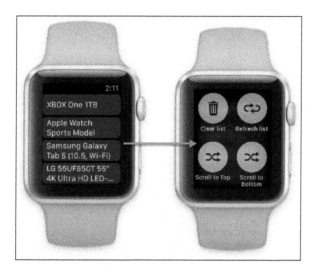

The preceding screenshot shows you the list of all the products that are read and populated from the `ProductsList.plist` file, and they are displayed within our `WKInterfaceTable` control.

To invoke our WatchKit context menu, you will need to press firmly on the Apple Watch device screen to initiate a deep press in order to display our WatchKit context menu to the right. Selecting a menu item from the menu should dismiss the context menu and perform the chosen action in the main scene to match the menu item selection.

> If you run this within the Apple Watch simulator, you will need to navigate to the **Hardware** | **Force Touch Pressure** | **Deep Press** menu option, or press *Command + Shift + 2* and then click on the screen before switching back to the shallow press mode by pressing *Command + Shift + 1*. The context menu should appear as shown in the preceding screenshot.

Summary

In this chapter, you learned about WatchKit context menus and how you can go about adding them to an existing Apple Watch application. You also learned about the differences between the `WKInterfaceMenu` and `WKInterfaceMenuItem` classes and how you can go about adding WatchKit menu items through code and respond to those actions when pressed.

You learned about Taptic Engine, which is integrated in Apple Watch, and how to go about integrating haptic feedback as well as understanding all about the Force Touch technology of Apple Watch. We also discussed how this technology is sophisticated enough to determine the difference between a tap or more forceful long press on the device screen to display the context menu associated with the current scene.

Each of the scenes within a WatchKit app can have a single context menu, each of which can present up to four menu items available for selection by the user and consist of a menu item that contains an image and title.

In the next chapter, you will learn how to incorporate Glances, which is part of the WatchKit platform, within an existing app. You'll learn how to add it and how to create a custom class that will be used to display and update information within the Glance user interface once it is displayed onscreen. You will also learn about Apple Human Interface Guidelines and the guidelines that need to be followed when designing your Glance user interface.

8
Incorporating the Glance Interface in Your App

Glances were first introduced in WatchKit 1.0 and are basically a way in which your users can view important information from within your app. A glance is a means of providing relevant information immediately in a timely manner.

Glances are basically an extension of your Apple Watch app that can present information to the user without the need of launching your Apple Watch app and are basically the equivalent of the **Today** extension in iOS.

Since glances inherit from the `WKInterfaceController` class, they don't require you to include any delegate callbacks within your code, so you can easily create these using Interface Builder and then connect each of the Interface Builder objects to their respective Outlets.

In this chapter, we will begin by providing an overview of WatchKit glances and their life cycle before working through an application that builds upon our *Shopping List* application, which we built in the previous chapter, involving the use of the WatchKit glance controller using the `WKInterfaceController` class.

This chapter includes the following topics:

- WatchKit glances and the WatchKit glance life cycle
- Adding a glance to our *Shopping List* application
- Customizing the glance controller using different templates
- Implementing and updating the glance interface controller
- Understanding Apple Watch glance interface guidelines

We have an exciting project ahead of us, so let's get started!

Introduction to working with WatchKit glances

Before we can begin adding and using glances within our *Shopping List* application, we need to get a better understanding of how they work within the WatchKit framework. We did talk a bit about this in an earlier chapter, *Chapter 2, Understanding Apple Watch*, so much of this will be quite similar.

In the next section, we will talk a bit about the glance controller life cycle, and you will note that the glance controller inherits all of the existing functionalities of the WKInterfaceController class and contains a variety of methods and calls that help determine whenever a glance becomes active or the controller context instance becomes awake.

Understanding the glance controller life cycle

The WatchKit glance interface controller is initialized at an early stage within your application so that it can be delivered to the user much more quickly. The glance interface controller is basically pretty much the same as any other view controller that comes with a number of methods to check when initializing.

Whenever a WatchKit app is launched on the device, an initial scene is loaded from within the storyboard file. Once the glance scene is successfully loaded, the WatchKit framework requests that the WatchKit extension corresponding to the app be launched and creates the interface controller associated with the glance scene that was loaded.

Once the WatchKit extension detects that the user is no longer interacting with Watch or the user suddenly decided to exit your app, the glance interface controller is deactivated and released from memory, and the WatchKit extension is terminated. The following table explains the key methods of the WKInterfaceController class, which is essentially WatchKit's UIViewController class:

Method	Description
init	This method initializes your interface controller. This is where the bulk of your interface initialization should still occur.
willActivate	This method lets you know that your interface will soon be visible to the user. You should only use this method to make small updates to your user interface; for example, you may want to update a label based on new data that is retrieved.
awakeWithContext:	This method lets you configure the interface controller using any available context data you provide to assist in the configuration of the new interface controller; for instance, when pushing data to the new interface controller, you need to specify a context object that contains the data needed to be displayed. You should also use this method to handle any updates to labels, image manipulation, tables, or any other interface objects in your storyboard scene.

The following table explains each of the processes and what happens when an action is performed by the user:

Action to be performed	Description
Launch WatchKit App	This tells WatchKit to automatically load the storyboard scene that is appropriate for the current user's action.
Load Initial Interface Controller	This tells WatchKit to load the glance scene from the storyboard.
Initialize UI and Display UI	This tells WatchKit to load the initial scene for your application. After the scene loads, WatchKit asks the WatchKit extension to create the corresponding interface controller object, which you can then use to prepare and display to the user.

Now that we have understood all of the theory behind WatchKit glances and their life cycle, we can move on to building our user interface for our *Shopping List* application.

Adding a glance to our Shopping List application – WatchKit

In this section, you will learn how to add a menu to our existing *Shopping List* application, which we created in from our previous chapter. Perform the following steps:

1. Select the `ShoppingList.xcodeproj` file from the `Chapter 07` folder, in the accompanying code bundle as shown in the following screenshot:

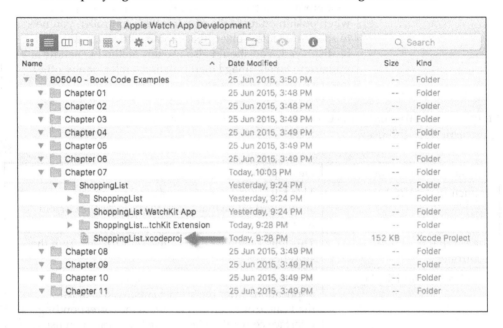

2. Next, ensure that the `ShoppingList` Xcode project file is open within the Xcode development IDE.

3. Next, select the **Interface.storyboard** file from the project navigation window, which is located within **ShoppingList WatchKit Extension** group in the project navigation window.

4. Then, from Object Library, drag a glance interface controller
(WKInterfaceController) control to the watch area canvas:

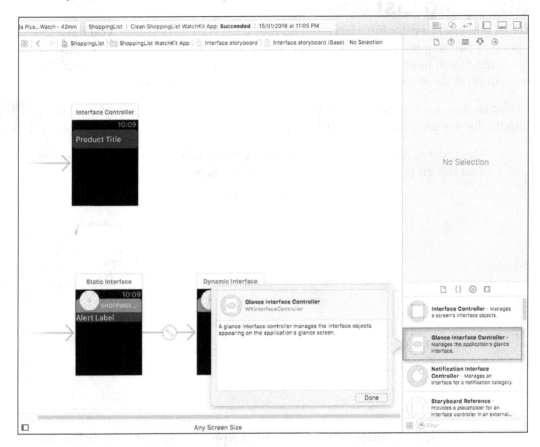

5. Once you add glance interface controller to your watch area canvas, it would
be good to save your project by navigating to **File | Save** or alternatively
pressing *Command + S*.

As you can see, incorporating WatchKit glance controllers within our *Shopping List*
application is a breeze. In the next section, we will need to create a new class that will
be responsible for displaying information within our glance.

In the next section, you will learn how to create a new scheme for our glance so that
we can test our glance directly within the Apple Watch Simulator.

Creating a glance build scheme for our Shopping List app

When you start developing glance functionality for your application, you have the option of running the glance directly to ensure that everything works correctly. This saves time from having to swipe up from the bottom of the watch face; by building and running the glance scheme, so you can see your glance appear.

In this section, we will take a look at how to go about creating a new scheme to handle this for us. Execute the following:

1. Open the **Scheme** menu and then select the **Manage Schemes...** option or you can go to **Product | Scheme | Manage Schemes...**:

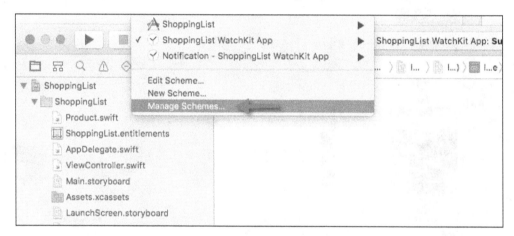

2. Next, select the **ShoppingList WatchKit App** scheme and then click on the cog icon at the bottom of the **Manage Schemes** pane.

3. Then, select the **Duplicate** menu option from the list of options, as shown in the following screenshot:

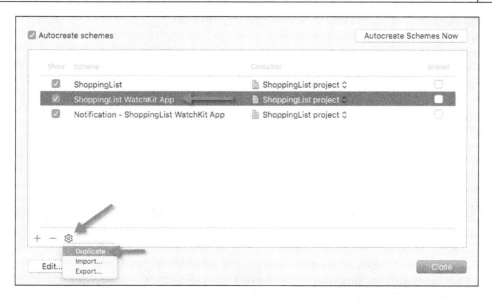

4. Next, modify the scheme name to **Glance – ShoppingList WatchKit App** and change the **Watch Interface** option to **Glance**, as shown in the following screenshot:

5. Finally, click on the **Close** button to commit the changes and exit from the scheme manager.

In this section, you learned how easy it is to create a new scheme for our glance. If you open the **Scheme** menu, you should see that our **Glance – ShoppingList WatchKit App** scheme has been created for us already.

If you change the scheme to **Glance – ShoppingList WatchKit App**, and build and run our application, you will then see our glance window appear within the simulator using our `WKInterfaceController` template that we added earlier.

In the next section, we will create a new class that will be responsible for displaying information within our glance.

Creating the glance interface controller WatchKit class

Now that we have added the glance interface controller to our `ShoppingList` WatchKit interface, we can start to create our glance controller class that will inherit from the `WKInterfaceController` class. This class will be responsible for displaying our glances when the user activates the glance. Perform the following steps:

1. From the project navigation window, select the **ShoppingList WatchKit Extension** group and go to **File** | **New...** or right-click on the group and select **New File...** from the list of options:

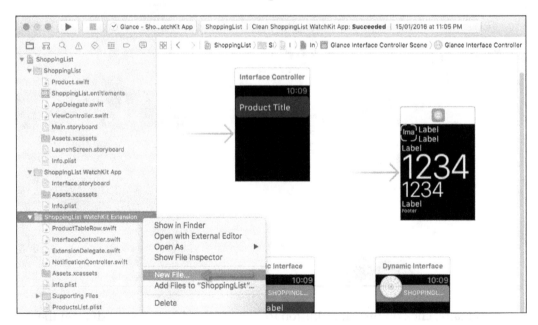

2. Next, select the **watchOS** group under the **Source** section and select **WatchKit Class** from the list of available templates:

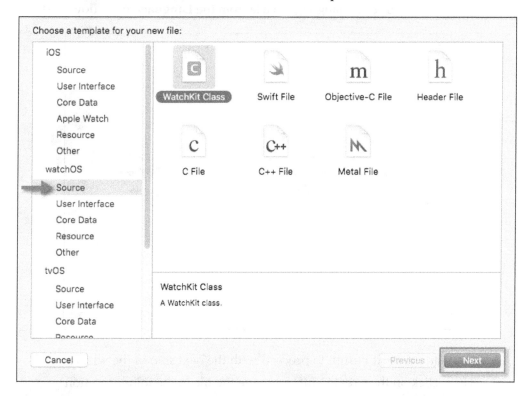

3. Click on the **Next** button to proceed with the next step within the wizard.

4. Enter `GlanceInterfaceController` as the name of the class to be created.

5. Ensure that you have selected **WKInterfaceController** (from which the subclass is to be created) from the **Subclass of** drop-down list, and ensure that you select **Swift** as the language to use from the **Language** drop-down list:

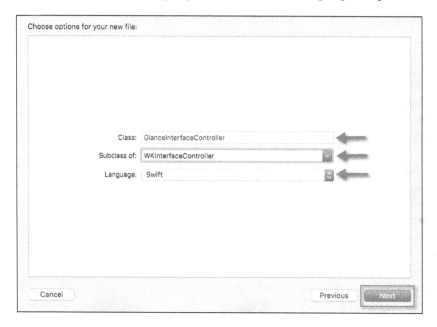

6. Click on the **Next** button to proceed with the next step of the wizard.

7. Then, click on the **Create** button to save the file to the folder location specified.

In this section, we successfully created a new `GlanceInterfaceController` class that will be used by the glance interface controller, and we will begin adding the necessary code later on.

In the next section, we will take a look at how we can configure our glance controller, changing its look and feel to suit our needs by choosing from a library of predefined designs that come as part of Interface Builder.

Configuring our glance controller using templates

Our next step is to set up our glance interface controller to use our newly created `GlanceInterfaceController` class that will be used to display information related to our chosen product item from the shopping list, which we will use later on to set up Outlets within this class.

Since glances are template-based, which basically means that you don't have full control over their appearance, you will notice that the interface is split into upper and lower layout group sections. Perform the following steps:

1. Select the `Interface.storyboard` file from the project navigation window.

2. Next, select **Glance Interface Controller** and click on the Show the Identity Inspector button.

3. Then, from the **Class** drop-down menu, select the **GlanceInterfaceController** class that we just created to use as our main class:

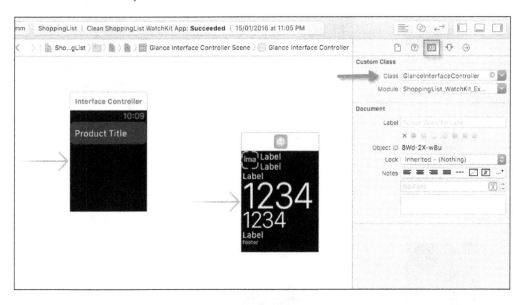

4. Next, click on the **Upper** layout group and select the **Image** template highlighted by the **A** icon reference.

5. Next, click on the **Lower** layout group and choose the **1234 Label Image** template highlighted by the **B** icon reference:

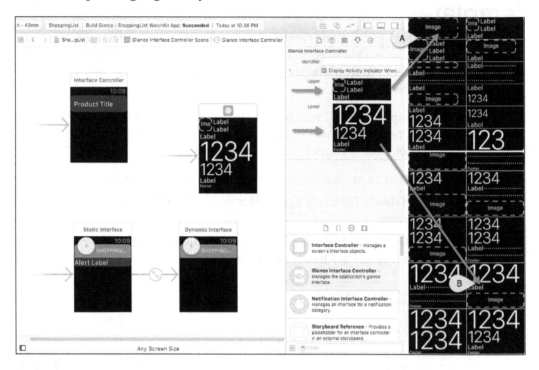

6. Next, we need to specify the minimum scaling for **Apple Watch 42mm**. Click on the + icon next to the **Min Scale** label under the **Label** group:

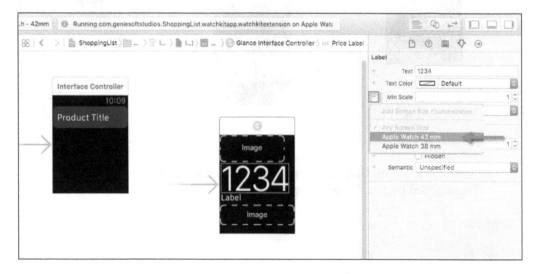

7. Then, modify the **42mm** property so that it has the value **0.3**:

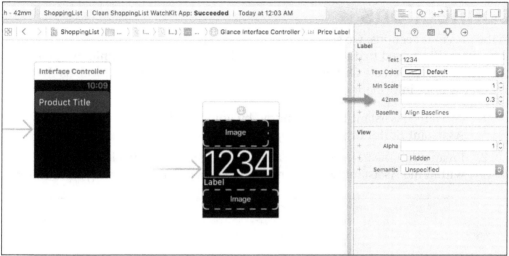

8. Once you modify the glance interface controller's properties to use the pre-defined glance templates, it would be good to save your project by navigating to **File | Save** or alternatively pressing *Command + S*.

In this section, you learned how to configure and set the custom class property for the glance interface controller (`WKInterfaceController`) so that it can make use of our `GlanceInterfaceController` class. You then learned how to configure our glance interface to use a set of template-based predefined templates that come with Interface Builder so that we can change the look and feel of our glances.

In our next section, we will start connecting up Outlets for each of our glance objects so that it will have the functionality to display our glance information when the user chooses an item from our shopping list.

Establishing glance interface controller connections

In the previous sections, we successfully created our `GlanceInterfaceController` class that will be used to display the selected shopping list item within our glance. Our next step is to create Outlets for our shopping list item name as well as the associated price information:

1. Open the Assistant Editor window by going to **Navigate | Open in Assistant Editor** or pressing *Option + Command + ,*.

2. Ensure that the `GlanceInterfaceController.swift` file is displayed within the Assistant Editor window, as shown in the following screenshot:

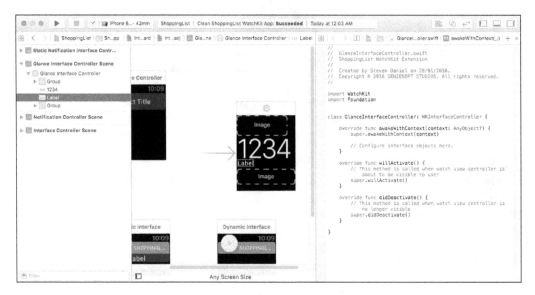

3. Next, select the **Label** (`WKInterfaceLabel`) control, then hold down the *Control* key, and drag it into the `GlanceInterfaceController.swift` file within the body of `class GlanceInterfaceController: WKInterfaceController` class body.

4. Select **Outlet** from the **Connection** drop-down menu for the type of connection to create and enter `titleLabel` for the name of the Outlet property to create.

5. Next, select **Weak** from the **Storage** drop-down menu and click on the **Connect** button:

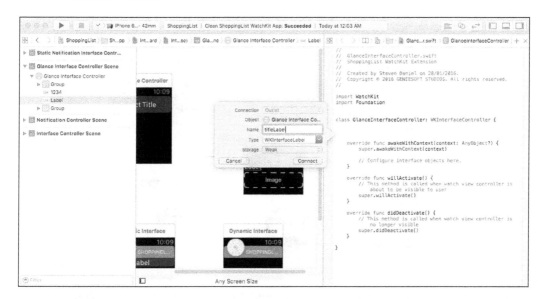

6. Next, select the **1234:** (`WKInterfaceLabel`) control, then hold down the *Control* key, and drag it into the `GlanceInterfaceController.swift` file, as we did for our `titleLabel` Outlet.

7. Then, select **Outlet** from the **Connection** drop-down menu for the type of connections to create and enter in `priceLabel` for the name of the Outlet property to create. Then, choose **Weak** from the **Storage** drop-down menu and click on the **Connect** button:

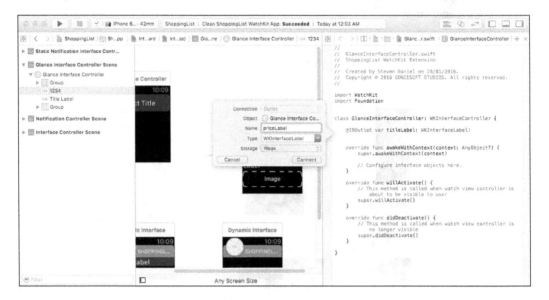

8. Once you create the necessary Outlets, it would be good to save your project by going to **File** | **Save** or pressing *Command + S*.

Whenever you create an Outlet, you must remember to create it within the `WKInterfaceController` class as these cannot be created outside this class body.

The following code snippet shows the complete implementation of our Outlets that we created in the previous steps:

```
//
//  GlanceInterfaceController.swift
//  ShoppingList WatchKit Extension
//
//  Created by Steven Daniel on 28/01/2016.
//  Copyright © 2016 GENIESOFT STUDIOS. All rights reserved.
//

import WatchKit
import Foundation
```

```
class GlanceInterfaceController: WKInterfaceController {

    @IBOutlet var titleLabel: WKInterfaceLabel!
    @IBOutlet var priceLabel: WKInterfaceLabel!
```

As you can note from the preceding code snippet, the Interface Builder created each of our Outlet control objects as well as the associated type of control we used. In our next section, you will learn how to store information within our NSStandardUserDefaults user database when an item is selected from the shopping items list so that we can display this within our glance later on.

Storing information to show within your glance controller

In this section, we will take a look at how we can use the NSStandardUserDefaults class to store the selected shopping list item when the user taps on a specific row within the WKInterfaceTable controller. This will then be displayed within the glance interface controller's WKInterfaceController class:

1. Open the InterfaceController.swift file located within the **ShoppingList WatchKit Extension** group in the project navigation window.

2. Next, locate the didSelectRowAtIndex method and enter the following highlighted code snippet:

```
// MARK: WKInterfaceTable Delegate Callbacks

// Handle when a row has been selected within our table
override func table(table: WKInterfaceTable, didSelectRowAtIndex
rowIndex: Int) {

    // Send the product to be charged by sending the product as
    // a dictionary object,
    // and then converting it to a 'Product' type value in our
    // application delegate.

    // We will then have our iOS app immediately display the
    // payment sheet when it is invoked.
    let purchasedItem = [
        "product": [
          Product.DictionaryKey.Name.rawValue:
                 ProductsList[rowIndex].name,
          Product.DictionaryKey.Price.rawValue:
                 ProductsList[rowIndex].price
```

```
            ]
         ]

         // Store the selected product from our Shopping List to be
      shown
         // within the Glance Controller.
         let userDefaults = NSUserDefaults.standardUserDefaults()
         userDefaults.setObject(ProductsList[rowIndex].name,
                            forKey: "productName")
         userDefaults.setObject(ProductsList[rowIndex].price,
                            forKey: "productPrice")

         // Writes any modifications to disk and updates any
         // unmodified information to what is on disk.
         userDefaults.synchronize()

         // The paired iPhone has to be connected via Bluetooth so that
         // we can display the Apple Pay payment controller on the
      phone.
         if WCSession.defaultSession().reachable {
            WCSession.defaultSession().sendMessage(purchasedItem,
            replyHandler: {
                     replyData in
                     },
                     errorHandler: { error in
                         // catch any errors here
                         print("Error occurred: \(error)")
               })
         }
      }
```

In the preceding code snippet, we started by creating a dictionary object and then grabbed the selected product from the ProductsList dictionary object for the chosen row by the user, which is returned in the rowIndex variable.

Next, we used the NSUserDefaults and standardUserDefaults methods to store the selected product into a dictionary object using the key-value pair information to hold each object. Next, we called the synchronize method, which is invoked automatically at periodic intervals to keep the in-memory cache in sync with the user's default database, which is in turn located within the WatchKit extension application bundle.

In our next step, we checked whether our WCSession object for the current session is reachable on the iPhone counterpart and then used the sendMessage method to notify the iOS application's didReceiveMessage method, which is located within the iOS apps view controller.

The `sendMessage` method also declares the `replyHandler` and `errorHandler` closures, which will be called and passed back by the iOS application once the message request is handled.

Displaying information within your glance controller

In the last section, we modified our interface controller class so that it can store information within our `NSUserDefaults` class and display the chosen shopping list product information within the Apple Watch glance interface controller.

In this section, we need to create the necessary code that will be responsible for retrieving information stored within our `standardUserDefaults` repository database and display the chosen shopping list product item within our glance. Perform the following steps:

1. Open the `GlanceInterfaceController.swift` file located within the **ShoppingList WatchKit Extension** group in the project navigation window.

2. Next, locate the `willActivate` method and enter the following code snippet:

```swift
override func willActivate() {
        // This method is called when watch view controller
        // is about to be visible to user
        super.willActivate()

        let userDefaults = NSUserDefaults.standardUserDefaults()
        let productName: String? =
            userDefaults.stringForKey("productName")
        let productPrice: String? =
            userDefaults.stringForKey("productPrice")

        if productName != nil { titleLabel.setText(productName) }
        titleLabel.setTextColor(UIColor.whiteColor())
        if productPrice != nil { priceLabel.setText("$" +
            productPrice!) }
        priceLabel.setTextColor(UIColor.greenColor())
    }
}
```

In the preceding code snippet, we started by invoking our NSUserDefaults class to provide the WatchKit extension with the ability to read default information from the user's default database, as denoted by the standardUserDefaults method. The NSUserDefaults class provides convenience methods to access common types of information, and values that are returned from the NSUserDefaults class are immutable. Next, we used the stringForKey method to access both the productName and productPrice dictionary items and checked whether neither are nil before assigning them to our titleLabel and priceLabel Outlets, and set the colors for each accordingly.

For more information on the NSUserDefaults framework class, refer to the Apple Developer documentation at https://developer. apple.com/library/mac/documentation/Cocoa/Reference/ Foundation/Classes/NSUserDefaults_Class/#//apple_ref/ occ/clm/NSUserDefaults/standardUserDefaults.

Understanding the glance interface guidelines

When designing apps for Apple Watch, these need to be designed differently than how you would go about designing apps for phones or tablets as they contain a different user experience.

It is extremely important to keep in mind and follow the Apple Watch interface guidelines documentation that Apple provides. This document describes guidelines and principles that help you design consistent user interfaces and experiences for your Watch apps as well as ensure that your applications run efficiently within the Apple Watch platform. You need to consider the screen sizes for your custom layouts as well as the ease of use your app brings to the platform.

Other areas are covered to ensure the consistency of your application while navigating from screen to screen as well as the principles of designing good user interfaces. There is also information related to the proper use and appearance of views and controls for navigation, alerts, notifications, table views, buttons, images, as well as the creation of custom icons and images.

Some of the Apple Watch glance interface guidelines are as follows:

- Each WatchKit extension can only contain a single glance instance.

- Glances should be designed appropriately so that they make use of graphics, colors, and text that convey information to the user clearly.

- Glances are similar to Today extensions in iOS, with the main difference being that they are read-only and provide the user with relevant information about the Apple Watch extension.

- As content within a glance is read-only, you are prohibited from including any form of interactive controls within your glance interface, such as buttons, switches, sliders, and menus.

- Glances are not scrollable, so when designing your glances, you need to ensure that all the content fits within a single screen. This means that you need to be selective about what information you decide to display to your users and ensure that it should be relevant to the content being displayed.

 To obtain further information about the glance interface guidelines, it is worth checking out the *Apple Watch Human Interface Guidelines* documentation at `https://developer.apple.com/watch/human-interface-guidelines/app-components/`.

Running the Shopping List application – WatchKit

In this section, we will take a look at how to compile and run our *Shopping List* application to display the Force Touch WatchKit context menu. Perform the following steps:

1. To run the app, select the **ShoppingList WatchKit App** scheme and choose your preferred device from the **iOS Simulators** section, as shown in the following screenshot:

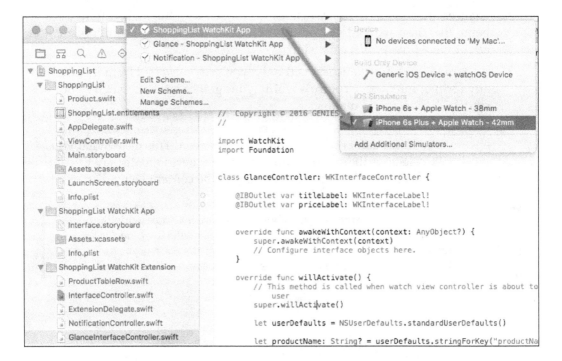

2. Next, build and run the application by going to **Product** | **Run** from the **Product** menu or pressing *Command + R*.

When the compilation is complete, the *Shopping List* app will be installed on the watchOS Simulator. The following screenshot shows you how to configure the *Shopping List* WatchKit application so that it has the ability to display glance information:

In the preceding screenshot, we showed you how to configure your *Shopping List* WatchKit app. In order to see your glance working, you need to launch the Apple Watch *Watch* app on your device, then choose the *Shopping List* WatchKit app, and then ensure that the **Show in Glances** option is switched on:

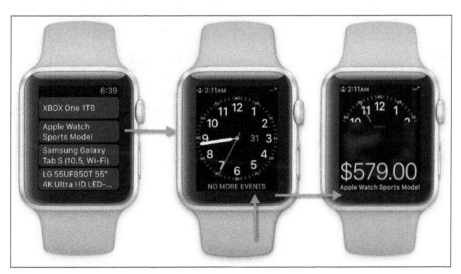

The preceding screenshot shows you a list of products that are read and populated from the `ProductsList.plist` file and displayed within our `WKInterfaceTable` control. When the user taps on an item within the list, the information is written to the `NSUserDefaults` and `standardUserDefaults` repositories. When the user swipes up from the bottom of the watch face, because we enabled the **Show in Glances** feature, you will see the chosen product as well as the associated price information.

In order to see your glance once you choose an item from the shopping list, you will need to hold down *Shift + Command + H* from the shopping list screen, which will take you back to the Home screen. You can then swipe up from the bottom of the watch face area to see your glance.

Summary

In this chapter, you learned about WatchKit glances and how you can go about adding these to an existing Apple Watch application. You learned how to create a custom `GlanceInterfaceController` class, which will be used to display information within the glance user interface once the glance is displayed onscreen.

Next, you learned that glances are template-based, which means that you don't have total control over their appearance when designing your glance user interface. You then moved on and learned about the interface guidelines that you need to follow when designing your glances, keeping in mind that each of the glance scenes within a WatchKit app can have a number of text labels and can incorporate an image and title.

In the next chapter, you will learn how to incorporate notifications, which comes as part of the WatchKit platform, within an existing app. You'll learn about the notification life cycle and the **Apple Push Notification service** (**APNs**) and how to work with both local and remote notifications as well as how to configure them. We will take a look at the differences between static and dynamic interfaces and how you can add action buttons to notifications and respond to them upon a user tapping on the button. You'll also learn about the interface guidelines that you need to follow when designing your notifications.

9
Incorporating Notifications within Your App

Notifications were first introduced in iOS 3 and have increased over the years with iOS 7 introducing silent remote notifications, which allow apps to wake up in the background to perform important tasks, such as meeting appointments, Skype notifications, or an incoming SMS or iMessage message.

With the release of iOS 8, Apple introduced **actionable notifications**, which allowed users to respond to an action within a notification message without the need of opening the app. In watchOS, your existing iOS apps that currently support notifications will still work on the Apple Watch without the need of making changes to your existing code. This is because watchOS uses the default system interface to show notifications, which inherits from the `WKInterfaceController` class, to make use of a number of method callbacks that handle responding to **local notifications** and **remote notifications**.

In this chapter, we will begin by providing an overview of WatchKit notifications and their life cycle before learning how to add a custom long look notification to our *Shopping List* application that we built in the previous chapter. You'll learn how to add Action buttons to notifications and how to respond when a user taps on the associated button.

This chapter includes the following topics:

- WatchKit notifications and the WatchKit notification life cycle
- Implementing and updating the notification interface controller
- Adding and responding to Action buttons in notifications
- Understanding the Apple Watch notification interface guidelines

We have an exciting project ahead of us, so let's get started!

Working with WatchKit notifications

Before we can begin using notifications within our *Shopping List* application, we need to get a better understanding of how they work within the WatchKit framework. We did touch on this in *Chapter 2, Understanding Apple Watch,* so much of this will be quite familiar.

In the next section, we will talk a bit about the notification controller life cycle; you will notice that the notification controller inherits all of the existing functionality of the WKInterfaceController class and contains a variety of method calls that help determine whenever a notification becomes active or the controller context instance becomes awake.

As we mentioned in the introduction to the chapter, notifications that appear on an iOS device will also appear on Apple Watch, which means that you don't need to physically take your phone out of your pocket whenever you feel it vibrating. You can simply just glance at your watch and respond to the action accordingly.

The WatchKit framework allows you to create a custom notification interface that allows you to add additional functionality to your notification messages. It takes the contents of the notification that the phone received and presents this to Interface Builder objects that you add to your interface design.

You can then choose to attach *actionable* buttons to your custom interface that enable your users to perform some task without having to unlock their iOS device. When working with notifications, it is important to understand that these can come from two different sources, which are explained in the following table:

Notification type	Description
Remote notifications	This type of notification is also known as a push notification and is delivered by the Apple Push Notification service to the Apple iOS device.
	The *Shopping List* Apple Watch app contains a sample ShoppingListNotificationPayload.apns file to test your custom notifications within the iOS and Apple Watch simulator.
Local notifications	This type of notification is scheduled by the iOS portion of your application without needing to communicate with the Apple Push Notification server.

In the next section, we will look at the life cycle of what happens when the notification controller receives a notification message and the events that get called when a notification of the appropriate type comes up.

Understanding the notification controller life cycle

The WatchKit notification controller is initialized at an early stage within your application, so that it can be delivered to the user much quickly. The notification interface controller is basically the same as any other view controller but comes with a number of methods to check when initializing.

Whenever a notification message arrives in the WatchKit app, an initial scene is loaded from within the storyboard file. Once the notification scene is successfully loaded, the WatchKit framework requests the WatchKit extension to instantiate the corresponding WKUserNotificationInterfaceController subclass.

Once the WatchKit extension detects that the user is no longer interacting with the watch, the notification interface controller proceeds to display the static notification interface controller instead of the custom notification interface controller.

The following table explains the key methods of the WKUserNotificationInterfaceController class, which is essentially WatchKit's WKInterfaceController class:

Method	Description
init	This method initializes your interface controller. This is where the bulk of your interface initialization should still occur.
awakeWithContext:	This method lets you configure the interface controller using any available context data you provide to assist in the configuration of the new interface controller; for instance, when pushing data to the new interface controller, you need to specify a context object that contains the data that is to be displayed.
	You should also use this method to handle any updates to labels, image manipulation, tables, or any other interface objects in your storyboard scene.
willActivate	This method lets you know that your interface will soon be visible to the user. You should only use this method to make small updates to your user interface; for example, you may want to update a label based on the new data that is retrieved.

Method	Description
`didReceiveRemoteNo tification:Complet ionHandler:`	After the notification interface controller is initialized, WatchKit delivers the notification payload data to it using either the `didReceiveRemoteNotification:WithComp letion:` or `didReceiveLocalNotification:WithComp letion:` methods.
	You should use this method to handle the display of each of the data elements that are contained within the `ShoppingListNotificationPayload.apns` payload file to provide updates to labels, image manipulation, tables, or any other interface object in your storyboard scene.

Now that we have understood all of the theory behind WatchKit notifications and their life cycle, we can move on to configuring our notification scheme so that it has the ability to display either our static or dynamic notifications depending on what is received.

Configuring the notification scheme for our Shopping List app

In this section, our next step is to configure our *Shopping List* app so that it has the ability to display custom notification messages within our dynamic notifications when an order is successfully processed for the chosen product item from the shopping list, which we will use later on to set up the Outlets within this class. Perform the following steps:

1. Select the `ShoppingList.xcodeproj` file from the `Chapter 08` folder in the accompanying code bundle, as shown in the following screenshot:

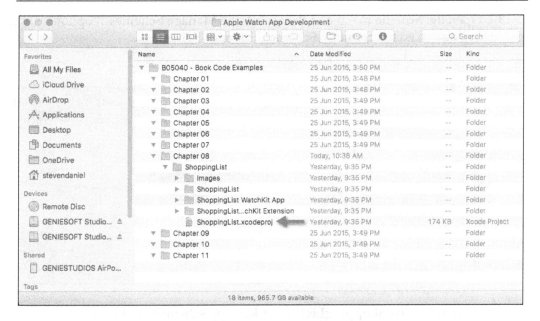

2. Next, ensure that the `ShoppingList` Xcode project file is open within the Xcode development IDE.

   When you start developing notifications for your application, you have the option of running the notification directly within the Watch simulator using the notification scheme to ensure that everything is working correctly. This saves time compared to having to swipe down from the top of the watch face, so you can see your notification appear.

   In this section, you will learn how to create a new scheme for our notifications so that we can test out our dynamic notification directly within the Apple Watch simulator.

3. Open the **Scheme** menu and then select the **Manage Schemes...** option, or you can go to **Product | Scheme | Manage Schemes...**.

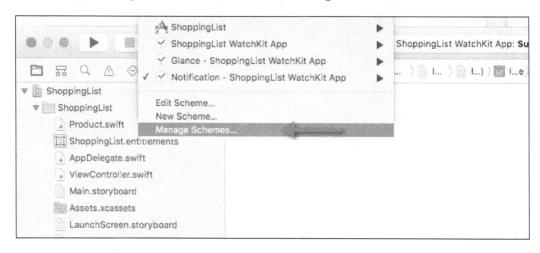

4. Next, select the **ShoppingList WatchKit App** scheme and then select the **Notification – ShoppingList WatchKit App** scheme.

5. Then, click on the **Edit...** button located at the bottom of the **Manage Schemes** pane, as shown in the following screenshot:

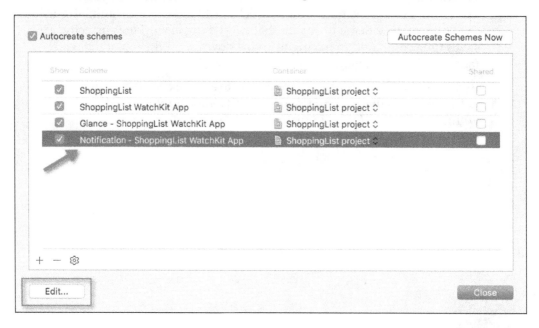

6. Next, ensure that the **Watch Interface** drop-down menu reads **Dynamic Notification** and the **Notification Payload** drop-down menu reads **PushNotificationPayload.apns**, as shown in the following screenshot:

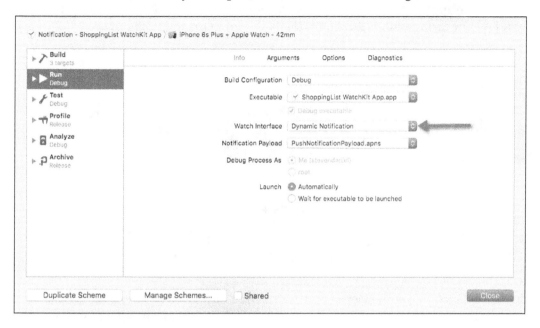

7. Finally, click on the **Close** button to commit the changes and exit from the scheme manager.

In this section, we proceeded through the steps to see how easy it is to customize an existing scheme to enable notifications for our *Shopping List* application. If you change the scheme to **Notification – ShoppingList WatchKit App** and then build and run the application in its current state, you should see a static notification window appearing within the simulator as shown in the following figure:

In the next section, you will learn how we can add buttons to our dynamic interface and the methods that we can use to handle remote notifications using the Apple Watch simulator so that we can respond to actions once they are tapped on by the user.

Adding Action buttons to your dynamic notifications

Apple introduced the ability to allow developers to test remote notifications on the Apple Watch simulator with the release of Xcode 6.2. This is achieved using a local file, `PushNotificationPayload.apns`, to mimic the JSON payload file information that is sent by the Apple Push Notification service. Here are the steps to perform:

1. Select the `PushNotificationPayload.apns` file located within the folder at **ShoppingList WatchKit Extension | Supporting Files** in the project navigation window.

2. Ensure that the `PushNotificationPayload.apns` file is displayed within the editor window, as shown in the following screenshot:

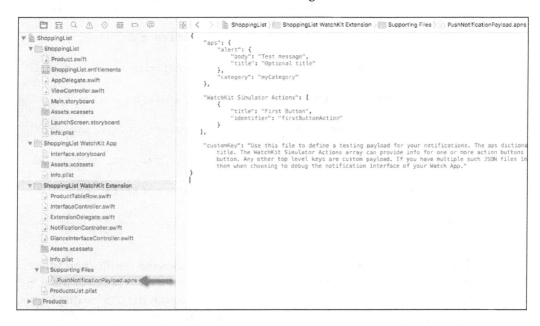

3. Next, modify the `PushNotificationPayload.apns` file by entering the following highlighted code sections:

```
{
    "aps": {
        "alert": {
            "body": "ShoppingList Test Message.",
            "title": "Custom Message",
            "receipt": "Custom Receipt"
        },
        "category": "ORDER_PLACED"
    },

    "WatchKit Simulator Actions": [
        {
            "title": "OK",
            "identifier": "okButtonAction"
        },
        {
            "title": "Cancel",
            "identifier": "cancelButtonAction"
        }
```

```
    ],

    "customKey": "Use this file to define a testing payload for
your
    notifications. The aps dictionary specifies the category,
alert
    text and title. The WatchKit Simulator Actions array can
provide
    info for one or more action buttons in addition to the
standard
    Dismiss button. Any other top level keys are custom payload.
If
    you have multiple such JSON files in your project, you'll be
able
    to select them when choosing to debug the notification
interface
    of your Watch App."
}
```

This JSON structure contains the aps dictionary that includes the notification title, the body of the message, as well as a category, which is optional. Whenever the iOS device receives a notification and the app is in the background, the device displays a banner showing the title as well as an accompanying message. The WatchKit Simulator Actions sections contain a dictionary that also includes a title as well as a unique identifier that is used to respond to the action chosen by the user.

It is worth mentioning that as the Apple Watch simulator doesn't have access to the iPhone applications' registered notification actions, the JSON payload file contains a special key that is used specifically for the testing purposes of **WatchKit Simulator Actions**, which we will begin to implement in the *Responding to actions within your custom notifications* section.

Since the notifications that we will build are based on local notifications for testing purposes, you can pretend that it's a remote notification as there is no difference between how the user interface functions in local and remote notifications.

If you change the scheme to **Notification – ShoppingList WatchKit App** and then build and run the application, you should see our dynamic notification window appearing within the simulator, showing the WatchKit Simulator Actions buttons, as shown in the following figure:

The preceding figure shows you our dynamic notification screen, which contains a list of predefined action buttons, which we created within the WatchKit Simulator Actions section in our `PushNotificationPayload.apns` file.

> For more information about the Apple Push Notification service, refer to the WatchKit framework reference documentation at `https://developer.apple.com/library/ios/documentation/NetworkingInternet/Conceptual/RemoteNotificationsPG/Chapters/ApplePushService.html#//apple_ref/doc/uid/TP40008194-CH100-SW9`.

Responding to actions within your custom notifications

In this section, we will look at how we can respond to an action when the user taps on one of our WatchKit Simulator Actions buttons within the dynamic interface controller. When a user taps on one of the Action buttons within your payload file, they can either be processed within the foreground or the background, with each being handled differently.

When actions are processed within the foreground, the chosen action proceeds to launch your WatchKit application, which then sends the identifier of the tapped button to either the `handleActionWithIdentifier:forRemoteNotification` or the `handleActionWithIdentifier:forLocalNotification` methods, which are contained within your interface controller.

Alternatively, when actions are processed within the background, these types of action proceed to launch your iOS application in the background so that it can process the tapped action. This information to be processed is then delivered to the `handleActionWithIdentifier:forRemoteNotification` or `handleActionWithIdentifier:forLocalNotification` application delegate methods. Simply perform the following steps:

1. Select the `InterfaceController.swift` file located within the **ShoppingList WatchKit Extension** folder in the project navigation window.

2. Next, with the `InterfaceController.swift` file still open, create the following `handleActionWithIdentifier:forRemoteNotification` method and enter the following code snippet:

```
// Handles Action buttons from PushNotificationPayload.apns file
// override func handleActionWithIdentifier(identifier: String?,
forRemoteNotification remoteNotification: [NSObject : AnyObject])
{

        switch (identifier! as String) {
        case "okButtonAction":
            print("OK button Pressed")
            break
        case "cancelButtonAction":
            print("CANCEL button Pressed")
            break
        default:
            print("Undefined action pressed")
            break
        }
}
```

In the preceding code snippet, we checked the identifier of the action that we want to process from the WatchKit Simulator Actions section of our `PushNotificationPayload.apns` file. Our `case` statement then checks each of the valid cases that match the chosen identifier and displays the relevant text to the console window of our Xcode IDE.

If it is determined that any action identifier doesn't match with our `switch` statement, it will fall to the default case, displaying an **Undefined action pressed** message to the console window of the IDE.

The difference between static and dynamic interface controllers

In the last section, we looked at how to create a dynamic notification interface that contains a number of WatchKit Simulator Action buttons, which is called a custom long look interface and contains at least one interface called a static interface. You also have the option of creating additional dynamic interfaces that are controlled by the WKUserInterfaceController class.

Static interfaces just show you an alert notification message that is contained within WKInterfaceLabel along with a list of actions. Within this interface, you have the flexibility of customizing the look and feel of the design by configuring the position and style of the alert label and the option of adding more labels (WKInterfaceLabel) or images (WKInterfaceImage).

On the other hand, dynamic interfaces are completely optional and inherit from the WKUserNotificationInterfaceController subclass. You need to include the didReceiveRemoteNotification or didReceiveLocalNotification methods so that you can receive the contents of the UILocalNotification object dictionary that your application receives.

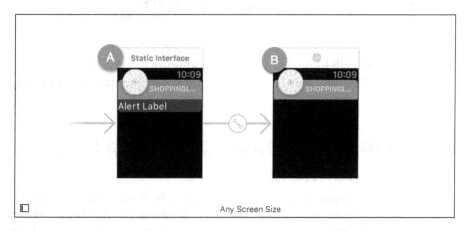

The preceding screenshot shows you the two interface controllers for a static and dynamic interface. The static interface is denoted by **A**, and you will notice that it contains our alert label to display the received notification message. On the other hand, our dynamic interface, denoted by **B**, doesn't contain anything at this stage, but we will customize this interface later on.

You will note from the preceding screenshot that static and dynamic interfaces are split into two separate controllers. The main reason behind this architectural design is mainly put down to the amount of CPU power consumption that is required when launching additional code that Apple Watch needs to execute, which has a huge impact on the amount of system resources needed to be loaded to run and manage the updating of the watch face area.

> Due to the amount of power Apple Watch consumes, or if Apple Watch is running low on power, it may decide to launch and display the static interface controller even if you have a dynamic interface controller present.

You should also keep in mind that when displaying local or remote notifications, you don't actually need to have a dynamic interface present within your storyboard, so you can decide whether you need to update your Apple Watch interface through code.

> For more information about the WKUserInterfaceController class, refer to the WatchKit framework reference documentation at https://developer.apple.com/library/ prerelease/ios/documentation/WatchKit/Reference/ WKInterfaceController_class/.

In the next section, we will look at how we can configure our dynamic interface controller, which will include a WKInterfaceLabel control to display our receipt information.

Configuring our Shopping List app's dynamic notification controller

Our next step is to set up our notification interface controller to use our newly created NotificationController class, which will be used to display a custom notification popup when the order is successfully processed for the chosen product item from the shopping list, which we will, in turn, use later on to set up the Outlets within this class. Perform the following steps:

1. Select the `Interface.storyboard` file from the project navigation window.

2. Next, choose **Notification Controller** and click on the Show the Identity inspector button.

3. Next, from Object Library, drag a `WKInterfaceLabel` control to the watch area canvas, and in the Attributes Inspector section, modify the **Text** property to read **ReceiptLabel**.

4. Next, modify the **Font** property to **Body** and the **Min Scale** property to **1** and set the **Lines** property to **5**.

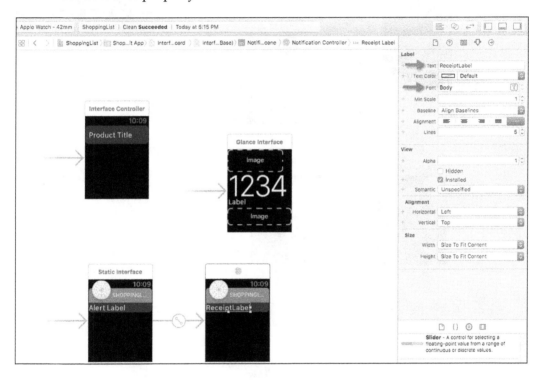

5. Next, we need to specify the minimum scaling for our **Apple Watch 42mm** device; click on the **+** icon next to the **Min Scale** label under the **Label** group.

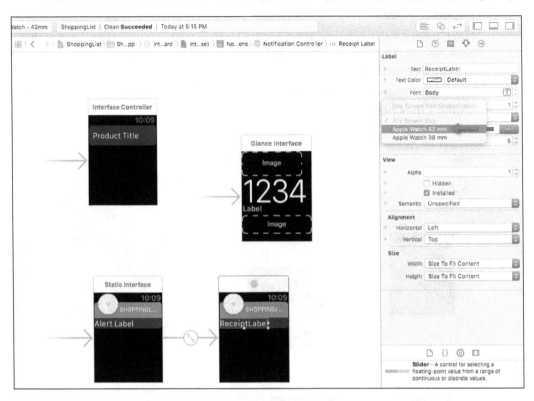

6. Then, modify the **42mm** property so that it contains the value **0.3**.

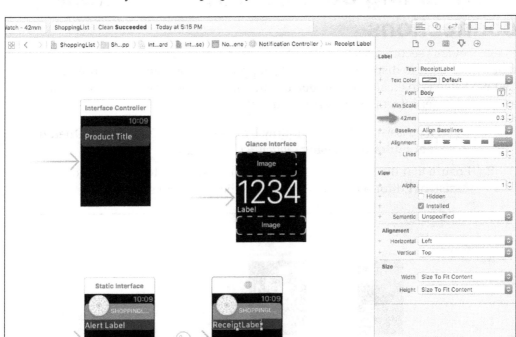

7. Once you modify the notification controller properties, it would be good to save your project by navigating to **File | Save** or pressing *Command + S*.

In our next section, we will start connecting the Outlets for each of our notification objects so that they will have the functionality to display our notification information when the order is successfully processed for the chosen item from our shopping list.

Establishing our notification controller connections

In the previous sections, we successfully created our `NotificationController` class that will be used to display the selected shopping list item within our notification. Our next step is to create the Outlets for our shopping list item name as well as the associated order information. Perform the following steps:

1. Open the Assistant Editor window by navigating to **Navigate | Open in Assistant Editor** or pressing *Option + Command + ,*.

2. Ensure that the `NotificationController.swift` file is displayed within the Assistant Editor window, as shown in the following screenshot:

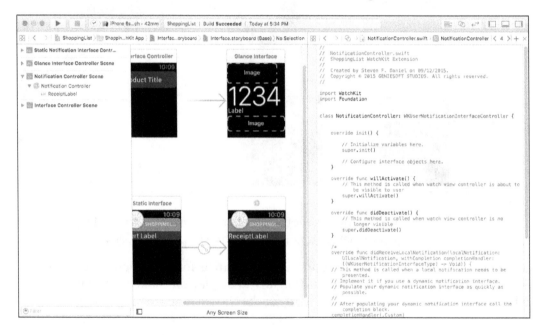

3. Next, select the **ReceiptLabel** (`WKInterfaceLabel`) control, then hold down the *Control* key, and drag it into the `NotificationController.swift` file within the body of `class NotificationController:` `WKInterfaceController`.

4. Choose **Outlet** from the **Connection** drop-down menu for the type of connection to create and enter `receiptLabel` for the name of the Outlet property to create.

5. Next, select **Weak** from the **Storage** drop-down menu and click on the **Connect** button.

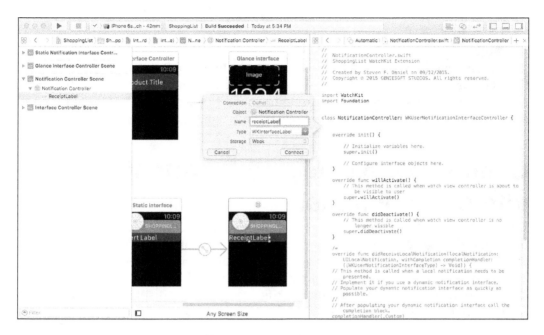

6. Once you create the necessary Outlets, it would be good to save your project by navigating to **File | Save** or pressing *Command + S*.

Whenever you create an Outlet, you must remember to create them within the `WKUserInterfaceController` class as these cannot be created outside this class body.

The following code snippet shows the complete implementation of our Outlets, which we created in the previous steps:

```
//
//  NotificationController.swift
//  ShoppingList WatchKit Extension
//
//  Created by Steven Daniel on 09/12/2015.
//  Copyright © 2015 GENIESOFT STUDIOS. All rights reserved.
//

import WatchKit
```

```
import Foundation

class NotificationController: WKUserInterfaceController {

    @IBOutlet var receiptLabel: WKInterfaceLabel!
```

As you can note from the preceding code snippet, Interface Builder created our Outlet control objects as well as the associated type of control that we used. In our next section, you will learn how to configure and set up a `Category` identifier for our static notification interface controller so that it can handle incoming notifications.

Configuring a category for our static interface controller

When working with notifications, each notification interface must be assigned a notification category that tells Apple Watch when to use it. If you remember, back in our `PushNotificationPayload.apns` file, within the `aps` dictionary object, we specified an `ORDER_PLACED` category string value within the payload that Apple Watch uses to determine which notification scenes to display within your `Interface.storyboard` file.

If Apple Watch determines that an incoming notification doesn't include a value for our category string, it will display the notification interface that is configured with the default category.

In this section, we will look at the steps involved in setting up a notification category for our notification interface controller:

1. Select the `Interface.storyboard` file from the project navigation window.

2. Next, choose **Static Notification Interface Controller** and click on the Show Attributes Inspector button.

3. Next, click on the **myCategory** property, and then from the **Notification Category** section of the Attributes Inspector button, modify the **Name** property to read **ORDER_PLACED**.

4. Then, ensure that the **Has Dynamic Interface** option is selected.

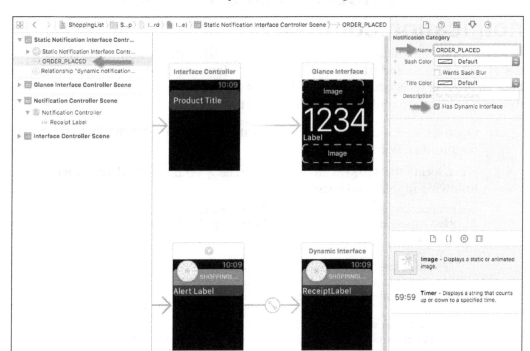

5. Once you configure the notification category for our static notification interface controller, it would be good to save your project by navigating to **File | Save** or pressing *Command + S*.

In our next section, you will learn how to schedule a local notification so that it has the ability to send push notification messages from the main iOS app to the notification controller when an item is selected from the shopping items list and we can display this within our dynamic notification controller later on.

Scheduling notifications with your notification controller

In this section, we will look at how we can set up and schedule notifications using the UIApplication and UILocalNotification classes to send notification messages once an order is successfully processed so that it can then be displayed within the dynamic notification controller class. Here are the steps:

1. Open the AppDelegate.swift file located within the **ShoppingList** group in the project navigation window.

2. Next, locate the didFinishLaunchingWithOptions method and enter the following highlighted code snippet:

```
func application(application: UIApplication,
didFinishLaunchingWithOptions launchOptions: [NSObject:
AnyObject]?) -> Bool {

    // Override point for customization after application launch.
    let notificationCategory:UIMutableUserNotificationCategory =
    UIMutableUserNotificationCategory()

    // Initialize our Notification Category
    notificationCategory.identifier = "ORDER_PLACED"

    // Register our Notification Settings to handle push
notifications
    let settings = UIUserNotificationSettings(forTypes:
    [UIUserNotificationType.Sound, UIUserNotificationType.Alert,
    UIUserNotificationType.Badge], categories:
    [notificationCategory])

    // Registers your preferred options for notifying the user.
    UIApplication.sharedApplication().
    registerUserNotificationSettings(settings)

    return true
}
```

In the preceding code snippet, the didFinishLaunchingWithOptions method is called once the main iOS application finishes launching. In our next step, we instantiated our UIMutableNotificationCategory class and provided it with an identifier before registering our notification settings once the category was created. We then initiated the UIUserNotificationSettings class object to tell iOS what we would like to see when the notification appears; here, we specified that we would like to hear a tone, an alert, as well as a badge icon, and a collection of category objects.

Once our `settings` object was prepared, we proceeded to make a call to our `registerUserNotificationSettings` method using the shared `UIApplication` class object. When the application is run, this will tell the system to display an alert dialog box to the user that will ask them for permission to display notification messages. If the user chooses not to allow this, then no notifications will be displayed.

3. Next, open the `ViewController.swift` file located within the **ShoppingList** group in the project navigation window.

4. Then, create the following the `initializeUserNotifications` code snippet after the `didReceiveMessage` method:

```
// This method is called to send a notification to the Apple Watch
func initializeUserNotifications(alertBody: String) {

    // Get a handle to our application delegate
    let app = UIApplication.sharedApplication()
    let notificationTime  = NSDate().dateByAddingTimeInterval(10)
    let notificationAlarm = UILocalNotification()

    notificationAlarm.fireDate = notificationTime
    notificationAlarm.timeZone = NSTimeZone.defaultTimeZone()
    notificationAlarm.soundName =
UILocalNotificationDefaultSoundName
    notificationAlarm.category = "ORDER_PLACED"
    notificationAlarm.alertTitle = "Shopping List"
    notificationAlarm.alertBody = alertBody

    app.scheduleLocalNotification(notificationAlarm)
}
```

In the preceding code snippet, the `initializeUserNotifications` instance method was called once a successful payment transaction by the Apple Pay payment server took place and a token was generated by the `orderCompleted` instance method. As both remote and local notifications are handled by the iOS application delegate, we first needed to get a handle to our application delegate using the `sharedApplication` method of the `UIApplication` class. Next, we called the `UILocationNotification` class to tell our controller that we were ready to receive local notifications.

We assigned the `fireDate` property to tell our notification that we would like it to appear ten seconds after we scheduled it and then specified our category property, which will call our static notification controller once the `fireDate` property counts down to zero. We then initialized our `alertTitle` and `alertBody` properties with the information that we would like to display once the notification appears within the watch interface. Finally, we called the `scheduleLocalNotification` method and passed in the notification details to schedule the notification.

5. Next, locate the `orderCompleted` method and enter the following highlighted code snippet:

```
// This method is responsible for displaying the order receipt
popup // dialog on the Apple Watch
func orderCompleted(paymentIdentifier : String) {

    // Create our confirmation message which will be send to
    // the Watch.
    let confirmationMessage = [
            "confirmation": "Order successfully Processed,
             your receipt#: \(paymentIdentifier)"
        ]

    // Display our Custom Notification to the Apple Watch
Interface
    self.initializeUserNotifications("Order successfully
Processed,
                your receipt#: \(paymentIdentifier)")

    // Send our order completed message to the paired Apple Watch.
    if WCSession.defaultSession().reachable {
        WCSession.defaultSession().sendMessage(confirmationMessage,
        replyHandler: {
                    replyData in
                },
                errorHandler: { error in
                // If an error occurred, we need to handle it
    here.
                print("Error occurred: \(error)")
            })
        }
    }
```

In the preceding code snippet, we began by declaring our confirmationMessage object variable that will contain the payment identifier once the order is successfully processed by the PKPaymentAuthorizationViewControllerDelegate protocol methods. In our next step, we called our initializeUserNotifications instance method, which accepts a string message that will be used for our local notifications alert, prior to checking whether our paired Apple Watch was reachable and capable of accepting sessions from the iPhone app, which is determined by the WCSession class.

Next, we created and configured an instance of our WCSession class and set the delegate object for our current session before activating the session object for our iOS app so that we could begin sending and receiving messages from our iOS App. Any errors that occur during the communication between the iOS app and the paired Apple Watch device would be handled by the errorHandler closure.

The sendMessage method also declared replyHandler and errorHandler closures, which will be called and passed back by the iOS application once the message request is handled.

For more information about the UIApplication class, refer to the UIKit framework reference documentation at https://developer.apple.com/library/ios/documentation/UIKit/Reference/UIApplication_Class/.

Displaying messages within the notification interface

In our last section, we modified the view controller class for our iOS app so that it could set up and schedule a notification message once the order is successfully processed; it could then display the receipt information associated for the chosen product within our Apple Watch notification controller.

In this section, we need to create the necessary code that will be responsible for displaying the notification information within our dynamic interface controller. Take a look at the following steps:

1. Open the NotificationController.swift file located within the **ShoppingList WatchKit Extension** group in the project navigation window.

2. Next, locate the `didReceiveLocalNotification` method and replace it with the following code snippet:

```
override func didReceiveLocalNotification(localNotificati
on: UILocalNotification, withCompletion completionHandler:
((WKUserNotificationInterfaceType) -> Void)) {
    // This method is called when a local notification needs to
    // be presented.
    // Implement it if you use a dynamic notification interface.
    // Populate your dynamic notification interface as quickly as
    // possible.
    //
    notificationAlertLabel.setText(localNotification.alertBody)

    // After populating your dynamic notification interface call
    // the completion block.
    completionHandler(.Custom)
}
```

In the preceding code snippet, we began by overriding the `didReceiveLocalNotification` method, which is called whenever the Apple Watch device is about to receive a local notification, prior to displaying the notification controller interface. Next, we set the `text` property for our `notificationAlertLabel` to include the sent notification message as determined by the `alertBody` property. Finally, we called the `completionHandler` property and passed in the `.Custom` parameter to display the dynamic notification controller instead of the static interface controller. Passing in `.Default` would tell the Apple Watch app to display the static interface controller instead.

3. Next, locate the `didReceiveRemoteNotification` method and replace it with the following code snippet:

```
override func didReceiveRemoteNotification(remoteNotificati
on: [NSObject : AnyObject], withCompletion completionHandler:
((WKUserNotificationInterfaceType) -> Void)) {
    // This method is called when a remote notification needs to
    // be presented.
    // Implement it if you use a dynamic notification interface.
    // Populate your dynamic notification interface as quickly
    // as possible.
    //
    let aps = remoteNotification["aps"] as? NSDictionary
    let alert = aps!["alert"] as? NSDictionary
    let body = alert!["body"] as? String
```

```
let category = aps!["category"] as? String

if category == "ORDER_PLACED" {
    notificationAlertLabel.setText(body)
}
// After populating your dynamic notification interface call
// the completion block.
completionHandler(.Custom)
}
```

In the preceding code snippet, we began by overriding the didReceiveRemoteNotification method, which is called whenever the Apple Watch device is about to receive a remote notification, prior to displaying the notification controller interface. Next, we set up a NSDictionary object to match the passed-in remoteNotification dictionary object that matches the standard push notification payload of a remote notification.

We then extracted the category name from our push notification payload file PushNotificationPayload.apns and then compared it with our ORDER_PLACED category name before setting the text property for notificationAlertLabel to include the sent notification message as determined by the body property. Finally, we called the completionHandler property and passed in the .Custom parameter to display the dynamic notification controller instead of the static interface controller. Passing in .Default would tell the Apple Watch app to display the static interface controller instead.

For more information on local and remote notifications, refer to the WatchKit framework reference documentation at https://developer.apple.com/library/ prerelease/ios/documentation/WatchKit/Reference/ WKUserNotificationInterfaceController_ class/index.html#//apple_ref/occ/instm/ WKUserNotificationInterfaceController/didReceiveLoca lNotification:withCompletion.

Understanding the notification interface guidelines

The Apple Watch interface guidelines document describes guidelines and principles that help you design consistent user interfaces and experiences for your Watch apps as well as ensure that your applications run efficiently within the Apple Watch platform.

You need to consider the screen sizes for your custom layouts while ensuring the consistency of your application while navigating from screen to screen, and the principles for designing good user interfaces are also covered.

There is also information related to the proper use and appearance of views and controls for navigation, alerts, notifications, table views, buttons, and images as well as the creation of custom icons and images.

Some of the Apple Watch notification interface guidelines are as follows:

- Notifications should be designed appropriately so that they make use of graphics, colors, and text that convey information to the user clearly.

- When incorporating notifications within your WatchKit extension, they must provide a static interface but can contain an optional dynamic interface controller.

- You should avoid dynamically generating or downloading images within your dynamic interface controller.

- Notifications within your dynamic interface can have up to a maximum of four buttons plus an additional **Dismiss** button that is included by default.

- When designing your notifications, you need to ensure that all the content fits within a single screen. This means that you need to be selective about what information you decide to display to your users, and it should be relevant to the content being displayed.

 To get further information about the notifications interface guidelines, it is worth checking out the *Apple Watch Human Interface Guidelines* documentation at https://developer.apple.com/watch/human-interface-guidelines/app-components/.

Running the Shopping List application – WatchKit

In this section, we will look at how to compile and run our *Shopping List* application. We will run this within iOS simulator and WatchKit simulator so that we can see what happens when we receive a local notification and have this result displayed within our dynamic notification interface. Perform the following steps:

1. To run the app, select the **ShoppingList WatchKit App** scheme and choose your preferred device from the **iOS Simulators** section, as shown in the following screenshot:

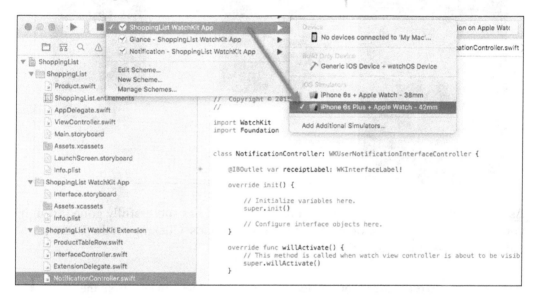

2. Next, build and run the application by navigating to **Product | Run** from the **Product** menu or pressing *Command + R*.

When the compilation is complete, the *Shopping List* app will be installed on the watchOS simulator. The following screenshot shows you the process of what happens when a product is successfully processed using Apple Pay; the user receives a notification dialog popup on the iOS device, and this same message is sent from the iOS device to the WatchKit extension.

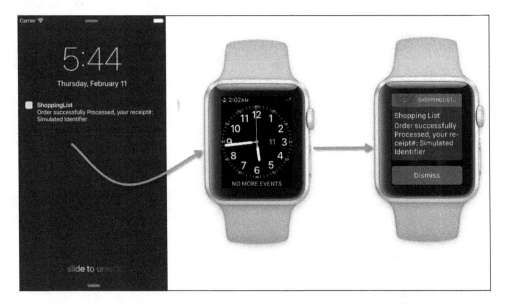

As you can note from the screenshot, once a payment has successfully gone through, you will receive a notification message after ten seconds. Clicking on the **Dismiss** button will close the notification dialog.

> In order to see your notification once you choose an item from the shopping list, you will need to hold down *Shift* + *Command* + *H* from the shopping list screen, which will take you back to the Home screen. You will then receive your notifications within the watch face area.

Summary

In this chapter, you learned about WatchKit notifications and how you can go about incorporating them within our existing *Shopping List* Apple Watch application. You then learned about WatchKit notifications and the notifications life cycle. We then looked at how to configure an existing notification scheme with the added benefit of being able to test your static and custom dynamic notifications within the simulator.

You then moved on to learning about the Apple Push Notification service and how you can go about adding buttons to a static interface controller and respond to Action buttons using the `handleActionWithIdentifier` method, which receives remote notifications.

After learning about the Apple Push Notification service, we talked a bit about the differences between static and dynamic interface controllers and how when developing notifications, you must at least have a static interface controller but the dynamic controllers are optional. You learned how to configure the static notification controller by assigning a category identifier, matching what was set up in the local payload file in the WatchKit extension.

Next, you learned about local and remote notifications and how to configure them before finally learning about the notification interface guidelines that you need to follow when designing your notifications, keeping in mind that each of the notification scenes within a WatchKit app can have a number of text labels and can incorporate an image and a title.

In the next chapter, you will learn how to create a new app that will show you how to add images to the assets catalog and how to animate these images within the WatchKit user interface. You'll learn how to handle and compress large images so that they improve performance.

10
Image Compression and Animation

When Apple released the original watchOS, the WatchKit platform provided you with a one-way solution to perform your own animations by flipping through each of the image frames. Now, with the release of watchOS 2, this software update provides you with an additional animation API that you can use to animate your images using the `animateWithDuration` method.

The WatchKit framework provides you with the `WKInterfaceImage` interface object class that you can add to your WatchKit app storyboard. You should consider using images that are in either the PNG or JPEG formats. Apple suggests that you should avoid using file formats other than PNG or JPEG as they may have an impact on performance when they are rendered to the WatchKit interface, and you need to take into consideration the size of these images, especially when working with large image files.

In this chapter, you will learn how to build a simple application that will showcase how to animate a series of images within the WatchKit user interface. You will learn how to add images to image assets catalogs and the best ways of handling and compressing large image files when they are downloaded from an external website so that they can improve performance.

This chapter includes the following topics:

- Setting up and adding images to the image assets catalog
- Configuring the project to use **App Transport Security** (**ATS**)
- Understanding how to animate images within the WatchKit interface
- Understanding the best approach to compressing large images that are downloaded from the Internet

We have an exciting project ahead of us, so let's get started!

Building the animation application – WatchKit

In this section, we will look at how we can go about designing our user interface for our *Animation Example* application. We will begin by developing the WatchKit portion of our application.

Before we proceed, we need to create our `AnimationExample` project, which is very simple to create using Xcode. Simply follow these steps:

1. Launch Xcode from the `/Applications` folder.

2. Choose **Create a new Xcode project** or go to **File | New Project**.

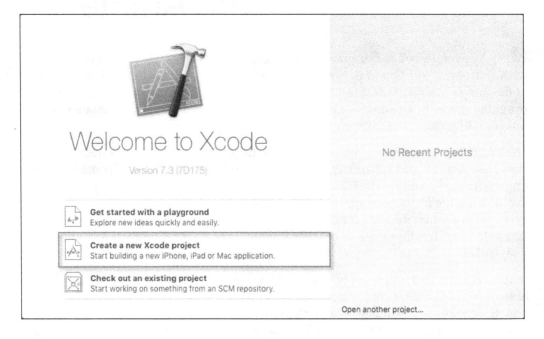

3. Select **iOS App with WatchKit App** from the list of available templates under the **watchOS** section, as shown in the following screenshot:

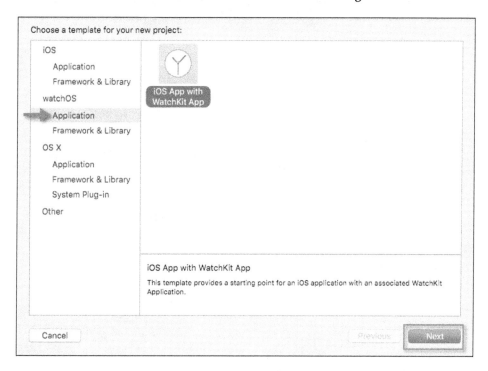

4. Click on the **Next** button to proceed to the next step in the wizard.
5. Next, enter `AnimationExample` as the name for your project.
6. Select **Swift** from the **Language** drop-down menu.
7. Then, select **iPhone** from the **Devices** drop-down menu.
8. Ensure that the **Include Notification Scene** checkbox is selected.

9. Click on the **Next** button to proceed to the next step in the wizard.

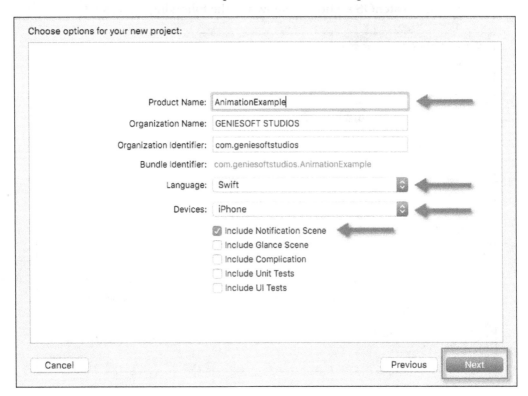

 The **Organization Identifier** input for your app needs to be unique. Apple recommends that you use the reverse domain style (for example, `com.domainName.appName`).

10. Specify the location where you would like to save your project.

11. Then, click on the **Create** button to save your project at the specified location.

Once your project is created, you will be presented with the Xcode development environment along with the project files that the template created for you.

Setting up and adding images to the assets catalog

Before you can begin animating images within the WatchKit interface, you will need to extract the individual frame from a GIF image. Fortunately, there is a free web app called *Gif Frame Splitter*, which I found online, that can extract each of these frames for you. Perform the following steps:

1. First, launch your favorite browser and go to `http://ezgif.com/split?url=http://www.animatedgif.net/computers/comp6_e0.gif`.

2. Then, click on the **Split it!** button, as highlighted in the following figure:

3. Next, click on the **Download frames as ZIP** button, as highlighted in the preceding figure. This will then proceed to download the compressed file to your Downloads folder by default.

4. Then, extract the contents of the ZIP file, as shown in the following screenshot:

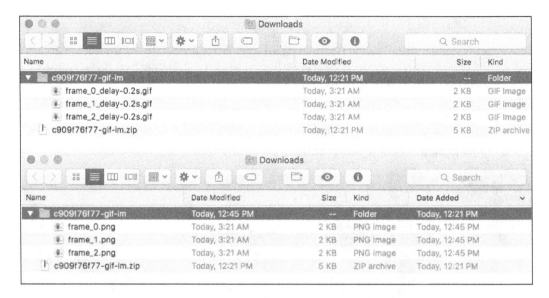

5. Next, rename each of the files to their respective names: `frame_0_delay-0.2s.gif` to `frame_0.png`, `frame_1_delay-0.2s.gif` to `frame_1.png`, and so on, as shown in the preceding screenshot.

6. Then, drag the contents of the `c909f76f77-gif-im` folder to the image assets catalog, as shown in the following screenshot:

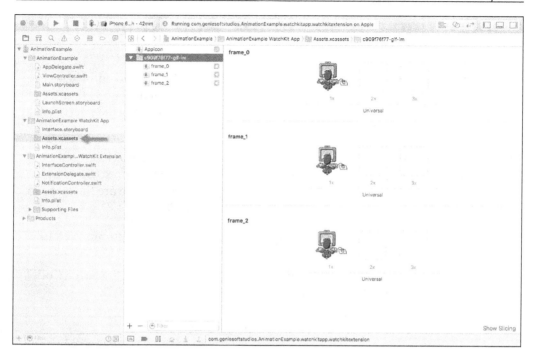

When adding files to the image assets catalog, these should end with @2x—for example, `frame_0@2x.png` to indicate to the asset catalog that the images are suitable to be displayed on the Apple Watch Retina display. The left-hand side panel contains a list of all the image sets that are currently contained within the catalog, and these images are grouped together with different sizes and resolutions so that we can refer to them within our code in later sections.

By default, the image asset catalog for a WatchKit app target contains a single image set named **AppIcon**, which contains the icon used to represent the WatchKit app in a variety of locations, such as the Home screen and Notification Center. Now that we have added our images to the assets catalog, our next step is to begin configuring our app so that we can access external websites to download images and they can be displayed within the WatchKit interface.

Configuring our app to use App Transport Security

Apple introduced the App Transport Security protocol with iOS 9 to enforce secure connections between Internet connections as well as your WatchKit apps that communicate using the HTTPS protocol. It requires that information be encrypted using the TLS version 1.2.

In this section, we will take a look at how to disable and opt out of ATS entirely by configuring our local `Info.plist` file within the WatchKit extension so that our application can communicate over HTTPS without any issues. Here are the steps to be performed:

1. Select the `Info.plist` file located within the **AnimationExample WatchKit Extension** folder in the project navigation window.

2. Next, right-click on the `Info.plist` file and go to **Open As | Source Code**, as shown in the following screenshot:

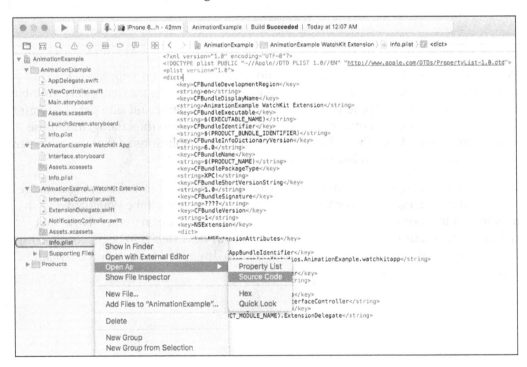

3. This will display the contents of our property list for the WatchKit extension. Next, with the Info.plist file displayed, enter the following highlighted code sections:

```
<?xml version="1.0" encoding="UTF-8"?>
<!DOCTYPE plist PUBLIC "-//Apple//DTD PLIST 1.0//EN" "http://www.
apple.com/DTDs/PropertyList-1.0.dtd">
<plist version="1.0">
<dict>
    <key>NSAppTransportSecurity</key>
    <dict>
      <key>NSAllowsArbitraryLoads</key>
      <true/>
    </dict>
    <key>CFBundleDevelopmentRegion</key>
    <string>en</string>
    <key>CFBundleDisplayName</key>
    <string>AnimationExample WatchKit Extension</string>
    <key>CFBundleExecutable</key>
    <string>$(EXECUTABLE_NAME)</string>
    <key>CFBundleIdentifier</key>
    <string>$(PRODUCT_BUNDLE_IDENTIFIER)</string>
    <key>CFBundleInfoDictionaryVersion</key>
    <string>6.0</string>
    <key>CFBundleName</key>
    <string>$(PRODUCT_NAME)</string>
    <key>CFBundlePackageType</key>
    <string>XPC!</string>
    <key>CFBundleShortVersionString</key>
    <string>1.0</string>
    <key>CFBundleSignature</key>
    <string>????</string>
    <key>CFBundleVersion</key>
    <string>1</string>
    <key>NSExtension</key>
    <dict>
      <key>NSExtensionAttributes</key>
      <dict>
        <key>WKAppBundleIdentifier</key>
        <string>com.geniesoftstudios.AnimationExample.
watchkitapp</string>
      </dict>
      <key>NSExtensionPointIdentifier</key>
      <string>com.apple.watchkit</string>
    </dict>
```

```
  <key>RemoteInterfacePrincipalClass</key>
  <string>$(PRODUCT_MODULE_NAME).
InterfaceController</string>
  <key>WKExtensionDelegateClassName</key>
  <string>$(PRODUCT_MODULE_NAME).ExtensionDelegate</string>
</dict>
</plist>
```

What we did in our property list is set up an array of dictionary items by specifying the <dict> tag at the beginning and subsequently creating each dictionary object as well as the associated key-value pairs for each item. This is so that we can opt out of ATS entirely by setting NSAllowsArbitraryLoads to TRUE.

For more information about App Transport Security and NSAppTransportSecurity, refer to the Apple Developer documentation at https://developer.apple.com/library/prerelease/tvos/documentation/General/Reference/InfoPlistKeyReference/Articles/CocoaKeys.html#//apple_ref/doc/uid/TP40009251-SW33.

Now that we have configured our project so that it can use App Transport Security, our next step is to begin designing the user interface for our AnimationExample WatchKit extension counterpart using the Interface Builder application.

Using Interface Builder to create the watch user interface

In this section, we will begin building the user interface for our *Animation Example* application using Interface Builder as well as all of the associated code for the AnimationExample WatchKit extension portion of our application via the following steps:

1. Select the **Interface.storyboard** file from the project navigation window.

2. Next, choose **Interface Controller** and click on the Show the Identify Inspector button, then from Object Library, drag a WKInterfaceImage control to the watch area canvas. Then, from the Attributes Inspector section, modify the **Image** property to frame_0.

3. Next, modify both the **Width** and **Height** properties to **Fixed** and set both the **Width** and **Height** values to **80**.

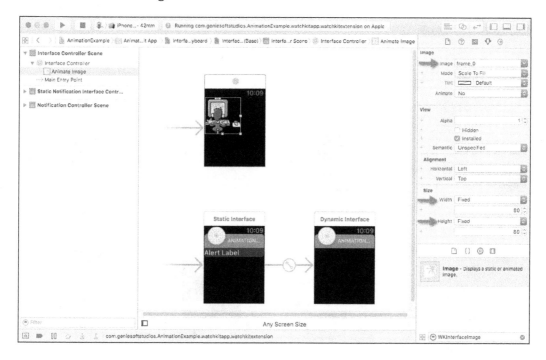

4. Next, from Object Library, drag a `WKInterfaceSlider` control to the watch area canvas and then from the Attributes Inspector section, change the starting **Value** property for our slider control to **0**.

5. Then, we need to set the **Minimum** property of our slider control to **0** so that it doesn't exceed the minimum set amount.

6. Then, we need to change the **Maximum** value property for our slider control to **1** so that we don't exceed the limit.

7. Lastly, we need to set the **Steps** property for our slider control to show **10** increments (as dashes) when we press the **+** and **–** buttons.

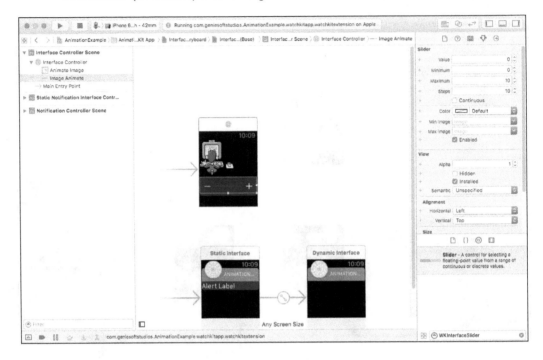

8. Next, from Object Library, drag a `WKInterfaceButton` control to the watch area canvas and place this under the `WKInterfaceSlider` control that we added previously.

9. Then, from the Attributes Inspector section, ensure that the **Size** property for **Width** is set to **Relative to Container** and modify the **Width** property to **1**.

10. Next, ensure that the **Size** property for **Height** is set to **Size to Fit Content**.

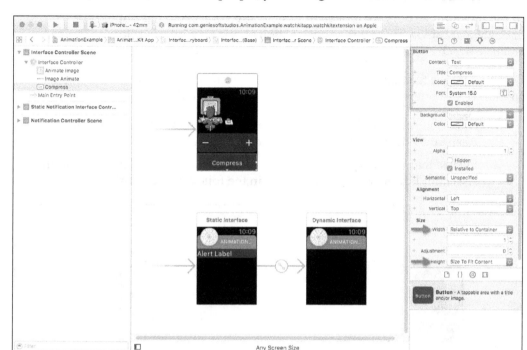

11. Once you modify the interface controller, it would be good to save your project by going to **File | Save** or pressing *Command + S*.

In the next section, we will start by connecting the Outlets for each of our interface controller objects so that it will have the functionality of animating our image within the WatchKit interface.

Establishing connections to our interface controller

In the previous section, we looked at how to add controls to our `Interface.storyboard` canvas to form the construction of our user interface for our *Animation Example* watch app as well as setting some properties for each of our controls.

Our next step is to create the Outlets for our *Animation Example* WatchKit application so that we can reference them through the code through the following steps:

1. Open the Assistant Editor window by going to **Navigate | Open in Assistant Editor** or by pressing *Option + Command + ,*.

2. Ensure that the `InterfaceController.swift` file is displayed within the Assistant Editor window, as shown in the following screenshot:

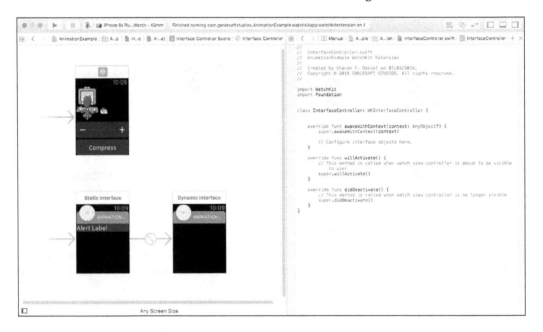

3. Next, select the `WKInterfaceImage` control, then hold down the *Control* key, and drag it into the `InterfaceController.swift` file within the body of `class InterfaceController: WKInterfaceController`.

4. Select **Outlet** from the **Connection** drop-down menu for the type of connection to create and enter `animateImage` for the name of the Outlet property to create.

5. Next, choose **Weak** from the **Storage** drop-down menu and click on the **Connect** button.

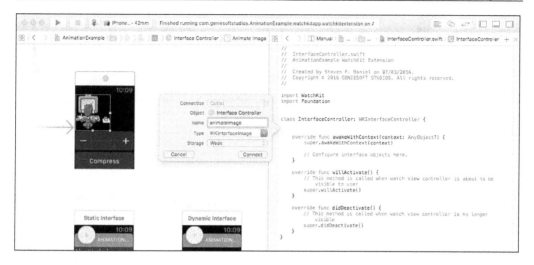

6. Next, select the `WKInterfaceSlider` control, then hold down the *Control* key, and drag it into the `InterfaceController.swift` file, as we did for our `animateImage` Outlet.

7. Then, select **Outlet** from the **Connection** drop-down menu for the type of connection to create and enter `imageAnimate` for the name of the Outlet property to create.

8. Next, choose **Weak** from the **Storage** drop-down menu and click on the **Connect** button.

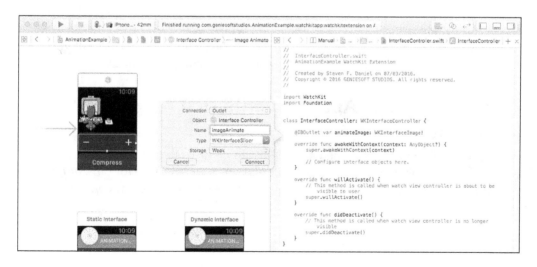

9. Once you create the necessary Outlets, it would be good to save your project by navigating to **File** | **Save** or pressing *Command + S*.

Whenever you create an Outlet, you must remember to create it within the `InterfaceController` class as these cannot be created outside this class body.

The following code snippet shows the complete implementation of our Outlets that we created in the previous steps:

```
//
//   InterfaceController.swift
//   AnimationExample WatchKit Extension
//
//   Created by Steven F. Daniel on 07/03/2016.
//   Copyright © 2016 GENIESOFT STUDIOS. All rights reserved.
//

import WatchKit
import Foundation


class InterfaceController: WKInterfaceController {

    @IBOutlet var animateImage: WKInterfaceImage!
    @IBOutlet var imageAnimate: WKInterfaceSlider!
}
```

As you can note from the preceding code snippet, Interface Builder created each of our control objects as well as the associated type of control we used. In our next section, we will take a look at how we can set up the Action events that will get executed when the user taps on the slider and how to compress objects.

Establishing our Action events that respond to user actions

In the previous section, we looked at how to add controls to our `Interface.storyboard` canvas to form the construction of our user interface for our *Animation Example* watch app and connected each of the Outlets for each of our controls.

In this section, we will look at how we can communicate with these Outlets when the slider and **Compress** buttons are tapped:

1. Open the Assistant Editor window by going to **Navigate | Open in Assistant Editor** or by pressing *Option + Command + ,*.

2. Ensure that the `InterfaceController.swift` file is displayed within the Assistant Editor window, as shown in the following screenshot:

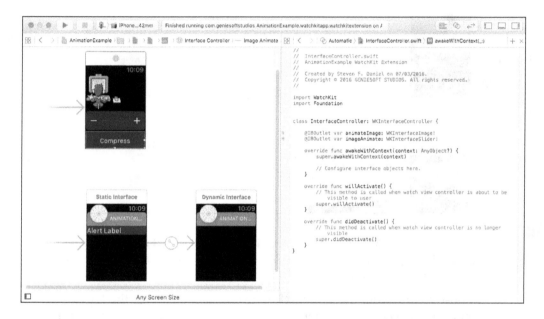

3. Next, select the `WKInterfaceSlider` control, then hold down the *Control* key, and drag it into the `InterfaceController.swift` file below the `didDeactivate` method.

4. Choose **Action** from the **Connection** drop-down menu for the type of connection to create and enter `animateTapped` for the name of the action to create.

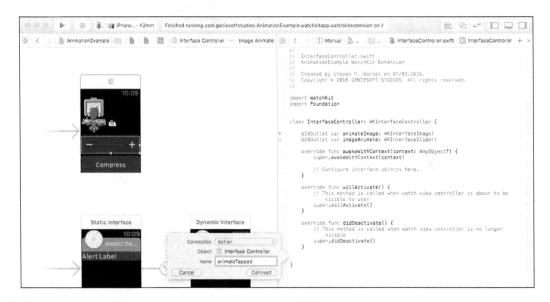

5. Next, select the `WKInterfaceButton` control, then hold down the *Control* key, and drag it into the `InterfaceController.swift` file below the `animateTapped:` method.

6. Choose **Action** from the **Connection** drop-down menu for the type of connection to create and enter `compressTapped` for the name of the action to create.

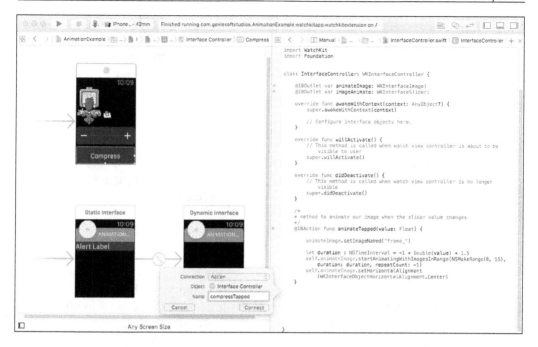

In the next sections, you will learn how to animate the image that we added to our image assets catalog within the WatchKit interface as well as how to download an image from the Internet, compress it, and then resize the image so that it fits nicely within the WatchKit interface.

Animating your images within the WatchKit interface

Animating images within the WatchKit interface is not that difficult, and you will shortly see how easy this is when using the new API that comes as part of watchOS 2. At the beginning of the chapter, we downloaded an image from the Internet that consisted of three GIF image files, which combined to make up an animation of a computer man typing at his computer screen.

We then renamed these images to frame_x.png and then imported them into the image assets catalog. In this section, we will take a look at how to animate these images within the WatchKit interface, so let's get started.

Open the `InterfaceController.swift` file located within the **AnimationExample WatchKit Extension** group in the project navigation window; locate the `animationTapped:` method and enter the following code snippet:

```swift
/*
 * method to animate our image when the slider value changes
 */
@IBAction func animateTapped(value: Float) {
    animateImage.setImageNamed("frame_")
    let duration : NSTimeInterval = -1 * Double(value) + 1.5
    self.animateImage.startAnimatingWithImagesInRange(NSMakeRange(0,
            15), duration: duration, repeatCount: -1)
    self.animateImage.setHorizontalAlignment(
        WKInterfaceObjectHorizontalAlignment.Center)
}
```

As you can note from the preceding code snippet, we began by setting a reference to the first image sequence from our assets catalog, and then, we calculated the number of seconds that we want our image to be animated, which is derived from our `WKInterfaceSlider` control. Then, we assigned the value to our `duration` variable.

Next, we called the `startAnimatingWithImagesInRange` method to animate our image, specifying the duration, the number of times we want to have our image animated, and the range that encompasses all of the images within the animation set. To have the animation repeat indefinitely, we specified the value of `-1`. In our final step, we called the `setHorizontalAlignment` method of our `animateImage` object to set the horizontal alignment and center the image object within the WatchKit interface.

For more information about the `WKInterfaceObject` class, refer to the Apple Developer documentation at `https://developer.apple.com/library/prerelease/watchos/documentation/WatchKit/Reference/WKInterfaceObject_class/index.html#//apple_ref/occ/instm/WKInterfaceObject/setHorizontalAlignment`.

Loading and compressing images within the WatchKit interface

When large images are displayed within the WatchKit interface, they can take a considerable amount of time before they get displayed within the Apple Watch display, and in some cases, they can take up to 2 or more minutes, which is an unacceptable amount of time to keep the end user waiting.

In reality, the largest image that can be displayed within the Apple Watch display for a 42 mm model is around 312 x 390 pixels. In this section, you'll learn how to download an image from an external website and then how to reduce the size of our image, in terms of both the dimension and storage space, using a scaling factor before it is displayed within the Apple Watch display.

Open the `InterfaceController.swift` file located within the **AnimationExample WatchKit Extension** group in the project navigation window; then, locate the `compressTapped:` method and enter the following code snippet:

```
/*
 * Method to handle loading the image from the Web and resizing it
 */
@IBAction func compressTapped() {

    // Declare the URL to our image that we want to download
    let imageURL = "https://www.packtpub.com/sites/default/files/
                    B05040_MockupCover_Normal_.jpg"

    // Download the image from the URL Specified and convert
    // this to a data object.
    if let data = NSData(contentsOfURL: NSURL(string: imageURL)!) {
        // Convert the data object to an image
        let largeImage = UIImage(data:data)

        // Calculate the new size for our image
        let reducedSize = CGSizeMake(largeImage!.size.width * 0.15,
                          largeImage!.size.height * 0.15)
        UIGraphicsBeginImageContext(reducedSize)

    largeImage!.drawInRect(CGRectMake(0, 0, reducedSize.width,
    reducedSize.height))
    let compressedImage = UIGraphicsGetImageFromCurrentImageContext()

    UIGraphicsEndImageContext()

    // Display our newly compressed image within the
    // WatchKit Interface
    self.animateImage.setImage(compressedImage)
    }
}
```

As you can note from the preceding code snippet, we began by declaring the `imageURL` variable that contains the URL reference for the image that we want to download. Next, we called the `contentsOfURL` property that accepts a NSURL reference that points to our `imageURL` location to download the image and then converts this into a data object.

Once we have a valid `data` object as determined by the `data` variable, we proceeded to convert the `data` object to an image using the `UIImage` class and then to calculate the new reduced size for the image using the `CGSizeMake` method. After this, we applied a scaling factor. In our next step, we made a call to the `UIGraphicsBeginImageContext` method to create a new image bitmap based on the newly calculated size.

In our final step, we called the `drawInRect` method to draw the entire image within the current graphics context and apply any scaling needed to fit within the specified rectangle, called the `UIGraphicsGetImageFromCurrentImageContext` method to return an image object containing the contents of the current bitmap graphics context, and assigned this to our `compressedImage` variable. Finally, we proceeded to call `UIGraphicsEndImageContext` to remove the image from the current graphics before assigning the newly resized image to our `animateImage` interface object and then displayed it within the Apple Watch display.

> For more information about the `UIGraphicsBeginImageContext` method, refer to the Apple Developer documentation at `https://developer.apple.com/library/prerelease/watchos/documentation/UIKit/Reference/UIKitFunctionReference/index.html`.

Building and running the Animation Example application

In this section, we will take a look at how to compile and run our *Animation Example* application within the WatchKit simulator so that we can take a look at what happens when an image is downloaded from the Internet, compressed, and then resized so that it fits within the Apple Watch interface. Perform the following steps:

1. To run the app, select the **AnimationExample WatchKit App** scheme and choose your preferred device, as shown in the following screenshot:

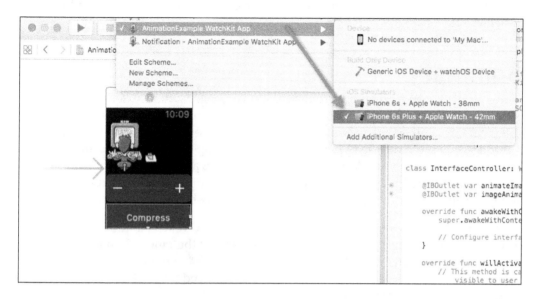

2. Next, build and run the application by navigating to **Product | Run** from the **Product** menu or by pressing *Command + R*.

When the compilation is complete, the *Animation Example* app will be installed on the watchOS simulator. The following figure shows you what happens when you change the value of the slider control and when the **Compress** button is pressed:

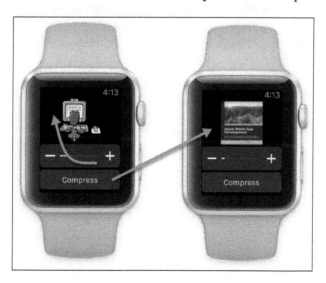

Simply use the **+** and **–** buttons to change the speed at which you want the animation to play and then click on the **Compress** button to download the image from the Internet. Then, this will be resized correctly so that it fits nicely within the Watch interface.

Summary

In this chapter, you learned how to download an image from an external website, extract the animation frames from the ZIP file, and then add them to the image assets catalog. You learned about the App Transport Security protocol that Apple introduced with the release of iOS 9 to enforce developers to provide secure connections between your Apple Watch apps and iOS apps that communicate over HTTPS, and learned how to properly configure our Apple WatchKit extension to allow our app to download images from external websites.

In our next step, we discussed Outlets and how we can connect and bind them to control objects within the Interface Builder canvas and then moved on to learning about creating Action events to our control elements that will be able to respond to user actions when tapped. To end the chapter, we moved on to discussing how to correctly animate an image within the WatchKit interface by cycling through each of the extracted frames and using the startAnimatingWithImagesInRange method. Then, you learned how to use the NSData class and the contentsOfURL property to download an image from an external website and reduce the size of this image so that it can be displayed within the WatchKit interface.

In our final chapter, we will explore how to set up your iOS development team, provisioning profiles, as well as the certificates for both development and distribution. You'll also learn how to effectively use the Instruments application to profile your application to eliminate performance bottlenecks and memory leaks. Finally, you'll learn how to package your Apple Watch app and deploy this to iTunes Connect so that you can download it and then test your app on your iPhone device so that it can be deployed to run on your Apple Watch device.

11

Packaging and Deploying Your App

You have now successfully built your application, and are ready to release it to the rest of the world. All you need to do is decide how to deploy and market your app.

In this chapter, we will look at what is required to submit your application to the Apple App Store, and share your creations with the rest of the community. You'll also learn how to set up your iOS development team as well as the certificates needed for both development and distribution.

Here, we will also explain how to use the **Instruments** application that comes with Xcode to effectively profile your application for eliminating performance bottlenecks. In the final sections, you will learn how to create the provisioning profiles for both development and distribution, as well as creating the necessary App IDs for your application, before finally learning how to register your iOS devices.

This chapter includes the following topics:

- Creating an iOS development certificate, and setting up your team
- Creating your application's App IDs and development provisioning profiles
- Using the provisioning profiles to install the app on the iOS device
- Profiling your app using Instruments to detect performance bottlenecks
- Using Xcode to submit your app to iTunes Connect

We have an exciting project ahead of us, so let's get started.

Creating and setting up your iOS development team

In this section, you will learn how to create and set up your iOS development team.

Before you can submit your application to the Apple App Store for approval, you will need to set up your iOS development team, so let's get started:

1. Log in to the iOS Developer portal at `http://developer.apple.com/`.

2. Click on the **Member Center** link that is located right at the top of the screen.

3. Sign in to your account using your Apple ID and password. This will then display the **Developer Program Resources** page, as we saw in the *Setting up and provisioning your app for Apple Pay* section in *Chapter 6, Implementing Tables within Your App*.

4. Next, click on the **iTunes Connect** button. This is where you will be able to check various things such as sales, trends, payments, financial reports, and app analytics:

5. Next, click on the **Users and Roles** button, as highlighted in the preceding screenshot. This will bring up the **Users and Roles** option pane from where you can add a new user, which is shown in the following screenshot:

 The **Users and Roles** screen allows you to add yourself or the authorized people within your organization to be able log in to the iOS Developer Program portal, test apps on iOS devices, and to add additional iOS devices to the account.

6. Ensure that you are within the **iTunes Connect Users** section, as highlighted in the preceding screenshot. Then, click on the **+** button to bring up the **Add iTunes Connect User** screen, shown in the following screenshot.

7. Next, fill in the **User Information** section for the person that you will be adding to your development team. Once you have finished, click on the **Next** button, as shown in the following screenshot:

8. Next, under the **Role** section, choose the roles that the user can perform from the list of roles available .

9. Then click on the **Next** button, as shown in the following screenshot:

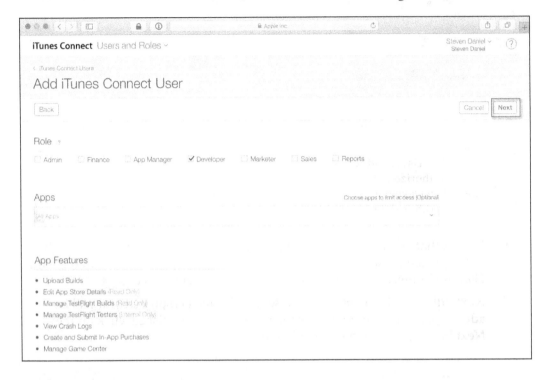

10. The **Notifications and Settings** section is where you can assign the ways in which you want the user to be notified. From this screen, you can also specify the information, related to a list of territories, that you want the user to be notified about. This is shown in the following screenshot:

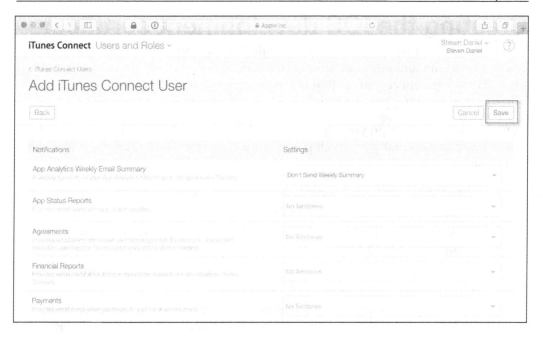

11. Once you have finished specifying each of the different types of notification methods, click on the **Save** button, as shown in the preceding screenshot. The new user account will then be created, along with a confirmation e-mail that will be sent to the user's e-mail account, requesting them to activate their account.

We have covered the steps required to create and assign roles to new users. We have also explained the steps needed to set up the user roles that are allowed to log into the iOS Developer portal for managing new and existing users, view sales and trends reports as well as payments and financial statements. We will now look at the steps involved in generating an iOS development certificate.

This certificate is encrypted, and serves as your digital identification signature. You must sign your apps using this certificate before you can submit your apps to the Apple App Store.

Creating the iOS development certificate

In this section, you will learn how to create the iOS development certificate that will enable you to run and test your apps on the iOS device. We will begin by generating the iOS development certificate that will be encrypted, and which will serve the purpose of identifying you digitally.

You will then need to sign your apps using this certificate before you can run and test any application that you develop on your iOS device. To begin with, follow these simple steps:

1. Launch the Keychain Access application, which can be found in the / `Applications/Utilities` folder.

2. Next, choose the **Request a Certificate From a Certificate Authority...** menu option from **Keychain Access | Certificate Assistant**.

3. Then you need to provide some information in the **Certificate Information** section before the certificate can be generated.

4. Next, enter the required information, as shown in the following screenshot, whilst ensuring that you have selected the **Saved to disk** and the **Let me specify key pair information** options:

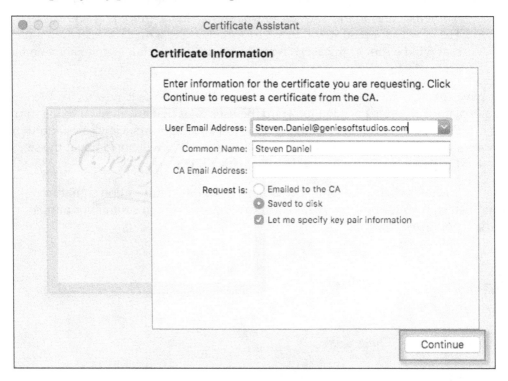

5. Once all the information has been filled out, click on the **Continue** button. You will then be asked to specify a name for the certificate; accept the default suggested name, and click on the **Save** button.

 At this point, the certificate is created at the specified location . You will then be asked to specify the key size and the algorithm to use.

6. Next, accept the default values **2048** bits and **RSA Algorithm**; we need to provide some information in the **Certificate Information** section before the certificate can be generated.

7. Click on the **Continue** button, and then click on the **Done** button when the final screen appears.

Up until now, you have learned how to generate a certificate request for iOS development, with the help of a **Certificate Signing Request** (**CSR**) file, using the pre-installed Mac OS X Keychain Access application. This enables you to code-sign your applications before deploying them to the iOS device for both development and testing.

In the next section, you will learn how to request a development certificate from Apple to enable you to code-sign your applications using the certificate information file that we created in this section.

Obtaining the development certificate from Apple

In this section, you will learn how to obtain the development certificate from Apple to enable you to begin developing apps.

Before you can begin submitting your applications to the Apple App Store, you will need to obtain your own copy of the iOS development certificate; this certificate is basically a unique identity for each of the apps that you submit for approval. So let's get started:

1. Log in to the iOS Developer portal at `http://developer.apple.com/`.

2. Click on the **Member Center** link that is located right at the top of the screen.

3. Sign in to your account using your Apple ID and password. This will then display the **Developer Program Resources** page, as we saw in the previous section.

4. Next, click on the **Certificates, Identifiers & Profiles** button, and then click on the **+** button that is displayed on the next screen.

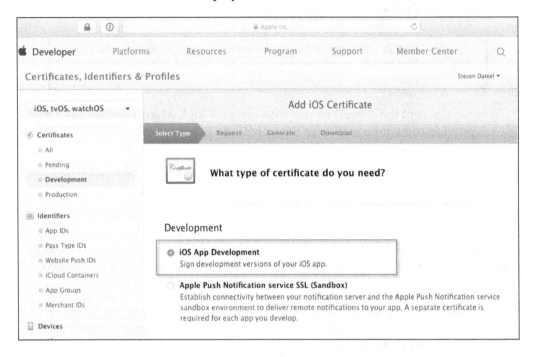

5. Choose the **iOS App Development** option under the **Development** section, as highlighted in the preceding screenshot.

6. Click on the **Continue** button to proceed to the next step of uploading your CSR file.

7. Next, click on the **Choose File...** button that is shown on the **Generate your certificate** screen.

8. Select the `CertificateSigningRequest.certSigningRequest` file that you created in the previous section, and click on the **Continue** button to proceed to the next step in the wizard.

9. After a few seconds, the page will refresh, and the certificate will be ready for you.

In this section, we looked at the steps involved in requesting a certificate from Apple, which will be used to enable us to code-sign our applications that are to be deployed on the iOS device and the Apple App Store. We then moved on to explain how to use the generated certificate request file that we created in our previous section for generating the development certificate.

Creating App IDs for your WatchKit applications

In previous sections, you learned how to request a certificate from Apple to provide us with the ability to code-sign our applications, and to use the generated certificate request file to generate our deployment certificate.

In this section, we will look at how to create the application's App IDs so that we can use them to deploy our applications for testing on an iOS device:

1. Log in to the iOS Developer portal at `http://developer.apple.com/`.

2. Click on the **Member Center** link that is located right at the top of the screen.

3. Sign in to your account using your Apple ID and password. This will then display the **Developer Program Resources** page, as we saw in the previous section.

4. Then click on the **Certificates, Identifiers & Profiles** button that is displayed as one of the options on this screen.

5. Next, click on the **App IDs** item located in the **Identifiers** group on the left-hand side of the page, and click on the **+** button to display the **Register iOS App IDs** section as highlighted in the following screenshot:

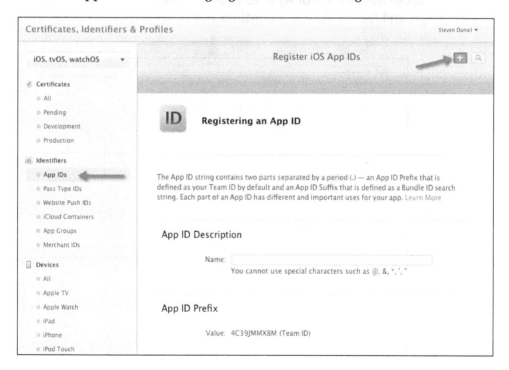

6. Next, provide a description for the **App ID Description** field that will be used to identify your app, as shown in the preceding screenshot.

7. Provide a name for the **Bundle ID** field. This needs to be the same as your application's **Bundle Identifier**.

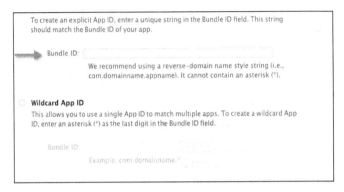

 The **Bundle ID** for your app needs to be unique. Apple recommends that you use the reverse domain style (for example, `com.domainName.appName`).

8. Next, choose from the list of **App Services** that you would like to enable for your app, and then click on the **Continue** button, as shown in the following screenshot:

9. In the **Confirm your App ID** screen, click on the **Register** button.

In this section, we covered the steps required to create the App ID for our application. Creation of an App ID is required for each application that you create, and must contain a unique application ID that identifies itself. The App ID is part of the provisioning profile, and identifies an app or a suite of related applications.

They are used when your applications communicate with the iOS hardware accessories or the Apple Push Notification service, and when data is shared between each of your applications.

Creating development provisioning profiles

In this section, you will learn how to create development provisioning profiles so that your applications can be installed on the iOS device, and you can deploy and test your applications prior to deploying your app to the Apple App Store:

1. Log in to the iOS Developer portal at `http://developer.apple.com/`.

2. Click on the **Member Center** link that is located right at the top of the screen.

3. Sign in to your account using your Apple ID and password. This will then display the **Developer Program Resources** page, as we saw in the previous sections.

4. Click on the **Certificates, Identifiers & Profiles** button that is displayed as one of the options on this screen. Then click on the **All** item under the **Provisioning Profiles** section on the left-hand side of the page.

5. Next, click on the **+** button to display the **Add iOS Provisioning Profiles** section, as highlighted in the following screenshot:

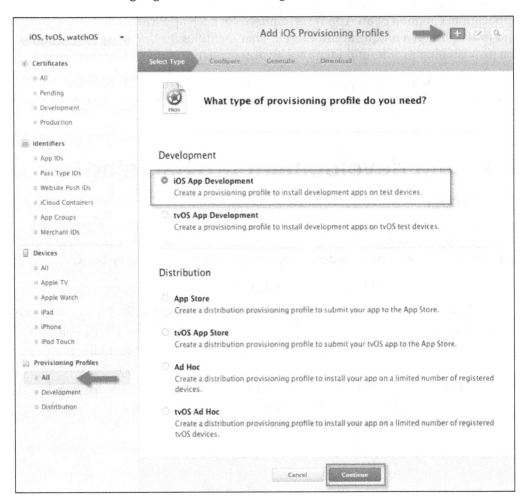

6. Choose the **iOS App Development** option from the **Development** section, and then click on the **Continue** button to proceed to the next step, as shown in the preceding screenshot.

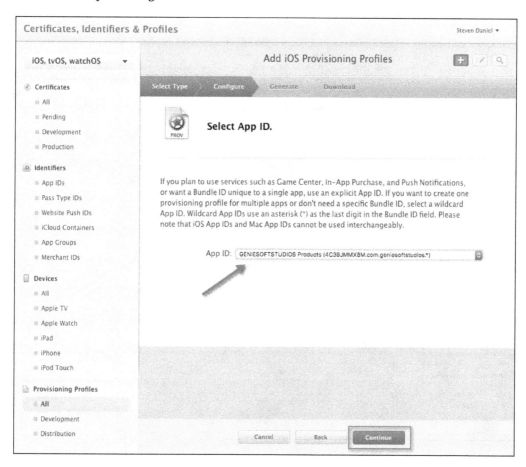

7. Next, select your **App ID** from the drop-down list available, and click on the **Continue** button to proceed to the next step in the wizard.

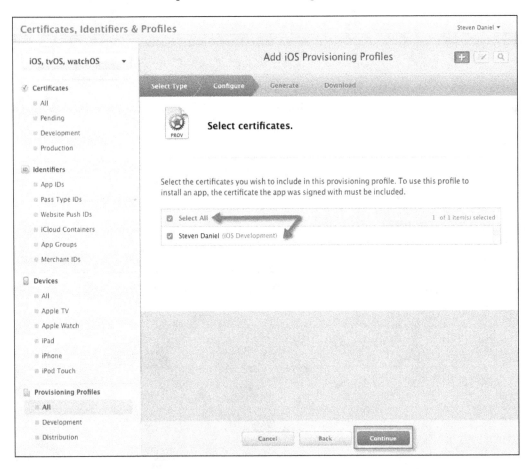

8. Then, choose your certificate from the list of available certificates that you would like to include to be part of the provisioning profile, and click on the **Continue** button to proceed to the next step, as shown in the preceding screenshot.

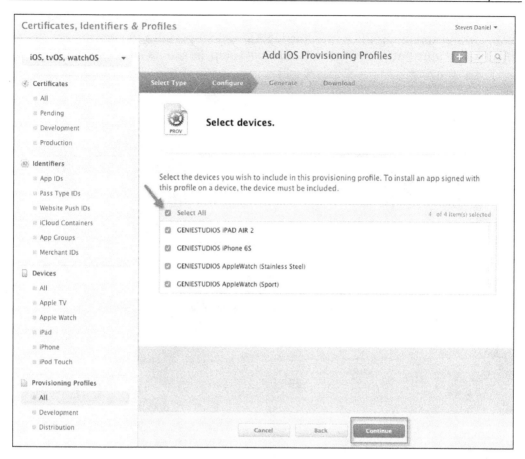

9. Choose from the list of devices that you would like to include as part of this provisioning profile, and click on the **Continue** button to proceed to the next step, as shown in the preceding screenshot.

For more information on how to register iOS devices using Member Center, please refer to the *App Distribution Guide* documentation at https://developer.apple.com/library/ios/documentation/IDEs/Conceptual/AppDistributionGuide/MaintainingProfiles/MaintainingProfiles.html#//apple_ref/doc/uid/TP40012582-CH30-SW10.

10. Specify a name for the **Profile Name** field to be used for identifying the provisioning profile within the iOS Developer portal, and click on the **Continue** button to proceed to the next step, as shown in the following screenshot:

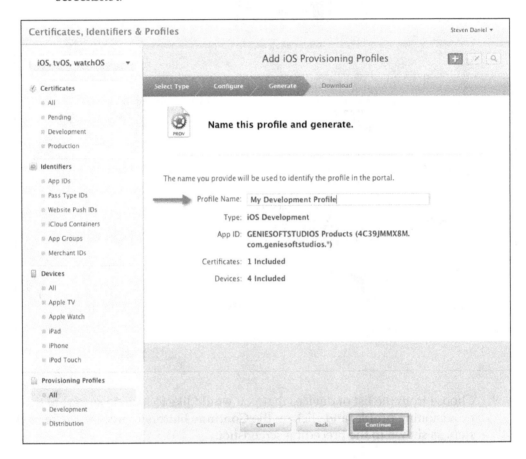

11. Finally, your provisioning profile has been created, and is ready to be used. You can choose to download your provisioning profile from here, or you can let Xcode handle this for you (we will cover this in the next section).

12. To close this screen, and to go back to the list of provisioning profiles, click on the **Done** button.

In this section, you learned how to create a provisioning profile that will allow your applications to be installed on a real iOS device. Once this is done, you will be able to authorize selected team members to install and test the application on each of their devices.

Whenever you deploy an application on an iOS device, it will contain the iOS development certificate for each team member as well as the **Unique Device Identifier** (**UDID**), which is a sequence of 40 letters and numbers that is specific to your device, and the App ID.

Profiling your application using Xcode Instruments

In this section, we will focus on how to effectively use Xcode Instruments within our applications to track down areas that could be affecting the overall running performance.

These types of issues could potentially cause an application to run slowly, or even crash on the user's iOS device. We will look at how to profile our *Animation Example* application using the **Leaks** instrument that will help track down any memory leaks within our code, which may not have been released correctly and may thus affect the application's overall performance.

To begin profiling your application using the Instruments application, follow these simple steps:

1. Select the `AnimationExample.xcodeproj` file from the `Chapter 10` folder in the accompanying code bundle.

2. Next, ensure that the `AnimationExample` Xcode project file is open within the Xcode development IDE.

3. Choose **Profile** from the **Product** menu, or alternatively, use the keyboard shortcut, *Command + I*:

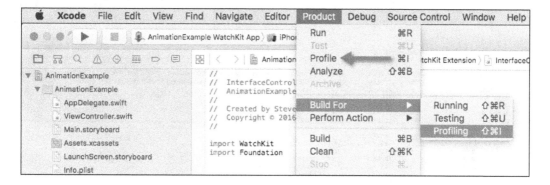

4. Once this option has been selected, your application will be compiled and then run; eventually you will see the Instruments application window displayed, as shown in the following screenshot:

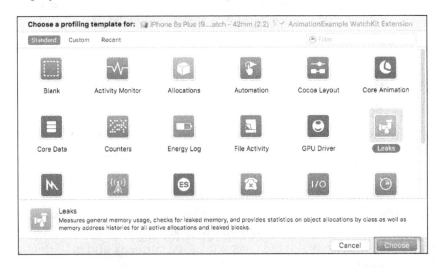

5. Then, select the **Leaks** item from the **Standard** list of available templates, as shown in the preceding screenshot.

6. Next, click on the **Choose** button to proceed to the next step in the wizard.

7. Finally, click on the **Record** button to begin profiling your application:

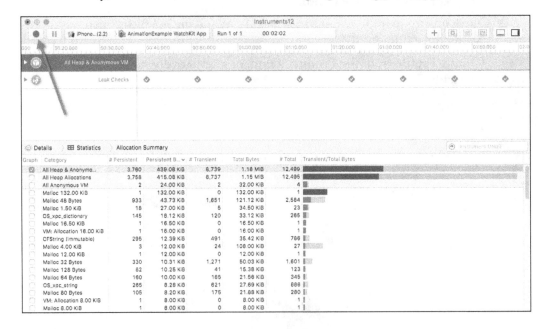

Through the use of Instruments you can gather information based on a variety of different types of data as well as view them side by side at the same time. This enables you to spot trends which would be hard to spot otherwise. This can also be used to see the running of code by your application along with the corresponding memory usage.

The following table provides you with a brief description of each feature within the Instruments application:

Instruments' feature	Description
Instruments pane	This pane lists all the instruments that have been added for those that you want to profile against.
	New instruments can be added by selecting and then dragging each one from the instruments library into this pane. Items within this pane can also be deleted.
Track pane	This pane displays a graphical summary of the data returned by the current instruments. Each instrument has its own track that provides a chart of the data that is collected by that instrument. The information within this pane is read-only.
Detail pane	This pane shows the details of the data that has been collected by each of the instruments. It displays the set of events gathered and used to create the graphical view within the track pane. Depending on the type of instrument, information that is represented by this pane can be customized to represent the data differently.
Extended detail pane	This pane displays detailed information about the item that is currently selected in the details pane. This pane displays the complete stack trace, timestamp, and other instrument-specific data gathered for the given event.
Navigation bar	This pane shows you your current position and the steps you took to get there. It includes two menus: the active instrument menu and the detail view menu. You can click on the entries within the navigation bar to select the active instrument, and the level and type of information in the detail view.

In this section, you learned how easy it is to launch the Instruments application to profile an application. You learned how to use the Leaks instrument to monitor your application, display information such as memory that is currently allocated, the user's performance, and the total virtual memory that is currently allocated.

In the next section, we will look at how to submit your applications to iTunes Connect, using the Xcode IDE.

For more information on Instruments, and how you can debug your apps, please refer to the Instruments reference documentation at `https://developer.apple.com/library/ios/documentation/DeveloperTools/Conceptual/InstrumentsUserGuide/`.

Preparing your app for submission using iTunes Connect

Now that you have tested your application to ensure that everything works fine and is free from errors, you should start preparing your application so that it is ready for submission to the Apple App Store.

To prepare your application using Xcode, follow these simple steps:

1. Ensure that the `AnimationExample` Xcode project file is already open within the Xcode IDE, and choose the **Preferences...** option from **Xcode | Preferences...** menu, or alternatively, by press *Command + ,*.

2. Next, ensure that the **Accounts** tab has been selected, then click on the + button and choose the **Add Apple ID...** menu option, as shown in the following screenshot:

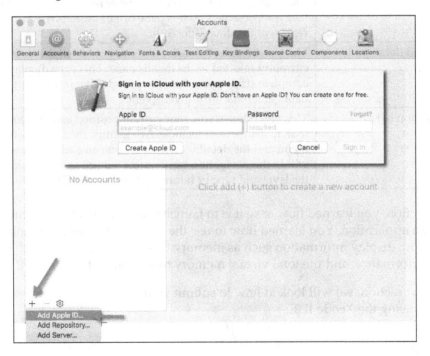

3. Enter your Apple Developer credentials by specifying both the **Apple ID** and **Password**.

> Once Xcode has validated your Apple credentials, you will be presented with a screen similar to the one shown in the preceding screenshot. This screen shows you the team that you belong to as well as your role within the team. You can also add multiple Apple IDs to this screen.

4. With the `AnimationExample` project still open within the Xcode IDE, select the `AnimationExample` from the project navigation window, choose the **Build Settings** tab, and scroll down to the **Code Signing** section, as shown in the following screenshot:

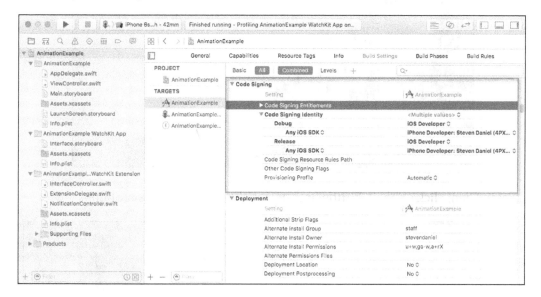

5. Next, select **Any iOS SDK**, and choose your certificate from the drop-down list.

> Your iOS provisioning certificate will be shown in bold, with your provisioning profile in gray. If you don't import a valid provisioning certificate, you won't be able to deploy or upload your iOS and WatchKit applications to the Apple App Store.

Now that you have modified the code signing entitlements for your project, the next step is to prepare your application for submission to the Apple App Store using iTunes Connect:

1. Log in to the iOS Developer portal at `http://developer.apple.com/`.

2. Click on the **Member Center** link that is located right at the top of the screen.

3. Sign in to your account using your Apple ID and password. This will then display the **Developer Program Resources** page, as we saw in our previous section.

4. Click on the **My Apps** button, as shown in the following screenshot:

5. Then, click on the **+** button and choose the **New App** menu option:

6. Proceed to enter the application details for the application that you are uploading. The **SKU** number field is a unique identifier that you create for your app:

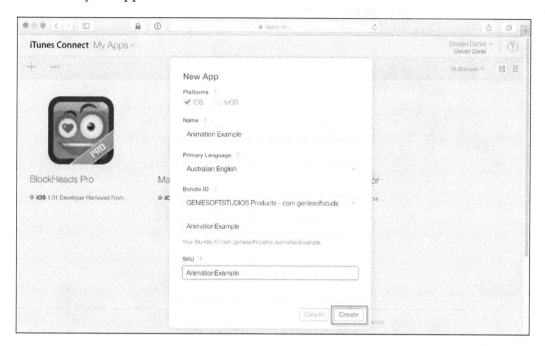

7. Then, click on the **Create** button to proceed to the next step.

8. Next, choose the **Pricing and Availability** menu option, located below the **APP STORE INFORMATION** section on the left-side panel.

9. Then, from the **Pricing and Availability** section, specify the values for the pricing tier as well as the availability date for your application. This will determine when your application will be made available for download. This is shown in the following screenshot:

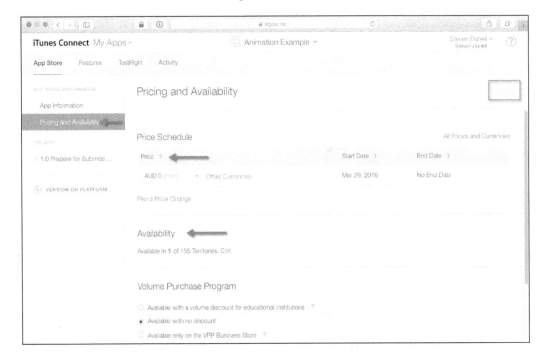

10. Next, click on the **Save** button to proceed to the next step.

There are more than 100 pricing tiers to choose from, including an option for selling your application for free. On clicking the **Save** button, your details will be updated.

In this section, you learned the steps involved in preparing your application for submission to the Apple App Store using iTunes Connect. You also learned that before submitting your apps for approval, you must ensure that everything works properly, and is free from problems, and the iOS Simulator is a good place to start that. Although not everything can be tested within the iOS Simulator, it proves a good starting point. Apple suggests that you should always deploy your apps to a real iOS device running the latest iOS release.

Next, we looked at how to create a new App ID for the application that will be uploaded to the Apple App Store, to provide detailed information about the application, and to specify the date when the application will become available.

For more information on how to submit and manage your apps using iTunes Connect, you can refer to https://developer. apple.com/library/ios/documentation/IDEs/ Conceptual/AppDistributionGuide/UsingiTunesConnect/ UsingiTunesConnect.html#//apple_ref/doc/uid/ TP40012582-CH22-SW3.

Submitting an app to iTunes Connect using Xcode

In this section, you will learn how to archive an app ready for submission to the Apple App Store, using the Xcode integrated development environment. To submit your application, follow these simple steps:

1. Ensure that the AnimationExample.xcodeproj project from the Chapter 10 folder in the accompanying code bundle is already open within the Xcode IDE.

2. Next, open the **Scheme** menu, and choose the **Manage Schemes...** option. Alternatively, you can use the **Product | Scheme | Manage Schemes...** menu option.

3. Then, select the **AnimationExample WatchKit App** scheme, and then click on the **Edit...** button located at the bottom of the **Manage Schemes** pane, as shown in the following screenshot:

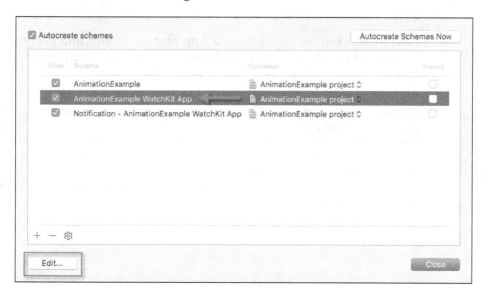

4. Ensure that the **Destination** option is set to use **iOS Device**, and that the **Build Configuration** option is set to use the **Release** scheme. Then click on the **Close** button to commit the changes, and exit from the scheme manager.

5. Next, choose the **Product | Archive** menu option from the Xcode menu, which will begin building your application, before finally displaying the application archive.

6. Now provide a description for your application, and then click on the **Validate...** button to make Xcode validate your app.

7. Once you have clicked on the **Upload to App Store...** button, and everything passes, you can upload your binary archive by clicking on the **Upload** button, as can be seen in the preceding screenshot.

 For more information on other ways to distribute your application, please refer to the *App Distribution Guide* from the Apple Developer documentation at `https://developer.apple.com/library/ios/documentation/IDEs/Conceptual/AppDistributionGuide/UploadingYourApptoiTunesConnect/UploadingYourApptoiTunesConnect.html#//apple_ref/doc/uid/TP40012582-CH36-SW5.`

Summary

In this chapter, you learned how to effectively debug your app, using Instruments to eliminate potential memory leaks. You also learned how to create and set up your iOS development team as well as the associated iOS development certificate that enables you to run and test your apps on an iOS device. After that, we moved on to describing the way to create App IDs for our apps; these App IDs are used within Xcode to associate your app with the one assigned as part of your provisioning profile.

Once we created all the necessary development certificates and provisioning profiles, we looked at how to profile our application using the Instruments application that comes as part of Xcode. You learned how to use the Leaks instrument to help detect any memory leaks within our *Animation Example* app; this instrument ensures that objects are allocated and released correctly.

Additionally, you learned how to package your app, deploy it to iTunes Connect in order to download and test your app on an iOS device, and install it on your Apple Watch device.

This was the final chapter. I hope that you had lots of fun going through this book, have learned a lot, and have got your Apple Watch wearable projects started off on the right foot. Now you have a wealth of experience with Apple Watch wearables and know what it takes to build rich and engaging apps for the wearable platform, by using a host of exciting concepts and techniques that are unique to Apple's wearable platform.

If, like me, learning about all these cutting-edge technologies and concepts has got you overflowing with ideas, then I can't wait to see what you build. Thank you so much for purchasing this book. I wish you the very best of luck with your Apple Watch adventures.

Index

Symbol

3D Touch 197

A

action buttons
  adding, to dynamic notifications 252-255
  responding to, within custom
      notifications 255, 256
  Shopping List app dynamic notification
      controller, configuring 258-261
  static and dynamic interface controllers,
      differences 257, 258
Action event
  creating, to handle our map zooming 93, 94
animation application
  configuration, for using App Transport
      Security 284-286
  images, adding to assets catalog 281-283
  images, setting up 281-283
  reference link 281
  WatchKit, building 278-280
App IDs
  creating, for WatchKit applications 309-311
Apple
  development certificate, obtaining 307, 308
Apple Developer
  documentation, reference link 179
  registering as 2-4
Apple Pay
  reference link 194
Apple Push Notification service
  URL 255

Apple Watch
  Activity 33
  Workout 33
Apple Watch haptics
  integrating, within app 213-218
Apple Watch interface guidelines
  about 41, 42
  action-based events 42
  digital crown 42
  Force Touch 42
  gestures 42
  glances 42
  notifications 42
  side button 42
application
  profiling, Xcode Instruments used 317-319
App Transport Security (ATS)
  about 277
  reference link 286

B

Bezel
  about 67
  reference link 67

C

category
  configuring, for static interface
      controller 264, 265
Certificate Signing Request (CSR) 307
Core Location
  using, with WatchKit extension 95-99

D

Dashcode 5
development certificate
  obtaining, from Apple 307, 308
development provisioning profiles
  creating 311-316
dynamic notifications
  Action buttons, adding 252-255

E

error handling 27

F

Force Touch 197
Foundation framework class
  reference link 175

G

gestures 198
glance controller
  configuring, templates used 231-233
  information, displaying 239, 240
  information for display, storing 237-239
glance interface controller connections
  establishing 234-237
glance interface guidelines
  about 240, 241
  reference link 241
Glances 33
Guessing Game application
  about 48-50
  building 65-67
  guessing 66, 67
  Interface Builder, used for creating watch
    user interface 50-52

H

Health Monitor application
  about 108-110
  Action event, creating for handling Start
    Monitoring button 135, 136

building 150, 151
HealthKit framework, integrating
    for handling updates 113, 114
hierarchical interface 112, 113
iPhone app, integrating 114, 115
modal interfaces 112
navigation 111
page-based interfaces 111
running 150, 151
used, for obtaining biological personal
    information 144-149
used, for obtaining heart rate
    information 137-144
used, for obtaining pedometer
    information 137-144
WatchKit, building 115-125

I

InfinitApps 67
Instruments application 5, 301
Integrated Development Environments
    (IDEs) 5
Interface Builder
  used, for creating watch user
    interface 286-289
  using, for creating Watch Tracker UI 87-90
Interface Builder objects
  Outlets, creating for 91-93
iOS Developer
  portal link 302-322
  reference link 157
iOS development certificate
  creating 306, 307
iOS development team
  creating 302-305
  setting up 302-305
iOS devices
  reference link 315
iOS Simulator 5
iPhone app
  integrating 114, 115
iPhone app and WatchTracker WatchKit
    extension communication
  performing 99

Watch Connectivity framework,
    integrating 100-104
iTunes Connect
  application submitting, Xcode used 325-326
  used, for preparing application for
      submission 320-324
  using, reference link 325

L

Leaks 317
local notifications
  URL 271

M

menu interface 198
messages
  displaying, within notification
      interface 269-271
methods, WKInterfaceController class
  awakeWithContext: 223
  init 223
  willActivate 223

N

navigation tracking application
  creating 70-72
Near Field Communication (NFC) 153
notification controller
  connections, establishing 262-264
  used, for scheduling notifications 266-269
notification interface
  guidelines 272
  messages, displaying within 269-271
notifications
  actionable notifications 245
  controller life cycle 247, 248
  interface guidelines, URL 272
  local 246
  local notifications 245
  remote 246
  remote notifications 245
  scheduling, notification controller
      used 266-269

scheme configuring, for Shopping list
    app 248-252
  working with 246
NSAppTransportSecurity
  reference link 286
NSUserDefaults framework class
  reference link 240

O

Outlets, for Interface Builder objects
  creating 91-93

R

remote notifications
  URL 271

S

Shopping List application
  building 154-195
  configuration, for working with Apple
      Pay 162
  dynamic notification controller,
      controlling 258-261
  glance, adding 224, 225
  glance build scheme, creating 226-228
  glance interface controller WatchKit class,
      creating 228-230
  menu, adding 205-209
  notification scheme, configuring 248-252
  payment requests, handling with PassKit
      framework 185-194
  product class structure, creating for holding
      product items 172-174
  ProductsList property list, creating 175-179
  product table row controller class,
      configuring 169-172
  provisioning, for Apple Pay 156-161
  response, setting on row selection within
      table 182, 183
  running 194-274
  setting up 156-161
  table controller, populating with row
      information 180-182

table row interface controller's class,
    creating 167-169
WatchKit, building 164-166
WatchKit, running 184, 185
WatchKit table object 163

Software Development Kits (SDKs) 5

static interface controller
and dynamic interface controllers,
    differences 257, 258
category, configuring for 264, 265

string interpolation 13

Swift 2.0
binding 29
error handling 27-29
features 27
protocol extensions 30

Swift language
about 10
Booleans 17-19
constants 12
numeric types and conversion 16, 17
semicolons 15, 16
string interpolation 23-25
strings 13, 14
Tuples 20-22
variables 10-12

T

Taptic Engine
design considerations 213

target 34

templates
used, for configuring glance
    controller 231- 233

throwing functions 27

Today extension 221

U

UIApplication class
URL 269

UIGraphicsBeginImageContext method
reference link 298

Unique Device Identifier (UDID) 317

W

WatchKit
App IDs, creating 309-311
building 115-125
Outlets for Interface Builder objects,
    creating 128-135
product class structure, creating for holding
    product items 175
product table row controller class,
    configuring 169
profile details controller class,
    creating 125-128
running 185

WatchKit classes
about 39
WKInterfaceButton 39
WKInterfaceDate 39
WKInterfaceGroup 39
WKInterfaceImage 39
WKInterfaceLabel 39
WKInterfaceMap 39
WKInterfaceSeparator 39
WKInterfaceSlider 40
WKInterfaceSwitch 40
WKInterfaceTable 40
WKInterfaceTimer 40

WatchKit context menu connections
establishing 209-212

WatchKit context menu gestures 198-201

WatchKit context menu icons
default WatchKit context menu actions 204
design considerations 202, 203

WatchKit context menu interface 201, 202

WatchKit extension
Core Location, using with 95-99

WatchKit glances
controller life cycle 222, 223
working with 222

WatchKit platform
about 34
limitations 40
projects 34
WatchKit application architecture 35, 36

WatchKit application life cycle 36-38
WatchKit classes 39
WatchKit Simulator Actions 254
watchOS 2
about 42
Activation Lock 43, 44
FaceTime audio 44
features 43
Mail 43
Maps 43
Nightstand mode 43, 44
Photo watch face 43
social features 44, 45
Time-Lapse face 43
Time Travel 43
watch faces 43
Watch Tracker application
building 104-106
Core Location within watchOS 2,
limitations 86
running 104-106
WatchKit extension, building 86
Watch Tracker application, iPhone
annotation placeholders, adding 81, 82
annotation placeholders, removing 81, 82
building 72-86
requests, handling for background location
updates 82-84
running 84-86
Watch Tracker UI
creating, Interface Builder used 87-90
watch user interface
Action events, establishing 292- 295
actions responding to user actions,
creating 60-65
Animation Example application,
building 298-300
Animation Example application,
running 298-300

connections, establishing to interface
controller 290-292
creating, Interface Builder used 51, 52
creating, with Interface Builder 286-289
images, animating 295, 296
images, compressing 296, 298
images, loading 296-298
labels, adding 52-55
outlets, creating to builder objects 55-60
text, adding 52-55
WKInterfaceController class
awakeWithContext method 38
init method 38
willActivate method 38
WKInterfaceObject class
reference link 296
WKInterfaceTable class
reference link 166
WKUserInterfaceController class
URL 258
**WKUserNotificationInterfaceController
class**
key methods 247, 248

X

Xcode
about 5
used, for submitting application to iTunes
Connect 325, 326
Xcode development tools, installing 5, 6
Xcode development tools, obtaining 5
Xcode Instruments
reference link 320
used, for profiling application 317-319
Xcode playgrounds
about 7
creating 8-10